D1561727

Black Life on the Mississippi

Black Life on the Mississippi

Slaves, Free Blacks, and the Western Steamboat World

Thomas C. Buchanan

The University of North Carolina Press

Chapel Hill and London

Designed by April Leidig-Higgins
Set in Ehrhardt by Copperline Book Services, Inc.

The paper in this book meets the guidelines for permanence
and durability of the Committee on Production Guidelines
for Book Longevity of the Council on Library Resources.

Library of Congress Cataloging-in-Publication Data
Buchanan, Thomas C., 1967–
Black life on the Mississippi: slaves, free Blacks, and
the western steamboat world / Thomas C. Buchanan.
p. cm.   Includes bibliographical references and index.
ISBN 0-8078-2909-9 (cloth: alk. paper)
1. African Americans—Mississippi River Valley—History—
19th century.   2. African American steamboat workers—
History—19th century.   3. River life—Mississippi River
Valley—History—19th century.   4. Mississippi River
Valley—History—19th century.   5. Mississippi River—
History—19th century.   I. Title.
F358.2.N4B83   2004
977'.020496073—dc22   2004009859

08 07 06 05 04   5 4 3 2 1

Portions of this book appeared earlier, in somewhat different form,
in Thomas C. Buchanan, "Black Life on the Mississippi: African
American Steamboat Laborers and the Work Culture of Antebellum Western Steamboats," in *The African American Urban Experience:
Perspectives from the Colonial Period to the Present*, ed. Joe William
Trotter, Earl Lewis, and Tera W. Hunter (New York: Palgrave, 2004)
(reprinted with permission of Palgrave Macmillan); "Rascals of the
Antebellum Mississippi: African American Steamboat Workers and
the St. Louis Hanging of 1841," *Journal of Social History* 34, no. 4
(Summer 2001): 797–816 (reprinted by permission of the publisher);
and "Levees of Hope: African American Steamboat Workers, Cities,
and the Slave Escapes on the Antebellum Mississippi," *Journal of
Urban History* 30, no. 3 (March 2004): 360–77 (reprinted by permission of the publisher).

for Bella and Daisy

always in my heart, always on my mind

contents

Contents

illustrations and maps

MAPS

acknowledgments

YEARS AGO WHEN I was a boy I visited my uncle Tommy Chantler. He lived on dredging boat docked on the Ohio River near Pittsburgh, and it was there that I first became charmed with the river and the people that worked on it. Later, when I decided to write my dissertation on river workers, it quickly became clear that dredging was exactly what I would be doing. This book is the result of many years of scouring the archives and libraries of the pan-Mississippi world for the records of people who inhabited the lower depths of nineteenth-century society. This kind of work requires digging in many places, asking plenty of questions, and receiving boatloads of generous aid. I've had a lot of help along the way.

The history department at Carnegie Mellon University paid my graduate stipend for two semesters without requiring me to teach, freeing up time that allowed me to begin my research. Later, once my dissertation was complete, a National Endowment for the Humanities Summer Fellowship and a Rockefeller Foundation Post-Doctoral Fellowship enabled me to continue this work. The University Center for Research at the University of Nebraska at Omaha funded a summer of research, and the history department's Martin Fund awarded me funds to defray the cost of obtaining illustrations. Together this funding made it possible for me to visit many archives. I am thankful to the staffs at the Inland Waterways Collection at the Cincinnati Public Library, the Filson Club, the Historical New Orleans Collection, the Missouri Historical Society, the Department of Special Collections at Hill Library at Louisiana State University, the State Historical Society of Missouri, the Special Collections at the University of New Orleans, the Southern Historical Collection at the University of North Carolina at Chapel Hill, the Special Collections at the Perkins Library at Duke University, the National Archives–Great Lakes Region, the National Archives–Great Plains Region, the National Archives–

Southwest Region, the Missouri State Archives, the Tennessee State Archives, the Mississippi Department of Archives and History, and the Missouri Department of Archives and History. I am especially thankful for the workers in the interlibrary loan department at Carnegie Mellon University who helped me discover many obscure documents, including the *Trials and Confessions of Madison Henderson*, which became the basis for Chapter 5. Of all the wonderful people who helped me find sources in these repositories, Marie Windell deserves special mention. Windell, an archivist in the Special Collection Department at the University of New Orleans, changed the course of this project when she introduced me to the records of the Supreme Court of Louisiana. Her passion for these sources, her thorough knowledge of nineteenth-century Louisiana and legal history, and her willingness to answer the same questions over and over, often years apart, have sustained this project.

I'll never be able to fully square my debts to the teachers I've had over the years. At Oberlin College, Gary Kornblith and Carol Lasser introduced a floundering sophomore to what was then the hot field of social history. It was a conversion experience, and I never looked back to the natural sciences again. They know tons of history, but it was the warmth, humanity, and sense of fun that they conveyed along with their knowledge that makes them the best teachers I've ever had. At Carnegie Mellon University, Wendy Goldman's seminars, particularly her course on comparative working-class formation, challenged me to think more clearly about my theoretical approach to history. Wendy has high standards and I'm thankful for it. David Miller, an early adviser to this project, mentioned that travel narratives might provide material about African Americans. I ignored him for two years and then wondered why I had. My dissertation committee, Peter N. Stearns, Joe W. Trotter Jr., Tera W. Hunter, and Marcus Rediker provided assistance whenever I asked for it. Peter N. Stearns gave me the freedom to define my own project and drew on his remarkable command of the field of social and cultural history to encourage me to reshape key parts of the argument. Joe W. Trotter quite simply taught me what I know about African American history. Without his support and guidance, this book would not have been possible. Tera Hunter joined my committee late in the going after she joined the faculty at Carnegie Mellon. She didn't know me at all but generously agreed to read the dissertation. Her copious and insightful comments inform many parts of this work.

Marcus Rediker deserves special mention for his contribution. *Between the Devil and the Deep Blue Sea* fascinated me when I first read it in the late 1980s and instilled in me an interest in the maritime world and working-class history that remains to this day. It was a stroke of good fortune that he was on the faculty at the University of Pittsburgh, just a short walk across Panther Hollow from Carnegie Mellon. Throughout my years in Pittsburgh he informally advised this project in innumerable ways as it moved from vague idea to finished dissertation. He gave me practical suggestions about how to research maritime laborers, but, most significantly, he made me feel the project was important even when it seemed to be going nowhere.

I've had help of all kinds from many friends and colleagues through the years that has made this a better book. In Pittsburgh, J. Trent Alexander, Li Ping Bu, Jennifer Geller, Bonnie Gorman, Hugh Gorman, Tim Haggerty, John Hinshaw, Dan Holbrook, David Jardini, John Jensen, Sigurdur Magnusson, Craig Marin, Kristy Michelson, Leisl Miller Orenic, Monserratt Miller, Jodie Minor, Michael Neiberg, Julia Roos, Breadon Mac Suibhne, Vernon Seguin, Lisa Seigel, Amy Trost, Jennifer Trost, Susannah Walker, David Wolcott, and Carl Zimring all were great fun. A special thanks goes to Mark Tebeau. We talked firemen and river workers for years, and I was enriched by his intelligence and good humor. I'm very thankful that Keith Allen was in graduate school with me and that he has remained a dear friend. He encouraged this project for years, and I am grateful for his keen insights and irreverent wit. In Memphis, Ken Goings (now at Ohio State University) and Barbara Ellen Smith funded this project when nobody else would. When I felt useless and aimless, I suddenly received word that they wanted me to come to Memphis for a year and be supported by their Rockefeller Fellowship Program, "Making Race and Gender in the Mid-South." Where would I be without you? When in Memphis I met Philip Zacair and Catherine Reinhardt, who took Amanda and me to the movies and for Mexican food. Our paths have diverged but I have not forgotten such dear people. At the University of Nebraska at Omaha I've been fortunate to have warm and supportive colleagues. Iain Anderson (now at Trent University), Maria Arbelaez, Marion Boulby, Harl Dalstrom, Bruce Garver, Moshe Gershovich, Lorraine Gesick, Charles King, Fred Neilsen, Jeanne Reames-Zimmerman, Mark Sherer, Jerold Simmons, Dennis Smith, Michael Tate, Tommy Thompson, and Sharon Wood all have had an impact on this book in one way or another. Peter Gierasch deserves a special thank you for getting me a work space in Cornell University's astronomy department in the summer of 2003, which helped me finish the book. Peter and Maida Gierasch were gracious hosts during this period.

Various scholars have helped with comments on this work at conferences and seminars. Eric Arnesen, Kim Butler, Leon Fink, Walter Johnson, Ari Kelman, Stephanie McCurry, Leslie Schwalm: thank you very much. Gary Kornblith, Craig Marin, Judith Schafer, Julie Winch, Sharon Wood, and the anonymous readers for the University of North Carolina Press read the entire manuscript and improved it dramatically. Thank you all for your labors. Mark Reuter, a graduate student at the University of Nebraska at Omaha, provided valuable comments for Chapter 5.

At the University of North Carolina Press, I've been fortunate to work with David Perry, who has been a steadfast ally of this project, even when it took years longer to complete than I thought it would. Mark Simpson-Vos helped move the manuscript into production. My copyeditor, Mary Caviness, deserves a special thank you. She helped make this a far better book, and I am very grateful to her.

My family has supported me throughout this project. If most people were like my brother, David R. Buchanan, the world would be a better place. Cousins Ted Anderson and Liza Anderson Kujovich feel like brother and sister for all the fun we've had over the years. They have helped this project along considerably. My aunt Sophie Buchanan taught me what "mad money" was and sent me some time and again when the "fun" funds were low, which was quite often. Larry Anderson graciously let me stay in his New Orleans house when I first started doing research and treated me to the best of New Orleans cuisine when I couldn't afford rice and beans. Megan Holmes Anderson, Rob Kujovich, Cindy Hummel, and Michael Boulas all provided me respite from thinking about river work at one time or another. Thanks to all my extended Buchanan relatives, especially Margo and Marissa, for all the reunions and more-informal fun gatherings.

My mother, Roberta H. Buchanan, has history in her blood, and she put it in mine. She left graduate school (her Ph.D. adviser was none other than Peter N. Stearns) to raise me with a curiosity and a tenacity that have helped me tremendously in my work in history. She has assisted me at every stage of the process, particularly in finding the core of this project as I was writing my dissertation. With her commonsensical genius she helped me see what was important and what needed to be left out. My father, John B. Buchanan, gentle of spirit and kind of heart, has also been a source of unwavering support throughout this project and my life.

Amanda Gierasch has been my companion since the early days of this project. We met at a New Orleans youth hostel during one of my many trips to that city, and we immediately moved into a disheveled, roach-infested apartment *filled with charm* off Rampart Street. Soon she was reading draft after draft of this work, improving every page. I appreciate all her love and support. More recently, the arrival of Bella and Daisy, our dear daughters, has filled me with joy and hope. The future looks bright.

Black Life on the Mississippi

The pan–Mississippi world, 1860

introduction

Race and the Antebellum Western Steamboat Economy

MARK TWAIN romanticized Mississippi steamboating. He marveled at the Mississippi's eminent basin, its fifty-four major tributaries, and its 4,000 miles of length, from its mouth in Louisiana to its headwaters up the Missouri. This magical landscape provided the setting for what he considered the most wonderful job in antebellum America. Piloting was "play—delightful play, vigorous play, adventurous play."[1] In a famous passage in *Life on the Mississippi* he proclaimed that pilots were the only "unfettered and entirely independent beings on the earth." He believed that "every man and woman" had a "master" but "pilots had *none*."[2] Mark Twain moved through the American West with authority and respect, high atop one of the revolutionary technologies of the era.

William Wells Brown lived and worked in a very different Mississippi world. He told of his experiences on the river in the *Narrative of William Wells Brown, A Fugitive Slave*, a story that launched his career as an antislavery activist and novelist. Instead of turning the pilothouse wheel with ease, Brown toiled as a waiter serving passengers and officers, including pilots, in the demanding confines of the steamboat cabin. Twain enjoyed respect when working; Brown's job was to be invisible. A good steamboat servant was supposed to loom, stationary and silent, on the outskirts of the cabin, waiting to descend to his labors whenever passengers had the slightest need. An empty glass? Filled. Mud on the cabin floor? Swept and mopped. While Twain glowingly wrote of his lack of accountability, Brown had masters seemingly everywhere. He had

William Wells Brown. Courtesy of the Missouri Historical Society, St. Louis.

masters in St. Louis who could order him to labor of their choosing, sell him at a moment's notice, or rent him away to steamboat owners who crowded around the city levee. The legal owners of his labor, however, were often the least of his worries. River stewards, captains, and passengers policed his daily life and were often rough and capricious. He could steam away from his owners, but whites were everywhere.

Mobility for Twain was unproblematic. He looked forward to new sights, people, and adventures with little worry about what was left behind. He knew he was free to return. For Brown, mobility was filled with remorse and sadness even as it created possibilities for freedom and independence. River voyages forced him away from his dearly loved mother, a St. Louis slave. Working on a steamboat made him all too aware that temporary separations could easily become permanent. While Twain "played" at the pilothouse wheel, Brown wept for the coffles of slaves he watched bound for New Orleans on the decks of river steamers, chained among the other cargo. His emotions were made more poignant by the fact that he knew their destinations. Mobility had educated him in the horrors of the sugar and cotton plantations of the deep South and the slave markets of New Orleans.

But the river was the focus of his dreams, too. The steamboats that moved up and down the Mississippi River carried the tentacles of slavery and racism, but they also carried liberating ideas and pathways to freedom. The river linked Brown to an African American Mississippi world that slaves, and their free black allies, created amid the attempts of masters to control their labor and family lives. By having so many different types of masters, Brown was freed from the personal domination that many riverside slaves suffered on the farms and plantations of the West. In between his masters' various demands, he was able to create moments of autonomy that allowed him to learn the West's social geography. This knowledge eventually made possible Brown's escape from slavery. Though he never steered a river steamer, Brown remembered that he "found great difference between the work in a steamboat cabin and in a cornfield."[3]

Mark Twain knew that this African American river world existed. The enduring image of Huck and Jim on that raft floating down the Mississippi shows the radical possibilities of river mobility in ways no historical source can. In *Huckleberry Finn*, the river allowed both a runaway slave and a young white boy to escape riverside conventions and to forge a forbidden friendship. By juxtaposing the freedoms of river mobility with the oppressions of riverside society, Twain's story memorializes the nation's historic fascination with liberty and independence while showing how dependent these ideas were on slavery to derive their meaning. But this linkage of the themes of freedom and bondage is curiously absent in *Life on the Mississippi*, Twain's account of steamboat life. His reminiscences reveal the freedoms of piloting but cast a blind eye to the experience of people of color like William Wells Brown who made his job possible. This book uncovers the Mississippi River experience personified in Jim but neglected in Twain's personal reflections.

The connections between piloting and slavery were not hard to see. The

Pennsylvania and the other boats Twain piloted along the lower Mississippi were strewn with slave-produced products. The intimate relationship of steamboats and slavery was evident each time roustabouts walked down the gangway to carry hemp, sugar, tobacco, and especially cotton from southern levees. The volume of this commerce was incredible. Fifty-five percent of the South's cotton crop, 1,915,852 bales in all, came down the Mississippi in 1860, bound for the textile mills of Liverpool and New York. The some one million riverside slaves of the western river valleys produced this cotton, but steamboat workers did the crucial work of helping get it to market. Deck workers rolled, lifted, and carried the 400-pound bales from river landings to steamboat decks and then unloaded them at New Orleans.[4] A letter published in *Debow's Review* from Missouri politician Edward Bates reflected the mood of accumulation that defined the era. "We say the Mississippi is our river," Bates pronounced, "and New Orleans is our storehouse. And we will bestow upon both whatever amount of labor and expense may be necessary to produce the greatest sum of good[s] to the proprietors."[5] The "labor bestowed," of course, was not Bates's but the labor of slaves like William Wells Brown.

The story told in these pages uncovers the hidden world of the slaves and free blacks of the Mississippi River world. This world included mobile workers, as well as people who never left the riverbank. African American steamboat workers helped make this world a community by connecting African American urbanites in both the North and the South with plantation-belt slave societies. Steamboats traveled the very veins and arteries of the slave system, and the importance of this commercial world to the economics of the slave regime meant that the pan-Mississippi black community was always being threatened. Disapproving masters seemingly lurked beside every levee consignment, boat officers watched clandestine river transactions, and the levee police patrolled the waterways. Commercial work was also simply dangerous. Maritime labor was one of the most treacherous jobs in nineteenth-century America. No matter if they worked on a high-seas brig or a Mississippi steamer, workers drowned, sustained crushed limbs, fell prey to disease, and suffered frostbite. In the antebellum period, still the age of sail on the oceans, such dangers were compounded on the rivers by the threat of boiler explosions and instant death.

These hardships did not prevent African American steamboat workers from seeking freedom on the Mississippi. Some used the Mississippi River to leave the world of slavery behind. The river and its black steamboat hands were an important, and underappreciated, component of the black networks that

"Hauling Cotton to the River." From *Harper's Magazine*, 1853–54. Courtesy of the Library of Congress, Prints and Photographs Division.

enabled slaves to reach freedom. Most slave steamboat hands, however, took advantage of the special opportunities of steamboat life to survive within the slave system. Slaves bargained for various wage payments, took part in trading, and developed a spending power that exceeded that of other bondsmen and -women. In addition, the ability to maintain contact with a broad slave community was a powerful incentive for many to keep working. Steamboat travel allowed slaves to stay in touch with far-flung family and friends and served as a grapevine of information for riverside slaves. Masters could control the flow of commodities on steamboats, but they could not manage the flow of information that accompanied steamboat cargo up- and downstream. Black networks sometimes nurtured the creation of outlaw bands of river rascals. The Madison Henderson Gang, a group of one slave and three free black rivermen, moved through the Mississippi world appropriating goods from unsuspecting riverside merchants. Their lives further illustrate the possibilities that river life offered African Americans. Networks of illicit trade, family communication, escape, and theft, all made possible by African American steamboat workers, gave slaves additional resources in their quotidian struggles with masters and overseers.

African American river workers were heroic figures in the slave community. Slaves gazed with wonder and envy at the cosmopolitan lives of men like William Wells Brown. They admired the way river hands could seemingly come and go from river landings and levees as they pleased. Alexander Kenner, a former Louisiana plantation slave, thought that this contact with various landed communities bred a certain sophistication among steamboat hands. "The negroes on the river," he said, ". . . are intelligent. . . . Those in the interior, away from the river, are stupid; they see nothing, know nothing, and are very like cattle."[6] Josiah Henson remembered that working on the Mississippi between St. Louis and Galena was "a sunny spot" in his life and was "one of his most treasured recollections." He felt that the job "was the most pleasant time he had ever experienced." Later, when forced to work in a St. Louis hotel, Henson found the job "as painful as his preceding employment was pleasant."[7] Washington Thomas commented to an interviewer, "I came from Kentucky. I was a slave there. I didn't have very hard times. I was on the river all my life, from the time I was old enough."[8] The slave Madison Henderson, who lived much of his life in New Orleans, recalled that he "preferred to be sold to a boatman, so that I might be kept on the [Mississippi] river."[9]

While steamboat workers clearly had liberties other slaves did not, their high status within western slave communities also stemmed in part from slaves' cosmology and their long-standing beliefs equating waterways with freedom. In slave spirituals like the "Old Ship of Zion," "Deep River," "Down by the River Side," and "Roll, Jordan, Roll," rivers and boats represented pathways to heaven. These songs may have had African origins, but they had particular meaning in the antebellum western steamboat economy. One former plantation slave woman told her family that when her mother first saw a steamboat, she thought it was the "Old Ship of Zion" come to take her away to heaven.[10] Although some slaves may not have made so conscious a connection between steamboats and the liberating aspects of their Christian belief system, and others were just plain scared of these huge, modern monsters of technology, the association of steamboats with freedom was pervasive throughout the slave community.

These hopeful visions grew along with the development of the western steamboat industry in the first half of the nineteenth century. The diverse array of builders, machine-shop workers, engineers, and gentlemen inventors that developed riverboats played an important though unwitting role in African American history. Beginning with Robert Fulton's 1811 launch at Pittsburgh's landing of the first commercially successful western steamboat, businessmen were interested in capturing the vast western river market that had been dominated by flatboats and keelboats since the eighteenth century. Steam power, recently adopted from England, offered the opportunity for improved speed—a key concern for shippers.[11] By the 1840s, wood-fueled, high-pressure engines revolutionized transport, particularly for upriver travel. The English traveler Basil Hall commented in 1829 that "the passage from New Orleans to Louisville, in Kentucky, before the introduction of steamboats, frequently occupied nine weary months of hard rowing and warping; whereas, it is now performed in little more than nine days."[12] Keelboats were nearly immediately put out of business on the larger rivers and were relegated to upcountry streams too shallow for the larger, steam-powered boats. Flatboatmen continued to compete with steamboats in the shipment of nonperishable goods throughout the nineteenth century, but they carried a smaller percentage of goods produced with each passing year. By the 1840s and 1850s, the major western river cities received several thousand steamboat arrivals a year. In cities like Louisville, St. Louis, Cincinnati, Pittsburgh, and New Orleans it was not uncommon for a hundred or more steamboats to be docked on city levees at one time. In a few short decades, steamboats revolutionized western transportation, becoming a key component of the industrial revolution that was quickly spreading through the region.[13]

The quick ascension of western steamboats stemmed not only from their speed, which came with steam power, but also their structure, which made them suitable both for the shipment of cargo and for passenger travel. While there was great diversity in the size and load capacity of steamboats, many hulls were over 200 feet long and 35 feet wide, capable of carrying over 400 tons of produce. Flatboats and keelboats did not cater to passengers, so steamboat owners made it a point to profit from the movement of people as well as commodities. In addition to the large hulls, owners commissioned builders to construct several decks for housing passengers and officers. The resulting tiered, three-deck structure—a wedding cake without the complications, Twain called it—gradually developed in the 1830s and 1840s and was the defining characteristic of the western steamboat. Cargo was stored in the shallow hold and on the main deck. Deck passengers, the poorest of travelers, slept on deck amid the cargo. Elite passengers traveled on the second deck, the boiler deck, which rose ten to fifteen feet over the main deck. As the structure of steamboats evolved, a smaller third deck, the hurricane, was added on top of the boiler deck to house officers. On top of all this was the pilothouse. Removed from social bustle that went on below, the pilothouse towered some forty-five feet above the river. By midcentury, the larger boats had living quarters behind the pilothouse in what was called the "Texas."[14]

African American workers like William Wells Brown provided a link between the revolutionary steamboat technology and the vast slave communities that were quickly forming on shore. The looming structure of the western steamboat housed a diverse labor force that numbered about 20,000 workers by midcentury.[15] If the 93 steamboat crews docked at St. Louis in September of 1850 are representative of the 700 to 1,000 steamboat crews on the western rivers by midcentury, about 2,000 to 3,000 slaves and 1,000 to 1,500 free blacks worked in the industry at any one time.[16] The crew lists of these 93 boats indicate that 230 free blacks (6 percent) and 441 slave workers (12 percent) out of a total workforce of 3,627 toiled on these vessels.[17] In addition, 43 percent of the workforce were native-born white, 24 percent were Irish-born, 11 percent were German-born, and 3 percent were born in other miscellaneous countries outside the United States. Twenty-two percent of the workforce were officers, 57 percent were members of the deck crew, 20 percent were members of the cabin crew, and 1 percent were independent proprietors, such as barkeepers and barbers. Men dominated the labor force, but about 2 percent of the workers were chambermaids. This diversity provided a complex social setting for African American resistance and oppression. (See Tables A1–A3.)

Although only a small percentage of the region's overall slave population worked on steamboats, river slaves were nearly as numerous as many other notable groups of nonagricultural slave workers. While figures for the western region are not available, Robert Starobin argued that the southern iron industry employed approximately 10,000 slaves, the hemp and tobacco industries each employed 15,000 slaves, and the cotton and woolen mills employed 5,000 slave workers.[18] Though estimating the number of maritime workers is difficult, it seems likely that the number of slaves working on the inland rivers, particularly the Mississippi River system, equaled the number working in Atlantic coastal and deep-sea sailing trades.[19]

The relatively small number of slave and free black Mississippi River workers that labored on steamboats at any one time does not adequately reflect the

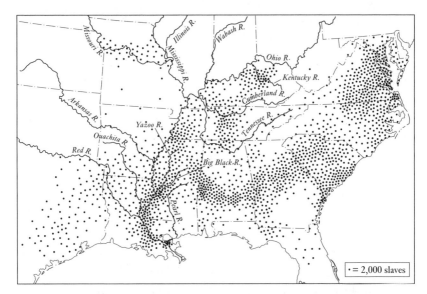

Slave population in the pan-Mississippi River region, 1860. Adapted from
Atlas of Antebellum Southern Agriculture, by Sam Bowers Hilliard. © 1984 by
Louisiana University Press. Reprinted by permission of the publisher.

overall importance of this work to the African American community, however. Most steamboat workers labored on the river for a few years in their
young adulthood before moving on to other jobs. According to the 1850 St.
Louis census, the average age of slave and free black steamboat workers was
twenty-six.[20] While older slaves were sometimes used by employers in other
southern industries to provide continuity and technical skills in mixed slave
and free labor forces, the difficulty of steamboat work led to regular turnover
and to more African Americans being introduced to the workforce. Over a
period of ten years in the late antebellum period, as many as 20,000 African
Americans labored on the western rivers.

One of the most important characteristics of slave and free black rivermen,
and the larger river labor force, was urban residence. By living in St. Louis,
William Wells Brown was typical of other rivermen and -women. The dramatic
population growth of western cities, and the rise to prominence of urban-based
western manufacturers and merchants, made western cities natural home ports
from which steamboat owners could simultaneously hire crews and contract
with shippers.[21] Just as eastern cities supplied the sailors for the country's
ocean ships, western cities supplied the region's inland mariners. Officers
most easily mustered crews, which sometimes totaled over 100 diversely skilled

persons, in large cities such as New Orleans, St. Louis, Nashville, Louisville, Mobile, and Cincinnati. To a lesser extent, smaller cities such as Memphis, Evansville, Baton Rouge, Shreveport, and St. Paul emerged as key labor markets. "I have lived here [in New Orleans] all my life," swore free mulatto Isole' D' arcole' in a typical statement from steamboat workers.[22]

Slaves and free black steamboat workers who lived in rural areas or smaller towns often traveled to cities to enter the new urban labor markets. Free black steamboatman Nelson Collins, for example, lived in Paducah but reported getting work in Louisville and New Orleans. Most enslaved steamboatmen migrated to city levees in New Orleans, Louisville, and St. Louis from small towns with their masters, who hired them out on steamboats.[23] A smaller number got work in rural areas. Former Tennessee plantation slave Will Long remembered, "W'en times wuz slack on the plantation, ole Marse 'ud hire me out ter de boats dat wukked up an' down de big ribber."[24]

The several thousand slaves that worked at any one time on western steamboats at midcentury comprised an important part of the urban workforce. In 1850, for example, 5,442 slaves lived in Louisville, just over 17,000 slaves lived in New Orleans, and only 2,656 slaves lived in St. Louis.[25] That 441 slave river workers were reported to be at St. Louis's dock at one time suggests that steamboat owners were probably some of the most important slave employers in that city. Similarly, the over 1,000 free black river workers in 1850 made up a sizable percentage of the employed male population in western cities. Most large cities housed a hundred or more free black river workers.[26] When the total number of free black river workers is compared to the small populations of free blacks in these cities it is clear that the river industry was an important employer for free blacks as well, especially for men. For instance, Louis C. Hunter argues that in Cincinnati, river work occupied 20 percent of the employed male free black workforce. Another survey of 1850 St. Louis found that nearly one-third of that city's employed free black males worked on the river.[27]

The history of the slave Mississippi is an urban history, but it is also a story of work in a racialized industry. William Wells Brown's exclusion from Twain's pilothouse was typical of other African American steamboat workers. African Americans were nearly entirely excluded from officer positions (captains, clerks, mates, engineers, and pilots).[28] Engineers' and pilots' professional organizations did not begin formally excluding African Americans until the postbellum period, but they had been barring them from the beginning of the steamboat era. Native-born whites dominated the higher-ranking positions through nepotism. Officers often recruited cub pilots, strikers (apprentice engineers), and second clerks from the sons of relatives and friends in riverside communities. "The minister's son became an engineer," Twain wrote. "The doctor's and the postmaster's sons became 'mud clerks'; the wholesale liquor dealer's son became the barkeeper on a boat; four sons of the chief merchant, and two sons of the county judge, became pilots."[29]

Below the pilothouse, African Americans worked in the cabin and deck crews, but more slaves than free blacks labored in deck positions.[30] Former slave Henry Clay recalled that "us negro boys worked as roustabouts to load and unload and [to] keep the fire going."[31] Just south of St. Louis, the traveler Charles Mackay noticed that "the crew and stokers were all negro slaves."[32] On the upper Mississippi, the Englishmen Arthur Cunynghame commented, "On board the *Lucy Bertram*, many of the waiters and a large portion of the crew, including all the firemen, were slaves."[33] The cabin crew was much smaller than the deck crew, but African Americans were particularly concentrated there. African Americans, mostly free blacks, filled about half of these jobs on the western rivers. Gender and class diversified the African American cabin population in ways that were not evident on deck. Free black stewards and barbers made two or three times as much money as common laborers, wages that earned them respect in riverside communities. While barbering was common on only the larger boats, few steamers could go without the labors of a chambermaid or two. Laboring above the river of deckhand masculinity, these women helped construct the homelike atmosphere that captains promised to their cabin passengers. African American rather than white women were favored for these jobs because they were particularly associated with domestic service. Edward and Herbert Quick wrote that African American chambermaids "gradually supplanted" white chambermaids during the antebellum period.[34] In 1850, of the 85 chambermaids working on the 93 St. Louis steamboats mentioned above, 22 (26 percent) were slaves, 41 (48 percent) were free blacks, and only 22 (26 percent) were native whites or European immigrants.[35]

Several factors contributed to the concentration of African Americans in service positions. The belief among native whites, both in the South and in the lower North, that African Americans were particularly suited to fill these jobs was probably the most important factor. These prejudices most likely influenced the hiring practices of boat officers. As one early free black riverman put it, "They [officers] wanted the people traveling on their boat to be served by one whose origin was unmistakable."[36] The lack of suitable alternatives to African American labor also encouraged the hiring of black workers.

Unidentified black man, ca. 1850s. Thomas Easterly, who made this daguerreotype, had an interest in river life, and this man may well have worked in the
steamboat industry. Courtesy of the Missouri Historical Society, St. Louis.

European immigrants often did not have the skills to work effectively in these
positions. Nearly all African Americans spoke English, and many had experience working in hotels and restaurants. The preferences of African Americans may also have contributed to their sizable representation in service positions. A *St. Louis Globe-Democrat* article claimed that among antebellum
African Americans, "the waiters and barbers of the boat regarded themselves
as immeasurably superior to the laborers on the first deck, and looked down
on them with sovereign contempt."[37] Though working in such close proximity with whites had many drawbacks, good cabin tips and freedom from the
most backbreaking labor and the most ritualized forms of labor discipline
made these desirable positions compared to the alternatives.

Introduction

While white workers often resorted to nepotism to secure the best jobs, slaves and free blacks navigated their own pathways to work. For free blacks, like for other laborers, getting work often meant being subjected to a levee shape-up, during which mates or stewards chose workers from the masses of laborers that congregated around steamboat landings. In the nineteenth century, urban labor markets had gradually supplanted the more family- and neighborhood-oriented labor pools that had long characterized the more agrarian-based flatboat economy. Free blacks who knew boat officers personally had an easier time securing berths, and recommendations from other common laborers could help as well, but in the industrial era, anonymity in labor relations increasingly became the rule. The market for slaves, in contrast, remained more individualized and personal. While, in some cases, steamboat officers owned the slaves who worked for them, in most cases, they leased slaves on behalf of boat owners from riverside masters, often people with whom they had other business dealings.[38] These leases could sometimes be a way for plantation owners to rid themselves of a troublesome slave. One Louisiana master leased out a slave because he "had a low opinion of him." The master complained that "he was addicted to drinking and was quarrelsome," and said he did not "wish him to work amongst his other negroes."[39]

Slave leases are good indications of how steamboat work depended on the rhythms of commerce. Fluctuations in labor demand generally corresponded to the agricultural cycle, with greater need for workers in the spring and the fall than at other times of the year.[40] Still, the labor requirements of steamboats did not fluctuate as much as those of the more seasonal flatboats that continued to ply the Mississippi during the antebellum years. The St. Louis merchant James Kennerly's leasing records, for example, suggest that steamboat officers demanded slaves in all seasons. He wrote in his diary on September 21, 1836, that he "called on Capt. Joe Small to hire negroes."[41] On October 18 of that year he recorded that the "*Vandalia* came up and my negroes [were] on board."[42] In 1837 he recorded receiving payments from steamboat owners in February, May, and July.[43] While other masters no doubt leased their slaves intermittently, for Kennerly, leasing steamboat slaves was a year-round proposition.

William Wells Brown worked intensively for several years on steamboats, which was typical of steamboat slaves. Steamboat leases suggest that slaves often accumulated extensive work experience during their youth. For example, the slave Joseph Jackson testified in federal court in 1863 that he spent two years on the *Louisville* alone.[44] Judy Taylor recalled that she had spent ten years as a slave chambermaid.[45] Another slave Henry Crawhion recalled that as soon as he was able to work his master hired him to a steamboat and that he "mainly followed steamboating" until his escape some years later.[46] The master of the Louisiana slave Wesley Holmes testified that between 1849 and 1854 "most of the time he [Wesley] was hired on steamers plying in the Ohio and Mississippi Rivers running from Louisville to New Orleans."[47] A New Orleans levee worker reported in another 1858 case that the slave Baptiste "was a steamboat hand" and that he "never knew him to be employed any where else but in a boat."[48] The account books of James Rudd, a prominent Louisville merchant who leased slaves to steamboats, further illustrates the extensive work experience some steamboat slaves accumulated. One slave, listed as "Big George," spent most of 1853, 1856, and 1859 on the river. Another slave, listed as "Little Charley," spent nearly the entire 1853–60 period working on river steamers.[49]

The African American workers discussed in this book are important in one sense because their occupational experiences were unique compared to those of plantation laborers, urban workers, and deep-sea maritime workers, all of whom they interacted with during their laborers. Their lives thus add richness to our existing knowledge of African American life during slavery. But while steamboats were a distinctive place to work, part of what defined workers' experience on them was their constant contact with society on the riverbank. They spent time in cities and journeyed to and from rural areas. The thousands of blacks who arrived in New Orleans landed at the intersection of domestic and international commerce and thus were at a crucial nexus of the Atlantic world. African American steamboat workers connected slave and free black communities through their jobs and thus were vital to building a pan-Mississippi African American culture.

Despite the close economic ties between the lower North (Pennsylvania, Ohio, Indiana, Illinois), the upper South (Arkansas, Tennessee, Kentucky, Missouri), and the deep South (Louisiana, Mississippi, Texas), there has been no attempt to write the history of slavery in this region from the perspective of this economic and social system. By focusing on the commercial world of the western rivers, this book illustrates the way in which slavery in the West was shaped by its link to the western river system and its workers. While slaves in this vast region differed in many ways, they all had contact with steamboats and thus were connected to a broader western African American world. The perils and possibilities that came with access to the river world were a common element in the experience of the region's slaves. Historians have studied urban slavery, plantation slavery, and industrial slavery, but they have not fully explored the lives of inland transportation workers. Flourishing work on Atlantic slave and free black sailors has made important inroads into this deficiency, but inland workers still have not received the attention they deserve.[50] Western slave and free black steamboat workers, who composed the largest portion of these inland mariners, have received scant mention in the vast literature on the slave experience.[51]

This book highlights the work experience of African American river workers, their pan–Mississippi world, and the actions they took to better their condition. Chapter 1 places slave and free black river workers in the context of the rapidly growing western economy. It illustrates their role as connectors between disparate slave and free black communities. Chapter 2 looks at the demanding work culture of the steamboat and emphasizes both the opportunities and the dangers of river work. Chapter 3 explores how contact between the inland maritime culture of the western steamboat shaped the world of slavery. It argues that the river industry produced a slave market that destroyed African American families. But it also suggests that African Americans used the Mississippi River system to construct covert information networks that maintained family contact. Chapter 4 shows that contact between African American river workers and the larger slave community also facilitated networks of river escape. The discussion of the ways African Americans used the river to expand the slave community is continued in Chapter 5, which moves from large-scale patterns of racial struggle to the story of how one group of African American lawbreakers used the river to fashion rascal identities. Chapter 6 analyzes how the African American steamboat work culture, and its relationship to the survival mechanisms of riverside African Americans, changed during the emancipation process. It argues that with the end of slavery, the river system became less of a highway to freedom, but it still remained crucial to the economic health of African American communities along the inland waterways. The radicalism of the slavery era continued with the efforts of African American steamboat workers to reform the horrible conditions that defined their experience on western steamboats. In the context of the widespread efforts by freedpeople to redefine labor processes throughout the South, these laborers worked to defend and define their freedoms on the decks of steamboats.

Western rivers provided slaves and free blacks with opportunities to forge local, regional, national, and even international communities. Beneath the pilothouse, slave and free black steamboat workers worked to construct their own world beyond the sight of masters, captains, and plantation owners. Working in conjunction with riverside communities, they made steamboats an important site of contestation in both the eras of slavery and freedom. Riverboats have long been considered an icon of American success in the early phases of the industrial revolution. The romanticism of *Life on the Mississippi* is just one manifestation of how most white nineteenth-century Americans embraced the steamboat without considering the struggles that took place on their decks. Slaves and free blacks, and then their postemancipation sons and daughters, countered this myth and sought to make steamboats their own.

chapter one

From Plantation to Freedom

*African American Steamboat Workers
and the Pan-Mississippi World*

WILLIAM WELLS BROWN knew the pan-Mississippi world. While most slaves in the antebellum West were concentrated on plantations in Mississippi and Louisiana, Brown traveled thousands of miles through much of the United States. He worked on upper Mississippi packets and lower Mississippi boats, in the Missouri River trade, and on steamboats along the Ohio River. These voyages put him into contact with the heavy trading that took place along the Tennessee and Cumberland rivers in the upper and middle South, as well as with the deep South Red River trade to Texas. The plantations along these routes were an important part of his world. He knew the Missouri's emergent "Little Dixie," the tobacco and hemp plantations in Kentucky, the sugar plantations of Louisiana, and the growing cotton economies of Mississippi and Tennessee. He knew the cities of Louisville, St. Louis, Vicksburg, Jefferson City, Davenport, and New Orleans. Brown was a worldly slave indeed.

Brown was not alone in experiencing such mobility. His account reflects the experience of thousands of slaves and free blacks who circulated the rivers with liberties that made them the most widely traveled of southern slaves. Importantly, their movements spanned the regions of the West. Even as the country lurched toward Civil War and divisions between North and South became ever more acute, economic connections between the sections flourished. Along these economic networks, African Americans linked market vendors in New Orleans, plantation hands in Louisiana's cotton and sugar bowls, and slave fugitives and abolitionist activists in Cincinnati's Bucktown. These communities and others like them are often discussed in isolation from one another, but they were intimately joined by river commerce. Riverboats connected city and country, North and South, slavery and freedom.

The world of William Wells Brown and his free black companions has been for too long hidden from view. The western river world shaped African American steamboat workers' mentality and created the intellectual, psychological, and material bases for broad networks that helped African Americans survive slavery. It allowed black workers to create a pan-Mississippi community that nourished collective challenges to authority, as well as opportunities for individual gain. We will travel here from seedy docks, to neighborhood saloons and brothels, to the private landings where steamboat hands talked with plantation slaves about the latest news from the river. These were places where hidden communication networks sustained the slave community.

Before exploring the contours of this world it is important to understand the patterns of mobility, as well as the sorts of riverside contact, that slaves and free blacks variously experienced. Slaves and free blacks often labored side by side on steamboats and mingled in a riverside African American culture, but the contours of their mobility differed. Southern lawmakers restricted free blacks' movement in city and state statutes, and slaves' responsibilities to masters and agents limited their activities. Owners and their agents, for instance, often prevented them from shipping out on Ohio River steamboats, from which escapes frequently occurred. Steamboat owners most commonly employed slaves on deep South rivers, frequently used them in the upper South, and rarely employed them in the lower North. Many slave owners insisted that their steamboat slaves working on the Ohio River be jailed in Louisville or Covington while their boats docked on free soil. Some owners, however, took the risk and had their slaves work all the way to Pittsburgh. Steamboat historian William Tippitt noted the regional concentration of African American workers. "Deck crews were as a general rule [in the deep South] . . . Negro slave laborers on most boats."[1] Passenger Benjamin Latrobe noted that on his lower Mississippi steamer the crew members "were almost invariably athletic negroes, or mulattos."[2] On lower North steamers, on the other hand, cabin positions were filled by a mixture of native-born whites, European immigrants, and free blacks. Lillian Foster, traveling through the deep South, noted that all the waiters and attendants on the *Ingomar* were black.[3] Another traveler commented, "I must say that the stewards and waiters on the steamboats of Louisiana are all Negroes."[4]

While most slave steamboat workers did not work in trades that bordered on free soil, they did travel extensively within the South. The labor needs of steamboat owners, who contracted workers for short periods of time so that they could dismiss them when trade was slack, ensured broad mobility. Unlike in other southern industries, slave owners were generally unable to lease their hands for an entire year to one steamboat owner. Slave owners were forced to move their chattel from boat to boat, and often from trade to trade, in order to keep their hands occupied. By shifting from boat to boat, slaves often also shifted to different rivers and thus were exposed to broader geographical experiences. For example, from 1856 to early 1857, the Louisville merchant James Rudd recorded leasing "Big George" to four boats: the *David White*, which worked from Louisville to Wheeling, the *Fanny Smith*, the *A. L. Shotwell*, and the *Woodford*, which worked in the Louisville-to-New Orleans trade. Similarly, in 1859, Rudd hired "Little Charley" to at least three steamers, the *Alvin Adams*, which ran from Louisville to Cincinnati; the *Time and Tide*, which worked on the upper Mississippi; and the *Kentucky*, which traveled between Louisville and Memphis.[5]

While such shorter-term leases were often the rule, slave masters were always on the lookout for more efficient, longer-term boat leases. In a September 1, 1846, letter, James Lackland, a slave-leasing agent in St. Charles, Missouri, urged a master to place his slaves on the *J. M. White*, "where there would be pretty certain employment for them until spring." He added that, "as they are now, they work a few days on one boat and then off to another so that you in reality don't get wages for more than two thirds of their time."[6] Long-term leases often reduced the number of river trades that slaves worked along, but repeat trips strengthened their social networks. Because steamboat owners specialized in certain trades, slaves and free blacks with long-term leases strengthened riverside contacts.

Agents like James Lackland were central to the leasing process and, consequently, to the freedoms of steamboat slaves. Many agents were young entrepreneurs who rented slaves from masters before subleasing them to steamboats at a profit. One slave named William Richeson recalled that a man named Cook "had hired him from his mistress and then hired him, at Memphis, to the boat."[7] Other masters paid agents fees to collect steamboat slave wages.[8] Keeping track of the comings and goings of steamboats was not easy, and some masters were too involved in other business matters to engage in this tiresome task. In either case, slaves often worked far away from their owners. It was not unusual for an agent to collect wages in New Orleans that ended up in a master's pocket in Missouri or Kentucky. Elizabeth Peace, for example, lived in England while her agent managed the leasing of her two slaves, Simon and Dick, to Mississippi River steamers.[9]

Agents were men of opportunity and ambition. Most lived in cities and used their urban residence to serve rural masters, whether in managing their cotton crops or in leasing slaves. Memphis agent George Cook (to whom William Richeson referred) specialized in supplying both his own slaves and slaves of other masters, to the *Louisville*. The slaves' various masters were not widely recognized beyond the ledgers of the boat clerk. Instead, they all were known as "Cook's boys" on board. Family connections often facilitated agents' jobs as labor brokers. James Lackland, for example, had a niece and nephew in St. Louis and another relative in New Orleans. Each sent letters to Lackland reporting on the business of leasing slaves to Mississippi River steamboats.[10]

Slaves such as William Wells Brown hired their own time, thereby eliminating the role of masters and agents in the contracting process.[11] While state legislatures criminalized the practice and southern dailies regularly railed against self-hires, labor-hungry steamboat owners, slave owners' desire for a convenient way to hire out their slaves, and slaves' desire for less supervision conspired to make self-hire common on southern city levees. Simon, a New Orleans slave, had a pass that stated, "The boy Simon is authorized to hire himself on any good boat running between this port and St. Louis or in the St. Louis and Missouri River trade."[12] During her testimony in the federal case *United States v. Louisville*, the chambermaid Judy Taylor told the District Court of Southern Illinois that "she has no particular bargain with her [master] . . . that she comes and goes as she pleases."[13] Similarly, Stephen Ridgely, the master of another steamboat chambermaid, told the Missouri Supreme Court in *Ridgely v. Reindeer* that the woman "made her own bargains with the boats."[14] In another court case, which involved a drowned steamboat slave, a witness commented that "owners generally come with them [the slaves] or send an order for them to hire themselves."[15] Milton Clarke commented of his master: "[He] gave me a free paper, to pass up and down the river as I pleased, and to transact any business as though I was free."[16] These practices were often institutionalized during shape-ups, where officers asked slaves "with passes from their masters" to come forward to have their passes checked.[17]

Of course, in some cases, the line between self-hire and freedom became difficult to distinguish. Some steamboat slave self-hires paid their masters a monthly fee but lived on their own, and sometimes they were able to support their families in this way.[18] Agents and boat owners complained bitterly about these arrangements, even though they generally profited from them. Boat owners, for instance, protested when masters sued them for helping their slaves escape. Captain Thomas Baldwin claimed that a slave named Harrison was "permitted to run about in the City of St. Louis and out of the State of Missouri from place to place at his own will and pleasure and without any restraint, and that [Harrison's owner] . . . permitted [him] to make contracts or agreements for the hire of his own services to others."[19] How could he be responsible for Harrison's escape? Free man of color Solomon Lynchhart, testifying for boat officers who had been accused of helping the slave John Scott escape, saw Scott and recalled that he "seemed to have no master. He acted as he pleased and let himself on board any boat he chose. I supposed he had no master . . . because he said so."[20] Agents vented their own frustrations with self-hires. James Lackland complained to his uncle frequently about the liberties of a slave named Lewis, who hired his own time. "I have not seen Lewis since he called to see me when I was in bed," he wrote on one occasion. "Abe [another steamboat slave] says he is on the *Nimrod* but I have no means of knowing when he commenced or what he is getting [in wages]. . . . I will try to find out something about Lewis before I leave."[21]

Imprecise steamboat schedules and the crowds at levee districts made slaves' off-the-boat freedoms possible. With boats circulating in and out of ports, slaves were able to elude masters and agents. One St. Louis owner, missing her steamboat slave, simply assumed that the "boy" was "some where about and would return again."[22] Slaves George and Baptiste walked freely through New Orleans after their boats came into port. Their master had to send another steamboat slave—a friend of the missing men from yet another steamboat—to find them so that he could ship them out again.[23] One St. Louis agent reported in March of 1844 that he had to find a "boy" named David "who had been employed on the *Ben Franklin* and had left her."[24] James Lackland complained that when the slave Abe came into port on the *Tobacco Plant*, "he left without leave or license—says he [is] used to doing as he pleases." Abe came back the next day, to Lackland's relief, and was promptly off on the *Little Missouri*.[25]

Free black workers' mobility was also restricted. Southern masters were well aware that northern free black river workers, and their abolitionist ideas, threatened the tenuous control slaveholders held over their chattel, so they worked hard to restrict their movement. While southern cities had elaborate systems of legal and extralegal controls in place to discipline their own slave and free black populations, they were vulnerable to the infusion of masterless, foreign blacks who left city quays and freely circulated through urban environments. The more the southern economy flourished, the more this vulnerability —and the corresponding danger of a loss of racial control—challenged local elites.

In the same period that state legislatures in Alabama and South Carolina passed laws prohibiting free black sailors on ocean-going vessels from coming ashore in those states, western river city and state lawmakers passed laws restricting the mobility of free black riverboat workers.[26] Deep South lawmakers were the most oppressive. In Louisiana in 1841, for example, the state legislature required that all free black rivermen and sailors be jailed when they came into New Orleans. In 1852, the law was amended so that out-of-state free blacks no longer had to be jailed but instead were required to obtain passes from the mayor's office when they were in port. In 1859, the old law was brought back and free black rivermen were imprisoned when they docked at the Crescent City's levee.[27] In Mississippi, an 1842 law made it illegal for captains and owners of steamboats "to introduce or to bring into the limits of the state" free black passengers, cooks, mariners, stewards, or those serving "in any other capacity." After this law passed, boat owners and captains docking in Natchez, Vicksburg, or any other landing place in the state faced a $500 fine if their free black workers strayed off their boats.[28] In the upper South, Arkansas and Kentucky lawmakers protected the rights of their resident free blacks to work on steamboats, but the regulation of "foreign" free blacks was widespread.[29] Kentucky's state legislature passed a law in 1860 that made it illegal for steamboat captains to let free blacks residing in other states leave steamboats for the Kentucky shore.[30] The Missouri legislature passed a law in 1843 that prohibited free negroes or "mulattoes" "on board any steamboat" from coming into any port, harbor, or city in the state.[31] Captains were responsible for submitting to local authorities a list of their free black river workers, who were to be jailed within twenty-four hours of their arrival in the state. Steamboat officers were subject to a $200 fine if they failed to submit lists to local police. Just as under the 1841 and 1859 Louisiana laws, captains in Missouri ports were responsible for paying the jail fees. Tennessee's state legislature did not pass similar laws, but, in Memphis in 1849, the board of aldermen passed a local ordinance that prohibited northern steamboats with free black crew members from docking at the city levee for more than three hours. "Foreign" free blacks in Memphis who stayed beyond the three-hour period risked imprisonment for thirty days.[32]

These laws apparently did not regulate slave steamboat workers. Although the statutes often referred to "people of color" and "mulattos"—vague terms that might have provided a legal loophole to jail slaves—clearly free blacks were the focus. And while steamboat slaves may have been jailed under an 1855 Missouri statute prohibiting people from bringing into the state slaves whose masters were not residents, this legal restriction on slave mobility was unusual.[33] In general, southern state legislatures did not regulate out-of-state slaves because they were perceived to be less threatening than out-of-state free blacks. Louisiana required slaves to have written permission from their masters in order to ship on steamboats, but even this mandate was often overlooked in practice.

Laws requiring the incarceration of free blacks posed a real danger to arriving boat workers, but they were not always enforced. One unfortunate free black steamboat worker recalled, "Sometimes they would put us in jail in New Orleans. They had very mean laws about coming into the state. They put me in prison twice."[34] Most free blacks probably avoided this fate, however. Steamboat owners actively lobbied against the enforcement of jailing laws by using their economic clout with local businessmen to influence police. In the most comprehensive existing study of this legislation, Richard Tansey argues that Louisiana laws were ineffective in stemming the tide of free black watermen into New Orleans. While the extent to which this same dynamic occurred in other ports cannot be determined without local case studies, the response of boat officers to the New Orleans law suggests the difficulties local authorities in other cities faced in preventing the influx of out-of-state free blacks.[35] The public clamored for widespread jailings, but the centrality of the steamboat to the economy, and the corresponding power of boat officers and owners, made thorough enforcement of the laws unworkable in practice.

Slave and free black river workers took advantage of the weaknesses in the legal system to lead vibrant off-the-boat lives. Despite jailing laws and the efforts of agents and masters to control their movements, African American river workers had considerable opportunity to interact with riverside slaves and free blacks. During working hours, river laborers met urban slaves and free blacks who worked on city levees in various capacities. They also interacted with plantation slaves who sometimes helped load commodities on board. Stewards and cooks made frequent runs into cities for boat supplies, and other workers took advantage of lengthy loading periods to run errands for officers in the hopes of gaining leisure time in the bargain.[36] Some just left. Amos Warrick, for example, after a fight with his boat's steward in the late 1830s, "fell in with a girl called Hannah Simonds" in St. Louis and "staid [*sic*] with her two or three weeks."[37] John Hatfield, a Cincinnati free black barber, "went up and stayed with a friend" while his steamer loaded at New Orleans.[38] In between cities, free blacks could sometimes slip off steamers and go unnoticed into the surrounding countryside. Captain S. M. Boyd, who ran the *Ike Hammitt* on southern rivers during the Civil War, noted in his logbook during a short stop near the junction of the Ohio and Mississippi rivers: "Nigger Charlie went adrift in the skiff last night at 11, went down this morning and found him at the Packet Landing. Got back to the Boat at 11½ and just as the boat was turning out."[39]

In this manner, African Americans were exposed to the vast and diverse world of the American West. "It would take many days for me to tell even a part of the interesting things that I remember [on the river]," former slave cabin boy William H. McCarthy recalled.[40] Perhaps influenced by the passing of years, McCarthy remembered the Mississippi as a place of wonderment and adventure. African American roustabouts memorialized this world and the search for love in song. In one tune they sang:

Been all a-roun' the whole roun' worl', oh Babe,
Been all a-roun' the whole roun' worl', oh Babe,
Been all a-roun' the whole roun' worl',
Trying to find a brown skin creole girl, Babe.[41]

Going up and down the Mississippi felt like traveling "the whole roun' worl'" after working on land.

New Orleans was the center of this world and the heart of the pan-Mississippi community. It was the meeting point of domestic and international commerce and thus an important hub of the broader Atlantic world. By the 1850s, over 3,000 steamboats docked each year at the city's levee, joining thousands of ocean sailing ships at the nation's busiest port.[42] Boatmen and sailors rubbed shoulders and exchanged stories in the city's boardinghouses and levee districts. While slaves and free blacks often specialized in one sector of the maritime world, there was also considerable overlap between ocean and river work. Men like free black mariner Amos Warrick moved between inland and international commerce, shipping out to Caribbean and European ports, as well as up the Missouri River. While historians have not thought to include the Mississippi in Atlantic history, mariners at the time would have readily testified to the economic and cultural connections between inland and ocean maritime life.

The city had considerable appeal to African American steamboat hands. The slave Sella Martin had "for six or seven years" wanted to come to New

Orleans to live and lay her plans in.[43] Steamboat work fulfilled her dream. Free black James Thomas, who worked for part of his career as a barber and waiter on southern steamers, was similarly attracted by the city. Thomas remembered fondly the city's drinking establishments, its markets, and its leisure activities—from watching African dance to betting on the cockfights he saw throughout the city. But more than any one thing, the overall mood of the city attracted Thomas. New Orleans was a "city prepared to take all comers," he remarked. "It was the only city I ever saw where nobody seemed to care about tomorrow."[44]

New Orleans's levee was central to the world of western boatmen. Four miles long, with a quay that averaged 100 feet in width, the levee was an impressive sight. Steamboats docked in a one-mile stretch of the levee that centered upon Canal Street, the avenue that divided the city's French and American sections. In this place, free black boatman James Thomas noted, there was a "wilderness" of "vessels from all parts of the earth."[45] Travelers echoed Thomas's awe. C. A. Goodrich commented that "steamboats are coming and departing every hour; and it is not uncommon to see fifty lying in the harbor at one time. . . . No place in the United States has so much activity and bustle of commerce crowded into so small a place."[46] Traveler H. Didimus described New Orleans as "a world in miniature—where one may meet with the products and the people of every country in any way connected with commerce." Strolling along the levee, Didimus found commodities of every kind: cotton piled "story upon story," flour "by the thousand barrels," "pork without end, as if Ohio had emptied its lap at the door of New Orleans." He also saw lead from Galena and furs and peltry from the headwaters of the Missouri, "four thousand miles to the northwest."[47] On the levee, privately owned goods were strewn about with nothing but little colored flags marking ownership.[48] When boats came into port, local slaves and free blacks anxious to carry a bag for a small charge into the city, or just to hear news from upriver, descended upon them.[49] The English traveler Henry Latham commented, "Negroes on the Levee swarm like black ants, dragging bales of cotton, rolling hogsheads of sugar and trotting to and fro from the steamers, carting rice and Indian corn in little square bags, from which the grains drop as they move."[50] One levee overseer reported, "Slaves hired to steamboats . . . generally commence work about day light in the morning, and leave off about sunset."[51] The city's draymen, most of whom were Irish, carted away the goods bound for the city. Didimus reported draymen driving "two and fro . . . breaking all the ordinances at once, cursing and railing, lashing their poor beasts, and not infrequently, and with more propriety, lashing each other."[52] A northern traveler commented on the "four thousand drays" he saw, which were "moving in all directions on the Levee, till its whole surface is alive with a ceaseless maelstrom of motion, accompanied by a noise of hoofs, wheels, and voices, almost deafening in their aggregate thunderings."[53] Slave vendors, in town from plantations outside the city, completed a scene of work and commerce.[54]

The slaves and free blacks swarming the levee were just a portion of New Orleans's distinctive African American community. Nearly 25,000 slaves and free blacks lived in the city by the end of the antebellum period, easily the highest concentration of urban African Americans in the South.[55] This was not a monolithic community. Well-to-do river stewards and barbers, many of whom were mulatto, moved easily in the circles of the city's *gens de couleur*. The wealthy free blacks of New Orleans endured increasing attacks on their civil liberties during the antebellum period, but they continued to enjoy an elevated status, founded in the French and Spanish periods of colonial rule, that was the envy of free blacks throughout the pan-Mississippi world. Light skin, ownership of property, and rich cultural traditions, such as separate, black-only educational and religious organizations and Quadroon Balls, which facilitated social alliances between free blacks and whites, all distanced the free black community from the experience of darker-skinned slaves. Abolitionist-minded cabin workers from northern ports would have been troubled by the prevalence of slave owning among New Orleans's free blacks but would have been impressed by their material success.[56]

Most boat workers were more interested in working-class amusements than the more refined gatherings of the city's black elite. Many enjoyed the city's nearly 100 coffeehouses, most of which dotted the fashionable streets between Decatur and Bourbon. Slave boatmen came to coffeehouses to meet agents and masters, and to drink, if the proprietor was willing to ignore city ordinances against selling alcohol to slaves.[57] Time with the city's prostitutes, who labored on the French Quarter streets farthest away from the levee and the most respectable mercantile establishments, was probably a more popular pastime. On Dauphine Street, one boatman found women "behind the curtains of nearly every window."[58] It was probably this neighborhood that prompted one pious traveler to exclaim: "The extent of licentiousness and prostitution here is truly appalling, and doubtless without parallel, and probably double to that of any other place in the whole civilized world."[59] Another slave boatman frequently visited a white prostitute named Madam La Blair on Bourbon Street.[60] Irish workers crossed the color line in their sexual adventures, too.

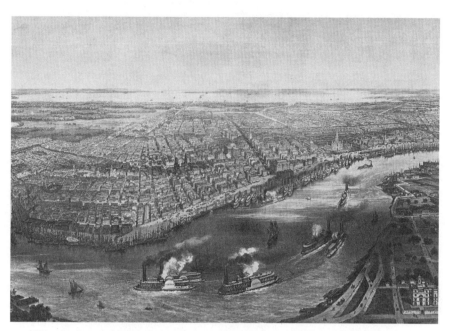

Thomas Muller's *New Orleans from Algiers in 1851*. Author's collection.

An Irish river hand recalled traveling to Dauphine to "visit" an octoroon woman, visits that, he said, "cost me very little—often less than a dollar."[61]

In the French Quarter, African American boatmen were familiar with several landmarks. Congo Square, also known as the *Place des Negroes* and, by the late antebellum years, Circus Square, was a center of African American life located on the backside of the Quarter, at the corner of Orleans and Rampart streets, near the swampy limits of the city. Here slaves from the city and nearby plantations came to sell their goods on Sundays, often to wealthy free blacks. In this economic context, slaves preserved African cultural forms much longer than elsewhere on the North American mainland—a situation that provided an education to visiting African American boatmen. James Thomas recalled seeing in the 1840s "blacks" dancing to "African" drum music in the square. A musician thumped on "the head of a barrel" while others beat on the sides with sticks. The sounds encouraged dancers, who wore tin on their legs to punctuate their rhythmic movements.[62] Another French Quarter landmark was less pleasing to the senses than Congo Square. On St. Peter Street was the famous Calaboose, the old Spanish prison that still functioned as the city jail. The Calaboose was the destination for steamboat slaves guilty of local misdemeanors and for free blacks arrested by levee police. Visitors frequently commented on the appalling conditions they found there: the crowded, unsanitary cells, the sickness among the prisoners, and the brutality of the prison guards. It was probably in the Calaboose that northern reporter James Redpath, on a southern tour in the mid-1850s, interviewed one former steamboat slave. Redpath went down "dark and filthy stairs, through a dark and dirty passage" to "a perfectly dark cell" that stank "as though the foul contents of a privy had been dumped there."[63] The outside was just as grim looking. The long, plain, plastered building loomed ominously over Chartres Street and was blackened from years of exposure to the city's soot. It was a symbol of the limits of freedom in New Orleans's urban landscape.[64]

A short walk away from the Calaboose, also on Chartres Street, in the lavish surroundings of the St. Louis Hotel and other competing firms, appeared another of the city's oppressive institutions: the slave market. Here, in front of crowds of wealthy French and English onlookers spilling out into the street, slaves from around the country were placed in hotel windows waiting to be "knocked down" by the auctioneer.[65] Slaves waiting for sale were housed in nearby slave pens where they were groomed for sale and inspected by prospective buyers. River workers had shared close quarters with many of these unfortunate souls on the decks of Mississippi steamers and were probably able to continue their relationships with them despite the seemingly impregnable jail walls. Slaves waiting to be sold, for instance, were often leased out to work on the city streets, which provided them opportunities for contact with the larger African American community.[66]

While there was much to occupy slave and free black boatmen in the French Quarter, they generally left this district for the nightlife in other parts of the city. James Thomas recalled that while the French Quarter "was very quiet at night," the American District "was all life."[67] This section, just beyond Canal Street, was notorious for its drinking dens where slaves could obtain liquor both day and night. A slave steamboatman named Peter probably was referring to this neighborhood when he reportedly "kept in the grog shops all day."[68] He might have also gone to underworld establishments on the city's outskirts. Boatmen would have known the "Black Rookeries," a small neighborhood of black-owned coffeehouses and taverns located in the city's third municipality to the east near the Pontchartrain Railroad. There were also a few choice spots near Elysian Fields by the swamps beyond the northeastern edge of the French Quarter. On Gallatin Street there were two blocks of bars and houses of prostitution that attracted workers from around the city. These social centers allowed for illegal mixing between slaves and free blacks and sometimes between the races—a fact that continually vexed city authorities.[69] For these elites, the specter of poor whites conversing in momentary equality with slaves and free blacks over a glass of upriver whiskey threatened the myth of southern herrenvolk democracy. While in the eighteenth century such interactions were exceedingly common in New Orleans and in cities throughout the South, by the antebellum years, interracial friendships had been effectively limited through increasingly virulent racist discourse and by laws that were intended to separate the races.

New Orleans was the center of a series of overlapping African American communities, both near and far. Long-distance steamers linked black workers in New Orleans with those in faraway northern cities like Cincinnati and Pittsburgh. New Orleans's boat workers also frequently traveled the few miles from the Mississippi levee to Lake Pontchartrain's docks in order to enter the coastal trade. And if they got as far as Mobile, western river workers could reship north, up the Alabama River, and into the heart of the state's cotton belt. But since New Orleans's merchants' strongest ties were to the "coasts," the plantation districts just upriver and downriver from the city—in 1860, nearly 60 percent of the 3,558 steamboats arriving in New Orleans came from places below Natchez, Mississippi[70]—New Orleans's slave and free black residents established strong bonds with deep South plantation communities.

One of these communities worked to produce sugar. The Louisiana sugar bowl, as it came to be known, spanned over 250 miles of riverfront territory from Baton Rouge to the Gulf Coast. The rich alluvial soils of the region, combined with its tropical climate, allowed planters by the 1820s to grow sugar in quantities unequaled on the North American mainland. Plantation houses, tucked behind the levee, could be seen from the upper decks of steamboats. More noticeable were the small docks at which boats periodically stopped to ship out products or unload supply orders. In some cases, sugar slaves even shipped their own products to market on these docks.[71] To maximize the number of plantations with access to the river, state governors had allotted planters long, narrow tracts of land with small riverfronts. The traveler Victor Tixier noted this land-use strategy. As he moved upriver to New Orleans he was "struck by the narrowness of the cultivated fields" that were "separated, one from the other, by fences built at right angles to the river."[72] Charles Mackay saw sugar plantations "bounded by right angles to the banks of the river and extending through the forest" with villas having "the usual porticoes, pillars, verandahs, and green blinds."[73]

Travelers also often commented on the slave culture that was in easy sight

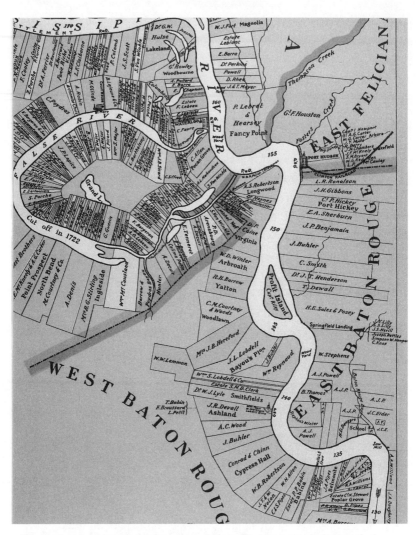

The land-use pattern shown here around Baton Rouge was typical along the lower Mississippi. Long narrow lots maximized the number of planters with access to the river. From *Plantations on the Mississippi River from Natchez to New Orleans*, by A. Persac. © 1967. Used by permission of the publisher, Pelican Publishing Company, Inc.

of the river. Mackay described "rows of whitewashed huts,"[74] and, in 1838, Harriet Martineau commented on the "groups of slave-dwellings, painted or unpainted, standing under the shade of sycamores, magnolias, live oakes [*sic*], or Pride-of-India trees. Many dusky gazing figures of men with the axe, and women with the pitcher."[75] Another downriver traveler found herself "fairly among the orange trees and the sugar canes: negro villages rose up on either

The Pan-Mississippi World

shore."[76] Fredrika Bremer noted the "caravans of black men and women" on their way to the sugar cane fields."[77] Daniel Nason saw "a great many fine sugar plantations" on which slaves were "ploughing and hoeing among the corn."[78] Slave boatmen also commented on the conditions they saw in the sugarcane fields, implicitly comparing the difficulty of sugarcane slaves' labor with their own freedom. "The sufferings of Louisiana slaves are awful," the Kentucky slave barber Isaac Throgmorton bluntly stated.[79] Allen Sidney, a slave from Memphis who claimed to have had a relatively easy time working on a steamboat, recalled "looking from the deck of his steamer" as slave drivers yelled and threatened 400 slaves "hoeing in the sugar cane."[80] A slave steward was equally moved. Every morning, from both sides of the river, he heard the "great bells" being rung and then soon thereafter the "crack of the overseers whip."[81] Another slave, who told an interviewer that he "was up and down the Mississippi a great deal," similarly remembered the great bells that rang each morning on the region's plantations and the cruel treatment that followed.[82] Even if these boatmen's accounts of plantation cruelty were exaggerated for the northern press, the contrast between their freedom and the condition of Martineau's "gazing" plantation slaves was apparent to both groups.

By the 1850s, more and more African Americans were passing through Louisiana's sugar bowl bound for the Red River trade. As sectional tensions rose, the Red River represented the southern slaveholders' hopes and dreams for the expansion of slavery. Slaves and free blacks had a far different perspective on a voyage to the frontiers of bondage. Working on a Red River steamer meant traveling for over 300 miles through the heart of Louisiana's and Texas's cotton economy. After passing Baton Rouge, at the northern edge of the sugar bowl, river hands could expect few urban diversions. Alexandria and Shreveport were provincial cities with little of the anonymity that the bustle of New Orleans provided.[83] Roustabouts knew there would be work for them when their boats reached Hempstead and Lafayette counties, crucial outposts of Arkansas's cotton industry in the southwestern corner of the state.[84] Farther upriver, along the northern border of Texas, river hands labored mightily in the counties of Harrison, Bowie, and Red River, where slaves made up approximately half the population. Slaves in this region were strongly influenced by Native American cultures north of the Red River in Indian Territory. They sometimes spoke Native American tongues, took Indian names, and braided their hair in native manner.[85] The mixing of African American and Native American cultures was the result of the frequent movement of slaves between Anglo and Native societies. Slave runaways enroute to Mexico took refuge in

"Gathering the Cane." From *Harper's Magazine*, 1853. Courtesy
of the Library of Congress, Prints and Photographs Division.

Native American communities that practiced a milder form of slavery than
was the norm in the Texas cotton fields. The Creek, Cherokee, and Alabama
nations were as likely to trade runaways back to Texas as to keep them, but
the Choctaw and the Chickasaw often took runaways as family slaves, who were
eventually incorporated into their societies.[86] But even in these communities,
the relative freedoms of Indian slavery were never secure. Texas planters made
unrelenting attacks in Indian Territory to reclaim their chattel. In this context, steamboats represented a distinct hope for fugitive slaves seeking to leave
the West altogether. But traveling undetected by water down the Red River to
the Mississippi was a formidable task.

While Texas represented the frontier of the cotton economy, the lower
Mississippi, between Memphis and Baton Rouge, was its heart. The Big Black

"Negro Quarters." River workers and travelers were able to see slave dwellings along the river from the decks of steamboats. From *Harper's Magazine*, 1853. Courtesy of the Library of Congress, Prints and Photographs Division.

and Yazoo rivers were profitable Mississippi tributaries that gave thousands of planters water access along the Mississippi Delta. River hands on steamboat decks watched as slaves cleared land before planting, hoeing, weeding, picking, ginning, baling, and storing acres of cotton.[87]

African American steamboat workers forged connections between river and land throughout this region, but the slaves and free blacks in Vicksburg and Natchez were the backbone of the region's African American community. The steady influx of steamboats from both upriver and downriver, and the constant movement of rural slaves running errands for rural masters, made possible considerable exchange of news and information. In Natchez, slave and free black river workers would have looked forward to the drinking and dancing that went on at a place called Under-the-Hill, by the city docks, below the planter mansions and mercantile establishments that lined the city's bluff.[88] In Vicksburg, slaves and free blacks met in the Kangaroo, a neighborhood named after its most famous brothel. Located just to the north of the business district, in a swampy dilapidated section of the city, the Kangaroo provided visiting workers a place to drink, fight, and gamble with an intensity that could not be controlled by the city's planter and merchant elite.[89] More respectable African American river workers had contacts in these cities, too. Steamboat barbers, for instance, knew well Natchez's William Johnson. Johnson's barbershop and others like it were meeting places for the white elite but also for a cosmopolitan group of skilled free blacks.[90]

Planters along the Louisiana and Mississippi deltas worried that these river connections would facilitate slave revolts. Most no doubt would have heard of the 1811 slave revolt that took place north of New Orleans, the largest revolt in North American history, in which hundreds of slaves marched down the Mississippi, burning plantations as they walked to the city. After quelling the uprising, vengeful planters decapitated the rebels and placed their heads on poles that lined the Mississippi. Slaveholder migrants from Virginia may have also known that Gabriel's Rebellion in 1800 and a sister conspiracy in 1802 were both organized in part by free black river workers. In 1835, four years after Nat Turner's rampage through the Virginia countryside, these fears boiled over in western Mississippi when a white outlaw, John Murrell, was accused of using the river to coordinate a mass slave rebellion and concurrent plunder of the countryside. In Madison County, between the Big Black and Pearl rivers, vigilante mobs hung two whites accused of being Murrell's ringleaders, as well as several slaves.[91] Later, during the insurrection panic of 1856, which swept from Kentucky to Texas, the Clarksville, Mississippi, vigilance committee urged steamboat captains to clamp down on the practice of employing self-hiring slaves. The committee further recommended that captains refrain from loading and unloading at night—the time at which dangerous communications could most easily be transmitted.[92] While the Murrell episode and the panic of 1856 were probably simply a product of planter hysteria, mobile slaves during the Civil War apparently did plan a revolt at Second Creek in Adams County, Mississippi, ten miles outside Natchez. While steamboat hands are not known to have been involved in the plan, historian Winthrop D. Jordan has argued that plantation carters used their freedom of movement to get word to different plantation communities and coordinate an insurrection that was hatched along the riverside.[93] At least twenty-seven slaves were executed during the panic that followed.

"Negro Camp." Slaves and free blacks often worked at levee landings throughout the South. They sold wood and provisions to officers and sometimes helped roustabouts load cargo. From *Emerson's Magazine*, 1857. Courtesy of Rare Books, Manuscripts, and Special Collections Library, Duke University.

The city of Memphis, the largest inland cotton-forwarding center in the country by the 1850s, defined the northern edge of the Mississippi Delta and its cotton belt. Its economic focus created a racial demographic that was more like that of the river landscape to the south than that of the land north of Tennessee. Day laborers from the plantations and free black river workers like Mathew Burton, Henry Gray, Jo Bell, and William Harrison joined with the city's nearly 4,000 slaves to create a sizable African American presence on the city's streets.[94] One of the more visible members of this street community was the local slave painter John Kay, who spent long hours painting colorful images of steamboats that later showed up for sale in his master's downtown studio.[95] River porters would have hurried past Kay to deliver baggage to hotels like the Gayoso, the Central, and the Commercial, which lined downtown streets just beyond the bluff that defined the city's geography. Such trips would have afforded boatmen opportunities to meander down Front Row, where many mercantile establishments did a thriving business and where thieves were known to do their work.[96] Boatmen could also stroll uptown to the Pinch, a neighborhood known for the safe houses that harbored runaway slaves. Steamboat workers in the know would have heard of the Pinch's Jacob Burkle, a white abolitionist with strong ties to the river community. Burkle allegedly hid runaways in the cellar of his Second Street home before taking them through secret tunnels leading to the levee.[97] Boat workers interested in more intoxicating pursuits headed toward the black gambling dens on Jefferson Street. Some of this excitement was found on Beale Street, the thoroughfare that would come to define the city's black popular culture.[98]

Perhaps even more than their male counterparts, slave and free black steamboat chambermaids docking in Memphis would have looked forward to the opportunity to rejoin friends and family. Chambermaids were very isolated among the nearly all-male workforce on steamboats, a situation that changed dramatically once they were on land. As in most other western river cities, women composed a majority of Memphis's African American population. Women headed about half the free black households in the city, and many chambermaids were important wage earners for their families. Life in the city promised a renewal of female networks that offered at least some extralegal protection from the threat of assault and rape that came with a berth on a steamboat. Long-distance mobility was even more rare for African American women than it was for men, and returning chambermaids knew that, despite the dangers of riverboating, they would be admired for their worldly experiences. They also knew that they returned with more money in their pockets than ordinary domestic servants and washerwomen would have earned in the city. Despite its dangers, the river was a place of opportunity for women.[99]

Although Memphis marked the northern urban hub of the cotton South, many of its steamboat owners traded with planters in Arkansas, another of the key growth areas of the western cotton economy. Working on western steamboats on Arkansas's rivers, however, was not a desirable job. Only 144 free blacks lived in the state in 1860, the smallest population of free blacks in the entire South, a situation due in part to the lack of a sizable city in the state. Boat workers passing through Arkansas would have had ample opportunity to think about the deteriorating plight of the state's slaves. In the early days of subsistence farming and small slave holdings, Arkansas slaves worked on a task system and their material conditions were not greatly different than the white pioneers they labored alongside. But by 1840, large planters increasingly dominated the Arkansas Delta east of the Ouachita and Ozark mountains and gang labor was in place. Boat workers would have seen these changes first along the Mississippi and Arkansas rivers and, by the later antebellum years, along the Red, the Ouachita, the White, and the St. Francis rivers. These were not pleasant rivers to work along for other reasons as well. The White River bottomlands, for instance, were swampy and clogged with obstacles that often required boatmen to plunge into water filled with water moccasins and mosquitoes that bred malaria. In addition, African American river workers knew that one betrayal could easily leave them building levees, clearing forests, and draining fields to fulfill the dreams of one of the region's young upstart masters. It was not unheard of for a master to tell a slave he had been leased to a steamboat when in fact he had been sold to a planter far away.[100]

Enslaved steamboat workers who traveled from Memphis to cities north along the Mississippi would have been pleased to see free land for the first time at Cairo, Illinois, though southern Illinois residents were rarely sympathetic to the plight of slaves. The Northwest Ordinance of 1787 officially banned slavery from future settlements of Illinois, as it did other territories north of the Ohio, but early proslavery migrants to southern Illinois discovered a way to get around the law. The territorial government, anxious to discourage slaveholding citizens from migrating to Missouri, passed legislation allowing slaves already in the state to remain in servitude. They also created a system of indentured servitude that permitted slaveholders to enter the state and then get their slaves to "voluntarily" sign indentures that often lasted a lifetime. These laws became a part of the state constitution when Illinois was admitted to the Union in 1818. Cairo may have been in a "free state," but most boatmen would have stepped cautiously onto its levee.[101]

Illinois was particularly unfriendly territory, but slaves "crossing the river Jordan" to freedom faced hostile black codes throughout the lower North. Anti-immigration laws aimed at restricting the influx of African Americans during the antebellum period were passed in Illinois, Indiana, and Ohio. African Americans who managed to avoid expulsion found that they were almost universally denied the vote, faced segregation in public establishments and schools, were routinely barred from testifying against whites in court, were excluded from jury service, and faced extralegal discrimination in employment.[102] Runaway slaves found that even the restricted freedoms these states allowed them were far from secure. Many white residents in southern Illinois, Indiana, and Ohio had migrated to these states from the South and were all too willing to return runaways to masters. According to historian Stanley Campbell, runaways to Illinois from Missouri and Kentucky were as readily returned as stolen horses.[103] Local sentiment toward African Americans changed somewhat after the passage of the Fugitive Slave Act of 1850 and with the gradual growth of antisouthern feeling in the North. The Fugitive Slave Act of 1850 toughened the Fugitive Slave Act of 1793 by criminalizing fugitive aid and forcing ordinary northerners to help apprehend fugitives. These provisions brought the abolitionist movement new supporters but had devastating consequences for many northern runaways.[104]

The marginalized status of free blacks in the North, and the strong proslavery climate in southern Illinois, made riverboat captains willing to employ slave labor on the trip upriver from Cairo to St. Louis. The strong economy in St. Louis also encouraged them to take the risk. By the 1840s, the city was clearly the most important port in the upper South. St. Louis merchants took advantage of the city's location just below the confluence of the Missouri and Mississippi rivers to trade with partners over a remarkably broad area. They controlled trade in the rapidly growing upper Mississippi region to places such as Alton and Galena, Illinois, Dubuque and Keokuk, Iowa, and St. Paul. They also traded with Davenport, which, by virtue of the Compromise of 1820, became part of free Iowa when the state entered the Union in 1846. It was the first free state west of the Mississippi that boat workers encountered as they journeyed up the Mississippi. St. Louis was also the home port for steamboats running on the lower Missouri River. By the end of the antebellum era, this trade area stretched through "Little Dixie," in the state's plantation belt near Jefferson City, to Council Bluffs, Iowa, 660 miles to the northwest, the jumping-off point for migrants seeking to go west on the Oregon Trail. St. Louis merchants supplied the commodities necessary to outfit the country's westward migrants and were essential to the growth of secondary river ports such as Leavenworth, Kansas City, and Fort Benton, Kansas. While frontier trade defined the city in many respects, the city's better classes also maintained firm contacts with the other main commercial centers of the western rivers. St. Louis boats ran frequently to New Orleans and to the Ohio River ports, further bolstering the city's rising economic status.[105]

Dred Scott, and his historic protest against slavery, was a product of the world of mobility and moneymaking that echoed outward from St. Louis's docks. After arriving from Virginia with his master, Scott lived in the city periodically from 1830 until his death in 1858. During this time, Scott used his ties to the city's abolitionist community to petition the Missouri Circuit Court and then the Federal Circuit Court for his freedom and the freedom of his wife. While not much is known about Dred Scott's life, his legal claim stemmed from his travel through the pan-Mississippi world. He based his petition for freedom on his travel up and down the Mississippi River with his master, John Emerson. In the 1830s, he journeyed to free land in Fort Armstrong, Illinois, and to Fort Snelling in Wisconsin Territory. Scott believed that his

The steamboat *Red Wing* at the St. Paul levee, ca. 1865. Photo by Charles
A. Zimmerman. Courtesy of the Minnesota Historical Society.

residence in free territory made him legally free. He arrived back in St. Louis
in the late 1830s committed to achieving his freedom.[106]

The kind of mobility through the Mississippi world that blacks like Dred
Scott enjoyed was evident every day on the city's docks. One can only imagine the conversations that took place in September of 1850 among the seven-
teen slaves and one free black who arrived from the lower Ohio and Mississippi rivers on the *Bostona*. Some of them would have told wondrous stories
of the steamers' decadent wealth, its fifty ornate staterooms, columned doors,
and richly gilded porticos, features that were so different from those of the
crude dwellings that most of the city's African Americans inhabited. On shore,
these African Americans would have met up with the thirty-three slaves and
five free blacks in from New Orleans on board the *Autocrat*, a massive, 846-

ton boat, which was known among deckhands for its backbreaking labor demands. Roustabouts working on this steamship would have well remembered one 1848 trip downriver when they were forced to hoist a record 4,407 bales of cotton. The sixty slaves and one free black on the *St. Louis* who also came ashore during this period would have had stories of death to share. Many would have survived the massive boiler explosion on board that had recently killed ten workers. Other slaves carried news from farther upriver. Eleven slaves and thirteen free blacks arrived on the sidewheel packet *Die Vernon* from Keokuk, while the 276-ton *Kansas* and the 454-ton *Iowa* brought a total of sixteen slaves and fourteen free blacks down from the Missouri River trade. Together, the African Americans on these boats, who made up but a small portion of the slaves and free blacks arriving in 1850 St. Louis, illustrate the tremendous breadth of experiences that free and slave steamboat workers carried with them to the city's levee districts.[107]

Many of these black boat workers were coming home. The free black Lewis Pope, a thirty-six-year-old steamboat fireman, came home on the *St. Ange*. Pope's boat arrived having just set a speed record on its Missouri River run, twenty-eight days round-trip to Fort Union. When he stepped off its deck he walked just a few miles to his family's residence in St. Louis's Fourth Ward. Similarly, the free black William Hamilton, a thirty-five-year-old steward, stepped off the *Mustang* to go to his Sixth Ward home. These men saw the city far differently than arriving boat workers who simply hoped for amusement. Returning to the city meant seeing loved ones who had existed only in their imaginations during their voyages.[108]

While the city was booming, the African American population remained fairly small, with 2,636 slaves and 1,398 free blacks in residence in 1850 out of a total population of 77,860.[109] In St. Louis, boat workers from the South saw more white faces than they were used to, but they found that the city's small African American community was very welcoming. When men like Lewis Pope came to the city he knew he was only steps away from his vibrant black neighborhood that constantly frustrated city officials. As early as the 1820s, John Peck commented that "there was an open space, of a square or more, between Main and Second Streets, and not far probably from Green Street. Here the negroes were accustomed to assemble in the pleasant afternoons of the Sabbath and dance, drink, and fight, quite to the annoyance of all seriously disposed persons."[110] Grog shops that lined the side streets leading away from the levee and were open well beyond African Americans' curfew served slaves and free blacks in open defiance of the law throughout the antebellum period.

St. Louis levee, ca. 1853. Daguerreotype by Thomas Easterly.
Courtesy of Missouri Historical Society, St. Louis.

African Americans congregated in places like Edward Matthew's oyster house in a section of the city near the wharves known as "Battle Row."[111] Here, dice players who knew free black Samuel Mordecal from his days on the river would have tried their luck with a man who would "bet his pile on anything that has the appearance of uncertainty."[112] Unfortunately for arriving river hands flush with cash, Mordecal usually won. Those who escaped with money in their pockets would have visited coffeehouses, grocers, barbers, and merchants, all of whom catered to the river trade. Passing by such establishments, William Wells Brown received "nods of recognition" from "several of my friends."[113] Well-to-do free black Cyprian Clamorgan certainly would have avoided a game of chance with Mordecal. The St. Louis African American community he knew and wrote about was a "noble class of men . . . whose good qualities are too well known to require any eulogy."[114]

Whether they were respectable barbers and stewards of Clamorgan's ilk or just ordinary hands, arriving boatmen knew that St. Louis was just as infected by racism as southern ports with larger slave populations. The upper South was known for its tense race relations, but St. Louis whites had a reputation for being especially violent, particularly during the city's frontier phase. Dred Scott claimed in his Missouri petition that his master had "beat, bruised, and ill-treated him."[115] William Wells Brown commented that "slavery is thought by some to be mild in Missouri, when compared to the cotton, sugar, and rice growing states, yet no part of our slaveholding country is more noted for the barbarity of its inhabitants than St. Louis."[116] Mobile river workers did not escape the cruelty of St. Louis's citizens. In 1836, a local mob, angry about the death of a city constable, wanted to find someone accountable. They found their victim in Francis McIntosh, a free black cook from Pittsburgh who had recently arrived on the steamboat *Flora*. The mob chained McIntosh to a tree at the corner of Tenth and Market streets and burned him alive. The flames ravaged his flesh for eighteen minutes before he eventually succumbed. The incident received national press and left a lasting impression on African Americans in the region.[117]

St. Louis boatmen in the Ohio River trade would have known several important river ports. Black Nashville, which was several days' journey down the Cumberland River, was James Thomas's town. Thomas was a slave barber and riverman who gradually earned his freedom, and middle-class status, with money he earned serving a mostly white clientele at his shop on Deaderick Street. He later made considerable money working as a barber on Cumberland and Mississippi river packets. Boatmen visiting from ports farther south would have noticed the relative prosperity of this black community in general. By 1860, the small city, which flourished in the rich plantation region of middle Tennessee on the northern fringe of the South's cotton belt, was home to over 700 free blacks. Together with the larger quasi-free urban slave population, these free blacks did a remarkable amount of community building. Boatmen could attend services at Baptist or Methodist colored churches, attend classes at Alphonso Sumner's colored school, or visit a variety of free black–owned establishments in the northern section of town, where black Nashvilleans congregated. Boatmen arriving in the city carrying one of the many diseases that plagued river hands could seek help from a slave root doctor named Jack who operated an independent establishment at 20 North Front Street. But while the city had much to recommend it, its white populace did all it could to dampen the enthusiasm of arriving river hands. The city was an active participant in the crackdown on free blacks that swept through the South in the late antebellum years.[118]

While Nashville was never a vibrant commercial hub of central Tennessee in the way that Memphis was in the western part of the state, there were strong economic ties between the city and local planters. Boatmen in the 1830s and 1840s were well aware of the region's leading planter, Andrew Jackson. Slave and free black steamboat workers were familiar with the Hermitage, located just upriver from the city, from the perspective of its Cumberland River landing. During the long hours spent loading goods at the river, some boatmen would have been able to slip onto the plantation and meet slaves like Alfred, Gracy, Sarah, and Sam who toiled for Jackson's wealth.[119] While Jackson was off fighting Indians, and being the champion of the common man, his slaves worked with roustabouts wrestling bales of cotton onto riverboats.

Steamboats that traveled up the Cumberland eventually wound their way back down it and returned to the Ohio River. From there it was about 200 miles, past several of the largest tobacco producing counties in Kentucky, to Louisville.[120] On the city streets of Louisville, African Americans, no longer subject to the suffocating political environment of Tennessee's cotton belt and within sight of free land, conversed about freedom. Historian J. Blaine Hudson cites Louisville Police Court testimony in which John Cain, a free man of color, "talked to [a slave girl named Mary] on the streets about freedom; and said he could take her off without any danger."[121] John Cain's confidence may have been misplaced, but his promises of freedom were not idle talk. Stewards, barbers, and ordinary river workers had extensive contacts with Indiana river towns such as New Albany, Madison, and Jeffersonville, where economic connections flourished despite the social divide the Ohio River represented. The city's growing free black population, which was nearly 7,000 by 1850 and concentrated in the western waterfront wards of the city, often helped slaves make the contacts they needed in order to escape. The abolitionist free black barber Shelton Morris used his position on a steamboat to coordinate escapes along the Ohio.[122] While one contemporary claimed that steamboat stewards "were compelled to use discretion in their intercourse with their slave brethren," many were willing to take the risk.[123]

Louisville was also known by African Americans as a city with white women willing to make what one steward called "a connection."[124] Historian Martha Hodes describes how black rivermen "shared information" about white women who would sleep with them. But, unlike most prostitution, in Louisville it was the African American men who were paid for their services. Free black steward Patrick Minor reported to a Union army commander during the Civil War that "the colored men on the river knew that the women of the Ward family . . . were in the habit of having the stewards, or other fine looking fellows, sleep with them when they were on the boats."[125] In one instance, one of the Ward women came to Minor's boat and paid him five dollars (two days' wages) to meet her while his boat was docked at Louisville's levee.[126] Such examples suggest an important way in which mobility unsettled sexual relations in the South. The Ward women probably chose rivermen not only because

Louisville in 1850. Courtesy of the Filson Historical Society, Louisville, Kentucky.

they were attracted to the masculine ethos of the job but also because of the greater possibility for anonymity that sex with a mobile labor force provided. In an era in which female sexual activity was highly suspect, it was safer to carry on occasional, clandestine relations with transient rivermen than to openly carry on multiple sexual relationships with the city's residents. The anonymity of these interactions was especially important in facilitating interracial sex.

African American boatmen like Patrick Minor who could tear themselves away from Louisville's charms were often headed to the Kentucky River—the gateway to the Bluegrass region and the home of most of the state's slaves. By the 1840s, this was the largest hemp-producing area of the United States. Hemp was used for rough clothing and as rope that could hold cotton bales together.[127] Boatmen no doubt dreaded the tedious work of hauling the coarse weed from the ubiquitous small farm landings that dotted the region anchored by Lexington and Frankfurt. These labors would have served a crucial function for the region's slaves, however. The river was a key means of transmitting information between Bluegrass slaves and free land, which lay just a few miles downriver.

The close proximity of the Bluegrass region of Kentucky to Cincinnati was the source of many conflicts over fugitive slaves. The most famous of these was the celebrated Margaret Garner case, which became the basis for Tony

Morrison's novel *Beloved*. Margaret Garner escaped from her Lexington, Kentucky, master with her three children, along with four other fugitives who left a neighboring Kentucky master. The party made its way to nearby Cincinnati but was tracked to a house near Mill Creek Bridge, where Garner attempted to kill her children so that they could not be returned to slavery. She killed her youngest daughter before slave catchers broke down the door and apprehended her. Garner was thereafter wanted for murder in the state of Ohio. Federal jurisdiction mandated in the Fugitive Slave Act won out, however, and Garner was returned to Kentucky, where she was eventually sold to the New Orleans market.[128]

Most slave river workers would have only heard of such cases since they were generally prevented from working on the Ohio levees. While slaves frequently worked on levees in Illinois and Indiana, many captains were more cautious in Cincinnati.[129] Worried about what southerners called "capture" by local abolitionists, captains often jailed their slaves in Covington, Kentucky, the city located directly across the river, before docking at Cincinnati's levee. When S. C. Slater, who was traveling the rivers with his own slaves in 1848, approached Cincinnati, for example, he "thought it prudent, from what we heard and saw to lodge the negroes on the Covington side overnight" because of "the spirit of abolition fanaticism" that was "so high in Cincinnati." The most cautious captains put their slaves ashore farther south, at Louisville, before heading upriver.[130] Despite the danger, some captains in need of slave labor risked bringing slaves to Cincinnati's docks. Allen Sydney recalled leaving the boat regularly: "Sometimes the boat lay in Cincinnati for two or three weeks and I was over the river a good deal."[131]

For these reasons it was mostly free black river workers who encountered the metropolis known as the "Queen City" of the Ohio River. By 1850, the city had 115,435 residents, a population second only to New Orleans among western river cities in that year. Cincinnati's vast population stemmed in part from the city's large manufacturing sector. Steamboats helped transform the slave economy of the lower South, making remote plantations economically viable, but they also enable capitalists to restructure urban commodity production in Cincinnati and to create racialized labor markets. Members of the city's African American community, one of the largest in the North in 1850, which numbered 3,172, held jobs as barbers, carpenters, cooks, waiters, and domestic servants. The demand for these kinds of workers grew as the city increased in size. The industrial revolution was transforming class relations in the city, but the city's black poor would have had little sympathy for white craftsmen who were losing status but continued to exclude African Americans from their ranks.[132]

Boat workers knew that the city's race relations were varied and unpredictable. Some of the nation's most progressive thinkers on matters of race lived in Cincinnati. In the 1830s, race rebels from the Lane Seminary and the city's indigenous radicals stirred up strong abolitionist sentiments in the city. They helped make Cincinnati a key stop for slaves who were escaping to northern Ohio, Michigan, and Canada. At the same time, the city's white populous was famous for its racial hostility. Race riots periodically swept the city. The white community had been concerned for a long time about black migration to the city, and tensions erupted when hundreds of African American boatmen came ashore in 1841 because of low water. In the pitched battle that ensued, white residents killed scores of blacks and destroyed enough property to hinder African American prosperity for years to come.[133]

Despite the city's contentious race relations, African American boatmen became part of a vibrant black community. Members of this community lived in every ward of the city, but gradually two important residential clusters developed. In 1828, Francis Trollope described "free negroes who herd together in an obscure part of the city, called Little Africa."[134] The neighborhood, one of the first destinations for boat workers arriving in port, was located along the central waterfront between Water and Third streets. By 1850, nearly a thousand free blacks clustered in this neighborhood, making up 5 percent of the neighborhood's total population. It was in Little Africa that a local observer interviewed old African American stevedores who could identify by sound each vessel on the Ohio River.[135] The other main concentration of African Americans was in the East End neighborhood of Bucktown, on Broadway between Fifth and Seventh streets. The 1,351 blacks who lived here composed just over 5 percent of the neighborhood's residents. The number of African Americans in Bucktown on a given day was larger than these figures indicate, however, as blacks from around the city frequently came to the neighborhood to visit its many churches and taverns.[136] Life in these black neighborhoods was hazardous, but many residents had slave families downriver and were reluctant to flee farther north.[137]

North of Cincinnati, boat workers labored for some 300 miles along the Ohio on the border between slave and free soil. They passed the small town of Ripley, Ohio, where the renowned abolitionist John Rankin owned a house overlooking the river.[138] They soon passed Kentucky and traveled the border between Ohio and Virginia. As the land grew increasingly hilly and sparsely

Public landing at Cincinnati. From the Collection of the
Public Library of Cincinnati and Hamilton County.

settled, they came upon Wheeling, the city that represented the most northern reaches of slavery. Slavery was never more than a small part of the social
fabric there, but this would not have been obvious to boat workers, given that
the city's vigorous slave market was in plain view. Virginia masters from as far
east as the Shenandoah Valley sent their slaves to Wheeling for transport south.
In 1800, Jack Ditcher, Gabriel Prosser's second in command in the Virginia slave
conspiracy of that year, traveled this route to the New Orleans slave market.[139]
Steamboat workers gradually saw fewer and fewer slaves as they made their
way farther up the Ohio River, but Wheeling was a reminder that the institution extended frighteningly far north.

One day's travel north of Wheeling lay Pittsburgh, the city with a populace
firmly committed to free labor. Antebellum Pittsburgh was also the home of
Martin Delany, the famous abolitionist and advocate for African American
self-improvement and moral reform who eventually became a strident emi-
grationist and pan-Africanist. In Pittsburgh, he founded the Pittsburgh *Mystery*, one of the nation's only black newspapers, with a readership throughout
the Ohio River valley. He was also leader of a philanthropic society that co-
ordinated efforts to help runaway slaves.[140] Incoming boatmen might well have
been skeptical of his temperance advocacy but would have respected him as
a towering figure in the community.[141] Delany's ideas and actions during his
Pittsburgh days were very much rooted in a pan-Atlantic identity and his
broad understanding of the working of the slave economy, which may well

have begun when he worked on the docks with other black workers, loading steamboats and barges headed south.[142] In 1839, perhaps in part inspired by the stories he had heard on the city levee, he traveled to Texas and Cuba, scouting out a possible refuge for black emigrants. During this journey, he would have traveled on deck, rubbing shoulders with slave and free black boatmen. In the end, he found Texas and Cuba unsuitable for emigration, but he came back to the Pittsburgh *Mystery* with a new appreciation of Mississippi steamboat economy and the possibilities for slave revolt. Years later, in 1859, he published a novel, one of the earliest written by an African American, titled *Blake; or, The Huts of America, a Tale of the Mississippi Valley, the Southern United States, and Cuba.*[143] In this novel, his protagonist is a runaway slave named Henry who uses the waterways to organize a slave revolt that encompasses the slaves living in the river valleys of the lower South. He moves on and off steamboats by displaying considerable knowledge of the boat culture in order to spread word of the coming insurrection. These plot lines reflect the reciprocal, nourishing relationship that Delany maintained with the river world. When black river workers came to Pittsburgh they would have admired his forceful leadership of the African American community, and Delany would have had great respect for their own broad horizons and protest traditions.

DELANY WAS BUT ONE product of the African American Mississippi world. From New Orleans to Pittsburgh, African American mariners linked Mississippi communities to a wider black diaspora. The impact of these links on southern slave communities was dramatic. Slaves like Dred Scott, James Thomas, and William Wells Brown were propelled to action by the connections of this world, connections that were created and maintained by the floating commercial laboring class on riverboats. Steamboats were central to the system of distribution that supported the slave economy and brought increasing revenues to urban merchants, plantation owners, and boat owners alike, but their functioning required employment of thousands of young, urban-living, quasi-free slave and free black laborers that often circumvented the region's system of racial controls and encouraged dangerous links to northern abolitionists. Boat workers who returned to riverside life after years on the river made these connections stronger. The experience of river work broadened their consciousness and even shaped the mentality of nonriver slaves and free blacks. Mobility nourished cosmopolitan identities that in turn created a sense of possibility among slaves.

The stories of mobility that steamboat hands shared were unusual, particularly for slaves. While slaves might be sold into another region or forced to follow their relocating masters, only seafaring offered the same kind of regular, broad patterns of occupational mobility that came with western steamboating. The interregional movements of steamboat slaves contrasted strikingly with the more restricted movement patterns of plantation slaves. Elite plantation slaves, such as drivers, carters, and other skilled workers, often moved around local areas during work, but most plantation slaves' working lives did not allow them to travel very far. Sunday leisure time, during which slaves frequently traded their own produce, allowed a wider range of plantation slaves to travel, but even on these days slaves' patterns of movement were distinctly local. Their mobility was generally confined to the distance they could travel on foot for a day or two. While the brutal workings of the internal slave trade ensured that slave communities in the West were far from provincial and that there was a regular influx of slaves from different regions, the day-to-day lives of plantation slaves did not generally involve interregional mobility.[144] Even urban slaves, the freest of slaves by many measures, rarely moved outside a particular city, unless they were sold, traveling with their master, or temporarily leased to the urban hinterland.[145]

The implications of the social connections between river and land, slave and free labor occupy much of the discussion in the pages that follow. First, however, it is important to consider the converse of the expansive world considered here. Unlike the diversity and breadth of communities connected by the rivers, steamboats themselves had a very distinct and contained work culture. While slaves and free blacks took advantage of every opportunity to leave boats and go ashore, most of their time was spent laboring in the tight, closely supervised confines of riverboats. The meaning of the black Mississippi cannot be separated from the harrowing conditions found in the wooden world of the western steamboat.

chapter two

Below the Pilothouse

The Work Culture of Steamboats

WILLIAM WELLS BROWN found working as a steamboat waiter "better than living in the city," but it was "anything but pleasant." "The Captain," Brown recalled, "was a drunken, profligate, hard-hearted creature, not knowing how to treat himself or any other creature."[1] Brown served passengers and offi cers in the cabin and was thereby exposed to the captain's watch and tyranny. Faced with the threat of beatings, as well as the oversight of wealthy cabin passengers, he knew that Mississippi steamboats were no haven of liberty. While he could come and go from steamboats at landings, most of the time he was confined to a limited world that ultimately rested on terror for its maintenance. Even though Brown's cabin job was in many ways less strenuous than deck work, the violence he experienced, which he encountered on land in St. Louis as well, made his life unbearable. Nineteenth-century white Americans sentimentalized steamboats, with their towering hurricane decks and awe-inspiring steam engines. Brown's dreams did not focus on these technological marvels but instead on the free states of Illinois, Indiana, and Ohio that he regularly passed while working.[2]

Historians have not listened to William Wells Brown's story of the Mississippi. Analysis of the steamboat work culture adds to our understanding of the various overlapping maritime cultures that enveloped the Old South. It is important to add Brown's western river inland maritime culture to existing studies of coastal fishing cultures and Atlantic deep-sea maritime work when examining the multiple ways in which African Americans experienced the

South's rivers and oceans. While African Americans in all these environments experienced varying degrees of mobility and independence, as well as dangerous and strenuous labor, the slaves and free blacks that worked on western steamboats were distinct in several respects. One difference was just the sheer variety of workers that labored on steamboats. No other maritime industry employed such a diversity of African American laborers. Another difference was that steamboat workers did not experience the more relaxed race relations that are often associated with maritime work, particularly on deep-sea sailing ships. W. Jeffrey Bolster argues that throughout the colonial and antebellum periods, long voyages, collective work, participation in "spinning yarns," and the ubiquitous sailor's tattoo combined to forge an integrated occupational culture on the forecastle. Steamboat voyages were similarly often long and the work collective, but riverside society was never far enough away for racism to loosen its hold on the minds of the industry's whites.[3]

Despite the differences between working on an Atlantic brig, a coastal fishing boat, and a western steamboat, the violence that William Wells Brown witnessed would have been recognized by any maritime laborer. Officers wanted an efficient and reliable labor force and were obsessed with labor discipline. Mates and engineers used a variety of techniques to enforce their will. Incessant cursing frequently gave way to kicking, pushing, and hitting—often with a piece of lumber picked up from a woodpile. One traveler, Mrs. Houstoun, was revolted by the "cruel and tyrannical manner in which the Irish and Germans on board were treated."[4] One free deckhand from St. Louis, for example, claimed that he was "dragged by the hair" to his work. Later he was beaten.[5] Watching a predominantly African American crew on the upper Mississippi, Arthur Cunynghame remarked that the "general demeanor of the chief mate . . . appeared the reverse of benevolent."[6] Another traveler felt that treatment of slave deckhands on his steamer "lacked humanity."[7] The crack of a whip often punctuated scenes of cargo loading and unloading. But passengers also took part in the abuse. One traveler reported using his "kane [sic] pretty freely" on the "insolent" African American who was carrying his freight on the New Orleans levee.[8] In a song titled "Roustabout's Refrain," African American rousters commented on the rough treatment. They sang,

> You hear dat whistle shoutin'
> You hear that little bell;
> Oh, swing around the derrick,
> We's got ter work a spell;

And dar's de mate a-comin',
De captain's up on deck,
Oh, hurry up, you rousters,
You'll cotch it in de neck![9]

Cabin workers faced no less abuse. Few were as lucky as Isaac Throgmorton, who claimed to have "never suffered any severe treatment."[10] There may have been times when cabin workers were protected from beatings by the shame attached to whites who were publicly cruel to servants, but evidence suggests this was apparently not a widely held emotion. Racist passengers were often violent. On one steamer, several passengers beat a black porter for accidentally bumping them with a piece of baggage.[11]

Chambermaids faced the harshest forms of violence. Isolated in an all-male work environment, chambermaids were vulnerable to sexual assault as an added exploitative component of officers' and passengers' efforts to control their labor. While native white chambermaids were vulnerable, the dominance of African American women in these positions and the larger social context of rampant sexual abuse combined to make steamboats a harrowing work environment for African American women.[12] Cabin rooms, officers quarters, and laundry areas at the back of the cabin all offered assailants fleeting moments of privacy in which to make their assaults. An African American firemen's work song alludes to the sexual exploitation of chambermaids. They sang,

I heard the captain say,
Shove her up my lively lads and get her in the way.
Shove her up, get her steaming hot,
I will pay you fifty-dollars to pass the *Alex Scott*.
(Chorus)

But everybody knows, and everybody says,
They know his tricks, they know his ways,
From time to time and never late,
They'll find him with the chambermaid.[13]

Just as women were particularly vulnerable to assault, especially in its most demeaning forms, evidence suggests that slaves were more likely to be attacked than free workers. Free maritime workers had traditionally been treated as bound laborers, but by the mid-nineteenth century, reformers challenged the physical abuses that flourished in maritime work culture. After 1850, when the federal government extended admiralty jurisdiction to the rivers, free river workers were protected by an 1835 statute prohibiting cruel treatment of sailors and by an 1850 statute outlawing flogging. Steamboat workers sued boat owners and officers somewhat frequently in several maritime courts under the 1835 statute during the 1850s. Workers brought no such suits to court under the flogging law. This does not mean free workers were never flogged, but it does suggest that it was not customary.[14] Even the threat of bringing a steamboat owner to court would have been a powerful weapon for free workers, since suits in federal court often led to boat attachment during trial and the loss of boat revenues.

Steamboat owners also had to be concerned about the possibility of lawsuits from riverside masters angry about overzealous driving of leased slaves. A Louisiana Supreme Court case details the story of a slave fireman named David who worked on the *Yalla Busha*, a Red River steamer. Sick for days with a fever, according to court testimony, he was unable to complete the final three hours of his four-hour shift heaving wood into the boat's furnace. Despite having a "droopy appearance," and his master's explicit instructions to the captain to let him rest until he was healthy, the captain ordered the engineers to force him to fire the engines. With these orders, the second engineer pushed David to the brink of despair. He "struck him three or four times" with a long cord, whipping him back to the boat's roaring fires. Some time later, David ended his agonies by jumping overboard and drowning himself. A local planter found him several days later on the riverbank "considerably mutilated and eaten by fish or something else."[15]

Although boat officers were anxious to avoid such suits, they apparently did little to change the tradition of slave driving on board. One traveler noted that overseers, with "whip in hand," drove slaves to exhaustion when loading and unloading at New Orleans.[16] Masters sometimes requested that boat officers discipline their hired slaves. One captain, allegedly acting upon the wishes of the master of a slave employed as a fireman, instructed his first engineer to "beat him [the slave] as the other boys and flog him if he refuses to do his duty."[17] One master, just as several of his slaves were shipping out from New Orleans, told several boat officers that "he hoped the mate would give Preston [one of his slaves] a good flogging; that he was always getting drunk and that he wanted to break him of it."[18] Another master told a captain to whom he leased his slaves "to take the negroes" and "make them behave themselves and work, and to whip them if necessary and to do with them as if they were his."[19]

The violence on steamboats was made worse by racial strife on board. On riverboats, racial conflict often contributed to the "rough culture" that characterized the less-skilled working-class of early industrial America.[20] On June 9, 1839, the *New Orleans Picayune* reported that "a coloured man casually employed on board the *Maid of Orleans*, was wounded with a knife and much beaten on Friday night. The cause, we learn, was his attempting to eat supper with the white 'hands' on board."[21] In other cases the causes of conflict were less clear. On February 14, 1864, the *Picayune* reported that an African American deckhand died when "one of the white hands undertook to beat the negro and that another one drew a knife and stabbed the negro."[22] African American boat workers clashed with native and ethnic whites on and off the job. As noted in Chapter 1, the Cincinnati riot of 1841 was started in part because low water had forced hundreds of white and black boat workers ashore together.[23] While skilled rivermen increasingly organized unions during the antebellum period, racial divisions among less-skilled workers, as well as the divide between free and slave laborers, made such efforts impossible for ordinary boat workers.[24]

An example of the dynamics of riverboat racial strife occurred in 1857 on the *Aunt Letty*. A petition for wages in federal court from the boat's free black crew documents a vicious fight that started at teatime on the banks of the Illinois River.[25] For reasons that are unclear, a white deckhand and a man from shore suddenly began to fight. A free black fireman watching nearby joined the scuffle and hit the deckhand. Three or four white deckhands then joined the fray and pummeled the African American fireman. At this point, a free black cook left the kitchen and pulled the deckhands off the fireman. As he did so he cried out, "I can whip any God damn white livered son of a Bitch on the boat if they would give me a white man's chance!"[26]

About ten minutes later, the fight resumed on the forecastle. Here the confrontation escalated. A white group, comprised of the deckhands, the mate, the watchmen, and either an engineer or a pilot, besieged a group of free blacks, including the cook, the steward, and several waiters. After an initial clash in which the mate and cook struggled with knives drawn, most of the African Americans scattered. The steward, armed with a sixteen-inch butcher's knife, was left to take on the white mob. The mob, armed with pokers and knives, quickly overwhelmed him. They struck him from all sides. Soon the mate had the butcher's knife at the steward's throat and was reportedly "sawing away." Only a thick collar and the quick action of several unidentified observers saved the steward from death. The clerk eventually warded off the mob, threatening to "shoot down" the first man that moved toward the steward.[27] Some time later, six African American workers quit when they heard the mate announce that "he would kill every nigger on board the boat."[28]

The sources of such violence stemmed from both the labor conditions within the industry and the broader trends in American race relations in the antebellum period. Although a variety of cultural factors in mid-nineteenth-century America encouraged European immigrants to take advantage of the privileges of whiteness, job competition was the key factor.[29] A Louisiana newspaper noted that "it is well known that there exists a great antipathy among the draymen and rivermen of New Orleans . . . to the participation of slaves in the industry."[30] According to historians Edward and Herbert Quick, "Even before the war there were enough negroes working on the river boats to make the whites in less important positions fear for their jobs."[31] The inland maritime work environment did little to bind African Americans to their fellow workers. Officers who were anxious to protect their jobs and make a profit had few interactions with slaves and free blacks that did not involve discipline. The fact that both black and white working-class laborers toiled under the same work conditions did little to create cohesion among them. The common experience of shipping out for weeks at a time did not ameliorate racial tensions, either. Interracial, class-based collective action was nearly impossible.

The violence that African American workers faced at every turn was made worse by the horrible conditions that threatened their lives. Steamboat workplace conditions were similar to those found in the worst kinds of early industrial environments. Boat snags, collisions, fires, loading accidents, and exposure to the winter weather together killed or injured hundreds of workers each year on the antebellum western rivers.[32] River workers traveled and worked amid the cargo, which could become deadly with the strike of a match or the slip of a barrel. In an era in which many workers did not know how to swim, even falling into the water could be fatal. Roustabouts and firemen often slipped on narrow loading planks, on wood piled too close to the guards (the railings at the edge of the decks), or on narrow decks and then fell into the river.[33] In one case, a cook drowned trying to draw water for his pots.[34] One traveler reported her steamboat striking a snag that "broke nearly all the glass" in the steamboat cabin. When the commotion subsided, the head cook, who was known to be "unable to swim," could not be found.[35] Because of these risks, masters often insured their valuable property.[36]

Boiler explosions posed a particularly dangerous threat. They became a national issue because so many passengers died in them, but it was the workers who were particularly vulnerable. Newspaper accounts of explosions illustrate that the casualties included a range of laborers, including members of the deck and cabin crews.[37] It was not unusual for a quarter of the slave workers on a steamboat to die because of one of these explosions. Firemen, who worked next to the boilers, were almost sure to die. Robert Starobin estimated that, altogether, several thousand slave workers lost their lives on riverboats during the antebellum period.[38] Alex Thompson, an African American waiter who was on the *Sultana* when the boiler exploded in 1865, recalled, "It was my duty as cabin boy to take a cup of coffee to the pilot twice a day. I was in the pilot house with his cup of coffee. . . . The next thing I knew I was in the river."[39] The former slave Betty Robertson recalled that her father died in a boiler explosion.[40] While innovations in boiler construction and government regulations improved conditions somewhat, antebellum workers all would have worried about this instant killer.[41]

Disease was also part of the day-to-day experience of river workers. Unrelenting work, primitive medical supplies, constant exposure to the elements, and contact with a variety of unsanitary urban environments led to recurrent illness among river workers. As they traveled up and down the western rivers, boat workers spread cholera, which became an increasingly common disease in the Mississippi Valley after the 1830s.[42] Other diseases such as measles, malaria, and yellow fever, as well as the more common flus and colds, frequently struck workers and kept them from their jobs for extended periods of time. One steamboat agent wrote to a master that "all of [his slave workers] were out of health—all had colds and looked badly."[43] Slaves remembered losing considerable time to illness. The slave Judy Taylor lost two months "to sickness" in her last year working on a steamer.[44] Another slave recalled, "If some disease broke out an' git a heap o' de crew sick we would have a time."[45]

While the terrors of physical violence and unsafe working conditions were broadly shared elements of all steamboat workers' lives, the experiences of cabin and deck crews differed. This disparity was one of the distinctive characteristics of inland maritime work. Although travel accommodations remained rudimentary on Atlantic ships, attentive service for travelers was a lasting innovation on the western steamboat. The impact of this innovation on the African American community was dramatic. Because porters, barbers, barkeepers, waiters, and chambermaids could find regular work in inland maritime employment, a broader cross-section of the African American community was tied to the river and steamboats than was the case in deep-sea Atlantic trades.

The full complement of steamboat jobs grew slowly during the antebellum period as the steamboat evolved structurally. Through the 1820s, steamboats

A steamboat waiter. Courtesy of the Filson Historical Society, Louisville, Kentucky.

were small, single-deck crafts with passengers and cargo together on deck. In these early days, each worker performed a range of tasks. A traveler on one of these smaller crafts commented on a "fine black man, who acted as barber, waiter, and man of all work."[46] Another traveler reported seeing a chambermaid waiting on passengers at the dinner table. By the 1830s, boat builders began constructing larger boats with the upper of two decks accommodating elite travelers. Shortly thereafter, builders added a third deck, the hurricane, which housed officers. The implication of these changes for workers was the development of distinct labor environments, one on the main deck and another on the upper decks. This basic division of labor continued throughout the steamboat era.

Members of the cabin crew labored amid elite culture. The steamboat interior, which was designed to attract passengers, became more ornate over the course of the antebellum period. By the late 1840s the larger steamers, particularly those operating on the lower Mississippi River, had dramatic stairways leading from the main deck to the grand saloon, where imported carpeting, chandeliers, long oak tables, and other fine furnishings could be found. The private staterooms that ringed the main cabin often included mattress beds, oil paintings, and glass windows affording views of the passing countryside. Commenting on these luxurious surroundings, one English passenger was moved to proclaim that river navigation in Europe "shrinks into nothingness, and worse than nothingness when compared to what has sprung into existence on the splendid streams of this youthful continent. Everything, too, upon the southern waters is cast in so much larger a scale as regards to size and comfort."[47] Other travelers described voyages ordered by bells rung four times a day for meals and afternoon tea. Leisure activities, which consumed nearly all of elite passengers' time, included drinking at the cabin bar, walking along the guards, or casually socializing in the comfortable chairs that lined the cabin walls.[48]

As with public conveyances in other parts of the antebellum economy, African Americans were not allowed to book cabin passage. Frederick Piercy described steamboats on the lower Mississippi as "floating palaces, open to, and for the use of, all who can pay, negroes excepted." "A coloured man," he continued, "however well educated or wealthy, dare not show his nose in the saloon, he must confine himself to the deck, with the deck hands and deck passengers."[49] In accordance with this policy, captains often required that passengers' slaves be kept on deck—a practice that seems to have been followed most closely in the deep South.

African American workers, of course, labored extensively in the cabin so long as they maintained a standard of dress fitting of their roles as public servants to the high society of the steamboat cabin. While cooks, hidden away in the main kitchen, were held to a lower standard, captains required other cabin workers to purchase clothes that fit with their surroundings. Chambermaids, who generally wore long cotton dresses with aprons and headbands in their hair, were known to wear silk on the finer Mississippi packets.[50] African American waiters and stewards wore suits, often with white coats, and were the "best dressed working-class" one Mississippi traveler had ever seen.[51] Porters were known to wear suit pants, fine shirts, green aprons, and badges, the last of which further clarified their status as servants. One Tennessee master wrote to his wife instructing her to get their slave Parker ready for labor in the cabin of a steamboat. "Tell him to get his best clothes ready," Gustavus Henry said, "for he will have to dress well everyday." Parker was also instructed to be "well-combed and as clean as possible" so that the captain would not think that Henry "had overrated him."[52]

Cabin workers had in common unusually fine dress, the duty to serve, and the multiple authorities to whom they had to answer, but their individual work assignments differed considerably. Waiters had jobs similar to those held by African Americans in the dining rooms of the West's finest hotels. William Wells Brown stated the job's requirements simply enough when he wrote, "My employment on board was to wait on gentlemen."[53] Waiters, under the immediate supervision of the steward, who generally hired between two and five of them, depending on the number of passengers to be served, prepared the dining table, served food and drinks, filled the coal stoves that heated the cabin, erected cots for cabin passengers when staterooms were overbooked, ran errands for provisions or other goods, helped cooks with dishes or slaughtering game, and cleaned the cabin—a task that included scrubbing the massive cabin floor.

Passengers frequently commented on the details of slave and free black waiters' jobs. Charles Latrobe, for example, reported watching two "supple-limbed black boys" perform some of these tasks. They drew out the twenty-foot-long folding table and covered it with cloth and silver, a chore that took nearly an hour to complete. After waiting on passengers during the meal, they cleared the dishes and then folded up the table, "straining with might and main till the ends met." "Before you could have believed it possible," Latrobe continued, the two were at it again for the next meal.[54] A. Oakey Hall also described African American waiters working on his Mississippi steamer. Early

A steamboat cook. From *Harper's New Monthly Magazine*,
1858. Courtesy of the Library of Congress.

in the morning, he saw "a heavy-eyelided negro" sweeping the cabin and another "shaking the large cabin bell," a task, Hall complained, "intended to di-
minish a passenger's quota of sleep."[55] He also saw "other sleepy waiters" emerging "from unknown parts of the boat" and working on the "complicated
machinery of the table." Minutes later, Hall recalled, the passengers crowded

around watching "with stomachic interest the evolutions of the waiters. They anathematize the laziness of this one, or commend the briskness of that one." They watched as one "cabin boy" put bread on each plate using a fork and a "dexterous" forefinger, as another came with a coffee urn, and as still others followed with more beverages and main courses. After the waiters placed all the dishes on the table, passengers slowly "edged up" and the meal began.[56]

On the larger boats, African Americans often filled jobs as cabin watchmen. Watchmen worked all night and were required to walk inside, through both the ladies' and gentlemen's areas of the cabin, and outside on the guards. In making these rounds they watched for fires and other hazards while the officers slept. In addition to performing these duties, boat watchmen were also sometimes required to wake during the daytime meals to trim the lamps in the cabin. Watchmen who were responsible for these tasks were able to sleep for only a few hours between meals.[57]

Porters were responsible for all baggage checked on board. Under the direction of the clerk, they received baggage from passengers, forwarded non-passenger freight to the clerk for entering into the boat's freight book, stored baggage in the lobby at one end of the cabin, issued baggage-claim tickets, and assisted passengers in carrying baggage off steamboats. Like their deck crew counterparts, their work was temporarily suspended when the boat was in motion. Their responsibilities resumed, however, at each country landing they stopped at as the steamer made its way up- and downriver.[58]

In cramped kitchens, often tucked behind the stairwell on the main deck, African American cooks performed the onerous tasks of planning, preparing, and cooking three meals a day for the cabin passengers and crew.[59] While the rich and varied food of steamboats was one of the distinguishing characteristics of travel along the major rivers, producing it took long, tedious hours. Working sometimes eighteen hours a day in searing heat, cooks labored in slightly staggered shifts from three o'clock in the morning, at the start of breakfast preparation, to midevening, when they washed the final pan from dinner. On smaller vessels, the first and second cook performed these tasks; three or four cooks often did the job on the larger vessels. In all cases, the first cook managed meal preparation and worked with the steward to obtain provisions. He also hired, fired, and paid—from wages given to him by the captain—the rest of the kitchen crew. On the larger boats, the kitchen crew included a cook specializing in baking bread and pastries, and another, the third cook, or "slush," who performed the most menial tasks: lighting the fires, washing the pans, and creating the pool of leftovers that was given to the crew to eat.[60]

Interior of the steamboat *Princess*. Courtesy of the
Louisiana State University Museum of Art.

Chambermaids were also part of the cabin crew. They were the river counterparts to the thousands of slave and free black women who filled similar positions in the hotels, boardinghouses, and inns of the western region. Because
of their gender and their intimate interactions with elites, they were the frequent subjects of passenger comment. Lady Wortley, for instance, traveling
near St. Louis, found that her "somnambula of a stewardess was a very handsome person" despite the fact that "her mouth was too wide." The quadroon's
"magnificently large" eyes reminded her by their "size and lustre, and their
languid expression, of the great dark orbs of the women at Constantinople."[61]

A chambermaid's work was extremely demanding. She performed a variety of tasks, sometimes with the help of a second chambermaid on the larger
boats. Chambermaids spent much of their working day in a small compartment at the rear of the ladies' cabin cleaning all the linen from the table, bed-
ding and towels from the staterooms, and frequently passengers' and officers'
clothes. They washed these items in long wooden tubs, hung them out to dry
along the guards or on the main deck, and, finally, smoothed out their wrin-
kles using coal-heated irons. When chambermaids completed these tasks they
returned clothes to their owners, returned linen to the steward, received more

dirty articles, and started the process again. Chambermaids were also required to clean staterooms, washrooms, and guards and to change passengers' beds, empty their washing bowls, and fill their water jugs. One chambermaid recalled having to draw fresh drinking water from the river for a passenger at maddeningly frequent intervals.[62] Chambermaids' duties took long hours to complete, frequently lasting from early in the morning until late in the evening. William Russell's chambermaid brought in his bath of Mississippi River water—which he claimed was "Nile like" in its heavy sediment—at five o'clock in the morning.[63] In other instances chambermaids were seen ironing late at night.[64] When the boat was not full, bedtime meant a berth in the ladies cabin. During full trips, accommodations were not so pleasant. In such cases, chambermaids would sleep on the floor of the cabin with the other cabin servants, after the passengers had retired to their staterooms. Sometimes they also slept on the main deck with the deck crew and with travelers' slaves.

Cabin labor was considered respectable both within the African American community and among steamboat slave leasers. Slave leaser Gustavus Henry, for example, assured his wife that their slave's "morals would be protected" in the refined environment of a steamboat cabin.[65] Free black cabin workers were often members of the small antebellum African American middle class. Although the job of first cook was a highly respected position among middle-class free blacks, the most sought after job among them was the steward's post. A supervisory job, but one that was still classified as a "service" position, it was the most prestigious position that African Americans could hope to obtain. African American waiters often labored for years in the cabin, hoping to earn the favor of the captain and be hired as steward, the "captain of the cabin."[66] Historian Carter G. Woodson called them the "fortunate few" among river laborers.[67] Quite a few river stewards were profiled in Cyprian Clamorgan's *Colored Aristocracy of St. Louis*, which includes biographical sketches of the city's prominent citizens. James Holmes, for instance, was a "hard-working" steward on the *Morton* who was worth "ten thousand dollars," according to Clamorgan. Another was James Nash, who displayed "easy and polite manners" and "kindness of his heart" while he accumulated a $5,000 fortune plying the Missouri River.[68]

The steward's job was multifaceted, demanding a broad range of skills. Captains required stewards to procure necessary foodstuffs from port cities and to coordinate the purchase of additional supplies during trips. These tasks took them off the boat and into a variety of settings. Well-networked stewards knew wholesale grocers and rural planters, as well as a range of foodstuff providers within the slave and free black communities. Frederick Law Olmsted, when steaming down the Alabama River, noted that "whenever we landed at night or on Sunday, for wood or cotton, there would be many negroes come on board from the neighboring plantations, to sell eggs to the steward."[69] Charles Williams, an Alabama ex-slave, recalled delivering possums to steamboat stewards every time they docked at his plantation woodpile.[70] Traveler William Russell reported watching from his Mississippi steamer as an "old negro," probably a waiter sent by the steward, rowed to Donaldsonville (a Louisiana town where slaves regularly sold their produce) and procured "fish, prawn, and red meat" for breakfast.[71] The traveler Mrs. Houstoun noted that steamboats frequently became "customers" for slaves selling their produce on the lower Mississippi.[72]

Stewards' responsibilities changed once boats were underway. They managed waiters and cooks and, to a lesser extent, supervised the other cabin workers. Also charged with assuring passengers' comfort, they planned leisure activities and made sure passengers adhered to cabin rules. James Thomas, a free black steamboat worker, commented that "the colored Steward was told to spread himself and spare neither pains nor money to make them [the passengers] comfortable."[73]

The scope of stewards' responsibilities, which gave these laborers a degree of authority that made them less than subservient, made many whites uneasy. One traveler reported great irritation that an African American steward with a "glistening face and bright teeth" woke him for breakfast one morning by suddenly drawing "unceremoniously back" the curtains of his stateroom.[74] Some white workers were unwilling to be supervised by African American stewards.[75] In other cases, passengers refused the steward's orders to obey cabin rules. One traveler reported that a fellow passenger rebuked a steward with the comment, "If it's the captain[']s orders, let the captain come and give them. I'm not going to obey a nigger like you."[76] Upon being told that he could not sit at the officer's table, another passenger struck an African American steward on the head with his cane. The man yelled, "No black bastard can tell me where to sit!" He then knocked the steward to the floor.[77] In another case, a steward who entered a white woman's cabin, which he thought was unoccupied, nearly started a gunfight.[78]

African Americans filled most of the jobs as barbers on the larger river packets. Four of the five barbers that census taker Ed Mulligan found on St. Louis's docked steamboats were free blacks.[79] This job differed from other types of African American cabin labor in that barbers were independent proprietors and were not on the clerk's payroll. They worked in small rented shops, generally at one end of the cabin, where they cut hair for fees and tips. Free black James Thomas, who often shipped as a steamboat barber, recalled "in antebellum times, when the large number of steamboats needed barbers, the shop keepers had hard work getting men to stick."[80] William Johnson, the free black barber and diarist from Natchez, Mississippi, often lost workers to steamboats. In 1850, he remarked, "My force at present in the shop is myself, Edd and Jim, for Jeff has left and taken the Shop on the S.B. *Natchez* and he is starting now for New Orleans." In another instance he wrote, "Claiborne leaves the Trade today to take a Birth on a Steam Boat."[81] For young journeymen barbers, working on steamboats was a way to see the world while saving money to start a riverside shop.[82]

Officers separated white and black cabin workers to the extent possible. The mix of Irish, German, white, and African American laborers who filled these jobs was always a potentially volatile brew. Many officers chose to hire either an all-white or an all-black cabin crew, thereby reducing the possibility for conflict. On boats with mixed crews, blacks and whites were segregated during meals. In most cases, African Americans ate last, following separate sittings for officers, cabin passengers, and white servants. One traveler reported on a lower Mississippi steamer that "the third service was for the servants on board and for the Negro passengers."[83] In the same region, another traveler reported that after the passengers' and officers' sittings, the table became "the scene of feasting for the black steward and coloured servants of both sexes."[84] Another reported the sequence of sittings as follows: "the passengers, one set after another, and then the pilots, clerks, mates, and engineers, and then the free coloured people, and then the waiters, chambermaids, and passengers' body servants."[85]

In order to combat the day-to-day indignities of their job, African American workers resorted to work slowdowns. Travelers complained that their servants in the cabin ignored them and brought them the wrong items.[86] One traveler remarked that her "languid and somewhat indolent" black stewardess "went slowly somnambulizing about, laboriously yawning, stretching herself industriously, and diligently doing nothing."[87] These efforts to control the workplace extended to African American's attempts to resist racist language. On the upper Mississippi, for example, one waiter refused to answer to "boy" —the universal term whites used to address slaves and free blacks on southern waters. On August 8, 1852, the English traveler Henry Arthur Bright recorded the incident in his diary:

The Work Culture of Steamboats

This morning we realized we were indeed on Free soil again in no pleasant way, viz, by the rudeness, and impertinence of one of the Free Blacks who wait on board. Loch asked him a question, and got no answer,—another, and the negro had still "lost his tongue" as completely as any village girl in England when you ask a question. Loch grew impatient, and pulling some things out of his hand, said, "Boy—what do you mean, —answer, sir." The secret was out—he had addressed the fellow as "Boy" at first, and with a malignant look, and a voice as spiteful as sulky, "I'll show you I'm a man," &c. &c. Loch of course complained to the steward, and he being also a "darkie" does not seem to have given much redress. The fact is, the term "boy" is only used in slave States, and *implies* a slave, a fact I never knew, believing it to be only another word for "waiter," and the same use of "boy" as of "garçon" in French. Loch had forgotten this too, or rather, as I think, he had forgotten that we were no longer in (or between) slave States.[88]

This revealing passage indicates the way claims to manhood were intricately related to the resistance of cabin workers to racism. Cabin workers were anxious to claim respectability and for their material and cultural efforts at advancement to be acknowledged. Asserting the right to be called a name of one's choosing was a basic way free blacks claimed their liberty.

Participation in reading networks was another way in which cabin workers struggled for liberty. These networks were particularly significant for steamboat slaves, for whom learning to read was a crime. By learning from each other or from free blacks during off-hours slaves effectively turned steamboats into a school. In such cases, the work environment, the site of the expropriation of their labor, became the site of cultural transfer and solidarity. Fredrika Bremer found her chambermaid "in her little cabin busily studying a large alphabet," where she "had seen her twice before so employed." "The steward," Bremer's chambermaid said, "had promised to teach her to read in secret."[89] Slaveholders were well aware of this danger. A *New Orleans Picayune* article tried to make light of the situation. The paper told the story of an African American steward who asked his captain for a note. Once he read it, he proceeded to correct the captain's spelling.[90] Free black cabin workers were often literate, and, by spreading literacy, they participated in a vibrant African American cultural tradition.

Cabin workers also asserted their culture when they played music during evening recitals. During these performances, African Americans drew on plantation musical traditions to entertain white audiences. Officers often sought out workers whose skills included musical talents. The former slave Will Long recalled, "Effen he could, de Cap'n allers hire deck hands an' cabin boys dat could play some kind ob insterment, dat how he git me."[91] One observer recalled one such group: "The upstairs band was composed of the barber, the head waiter and one of his subordinates. Laying aside their white jackets and aprons . . . these gentlemen assumed garments more appropriate to the evening, and an hour or two after the tables had been cleared away took their places in the cabin and struck up a lively tune."[92] While the demands of service required restraint during the day, these evening performances allowed for cultural expression, not to mention the chance for workers to earn additional tips.

Part of the cabin culture was the maintenance of a pipeline of information about escape networks that led from abolitionist organizations in the North to the plantation South.[93] Free blacks from Pittsburgh and Cincinnati relied on black steamboat workers to carry important messages to riverside slaves. Free black Cincinnatian John Hatfield used the mobility of his job as steamboat barber and his contacts within Cincinnati's African American community to tell runaways when pursuers were near. Free black leaders like Hatfield were crucial to the dissemination of underground news.[94]

Just down the steps from Hatfield's cabin barbershop, a much different African American culture flourished. On deck, the finery of the cabin disappeared and the goods of commerce were omnipresent. Every sort of commodity known to the antebellum West could be found on the decks of steamboats. When riverboats were fully loaded, boxes, bales, barrels, sacks, crates, and livestock were piled everywhere in a mass unordered to everyone except the mate. On the lower Mississippi, during the height of the cotton harvest, boats were piled high above the guards with the staple crop of the region's slave economy. Only the engines, the fire pits, the woodpiles at midboat, the main stairway, and the areas reserved for deck passengers at the stern were free of the myriad piles of merchandise. During the fall season, workers had difficulty moving about the main deck because of the sheer mass of cargo.

The deck crew's appearance matched their rough-hewn surroundings. Most dressed with their characteristic coarse pantaloons, boots, and old flannel shirts. In the winter, many added old suit jackets, mittens, overcoats, and whatever else they could find to brace themselves from the cold. During the warmer season, postwar traveler Julian Ralph commented on the diversity of clothing worn by a group of African American river laborers. They apparently disregarded conventional propriety, mixing and matching worn shirts, overcoats, and vests without covering the "oiled ebony" that was their flesh.[95]

African Americans on the deck crew were most often employed as firemen. Because the work of firemen was physically difficult, many officers considered it "negro" labor. Hired or leased by engineers, who supervised them on board, firemen carried fuel—wood or sometimes coal—onto the boat from shore and then, once the boat was underway, fed the fuel into the mouths of the furnaces.[96] Given the fact that antebellum steamboats often consumed six or more cords of wood a day, the work was time-consuming and physically exhausting, justifying the slightly higher wage firemen received compared to that earned by other members of the deck crew.[97] Officers required all firemen, and any deck passenger working for passage, to be on hand whenever more fuel was necessary. In long processions, firemen walked ashore, climbed the levee embankment, picked up several logs four or five feet in length, and walked back across the narrow boat staging. They then deposited the wood crossways in piles surrounding the fire pits at midboat. The piles surrounded the boilers and often rose high up onto the guards.[98] Firemen sometimes piled twenty to forty cords of wood on deck during a single stop. When boats were underway firemen worked in tremendous heat, feeding logs into the furnace every fifteen minutes, making sure to stir the embers to increase fuel efficiency. Fredrika Bremer watched the African American firemen on her Mississippi steamer perform this labor. "The immense engine fires are all on deck, eight or nine apertures all in a row . . . like yawning fiery throats," she wrote, "and beside each throat stood a negro naked to his middle, who flung in firewood. Pieces of wood were passed onward to these feeders by other negroes, who, standing on a lofty stack of firewood, threw down with vigorous arms food for the monsters on deck."[99] On his Red River steamboat, Frederick Law Olmsted also watched the firemen work the fires. Compensating for poor wood that did not produce enough heat, he saw them "crowding it into the furnaces whenever they could find room for it, driving smaller sticks between the larger ones at the top, by battering-ram method."[100] Charles Latrobe watched as "with a thousand grimaces" African American firemen "grasped the logs and whirled them into the blazing throat of the furnace."[101] Firemen were also required to haul away ashes and, when the boat was stopped for an extended period, to clean out the boilers, which frequently became filled with river sediment.[102]

In contrast to the fireman position, the job of deckhand was only occasionally filled by African Americans. Under the direct supervision of the mate and

"Coaling at Cairo." From *Every Saturday*, September 30, 1871.
Courtesy of the University of Iowa Libraries, Special Collections.

Wooding up on the Mississippi. Currier and Ives Lithograph. Author's collection.

"The Furnace." From *Every Saturday*, September 9, 1871.
Courtesy of the University of Iowa Libraries, Special Collections.

on call at every landing, these men were responsible for storing and retrieving cargo in the hold, where they spent considerable time.[103] Stacking cotton was a particularly important part of deckhands' work on southern rivers.[104] Until the late 1840s, and the advent of steam-powered lifts, this work was all done by hand. Considering that many steamboats could carry 100 tons or more of cargo, the amount of lifting involved in the job was truly prodigious.[105] In addition to these main tasks, deckhands also pulled the ropes of the capstan, the device that helped hoist cotton bales into place. They also cleaned the deck, pumped leaking water out of the hold, measured the depth of the river for the pilot, and took turns in shifts as deck night watchmen.

Whereas deckhands stowed the freight, roustabouts carried it on and off steamers. Mates generally instructed them to load from the "inside-out" and unload in the reverse pattern. Roustabouts frequently worked alongside dock stevedores, with whom officers sometimes contracted to help load and unload cargo in the major western cities, and plantation slaves, who hauled produce down to rural levees and sometimes helped load the boats as well. As one deep South plantation slave recalled, "We lived clos' to a boat landin' an' my father helped to unload de supplies from de boats when we wuz not workin' in de fiel's."[106] These duties required varying work rhythms. On smaller boats with fewer workers and less cargo, roustabouts were frequently on duty at every landing. On the larger boats, in contrast, the crew was divided into two watches. Each watch either worked a six-hour shift or was responsible for loading one side of the boat. Even on larger boats, however, all roustabouts were "on call" for large loads. Whatever the specific arrangement, the work was nearly continuous as boats frequently stopped to load and unload on their way upriver and down. One traveler observed that the "negro boatmen" were "hardly ever . . . permitted to sleep undisturbed upon their only beds, the cotton bales, and at all times are they summoned by the perpetually ringing bells to their severe labor."[107] Another commented that they ran ashore "like so many ants" at each landing.[108]

Roustabouts' labors required physical strength and cooperation among the crew, but the work also demanded a certain amount of skill. Loading cotton bales, which often weighed as much as 500 pounds, required the labor of two men holding cotton hooks, "the unmistakable badges of their profession," as one traveler put it.[109] Making sure not to get the cotton wet (moisture doubled its weight), the men rolled the bales across the gangway and pushed them into place—often high over the guards—to locations assigned by the mate. Loading other commodities required different techniques. Workers rolled barrels of molasses on board assembly-line style. Two men were needed to lift huge sacks of cotton seed onto the back of a third, who then carried it on board. Men heaved boxes of dry goods and slung hogs weighing well over 100 pounds over their shoulders, as teams of roustabouts drove larger animals on board. According to one traveler, roustabouts slowly persuaded mules, by pushing and pulling them, to cross a narrow plank bridging the boat to the embankment.[110] Such tasks epitomized the difficulty of steamboat work. One slave who worked on the deck crew recalled that it took two or three years before he mastered the work.[111] The skill required to perform these assignments was mostly lost on travelers who watched from the privileged perspective of leisure. One voyeur who apparently did appreciate these laborers' skills noted that although loading "was a great bore" to the traveler in a hurry, "to those who can take pleasure in witnessing athletic feats, or have a taste for the picturesque, it is full of interest."[112]

Slaves and free blacks labored on the same boats with native white and ethnic workers, but racial segregation was customary, particularly on larger boats where keeping the races apart was more feasible. The surgeon for the Marine Hospital in New Orleans noted that on large Mississippi steamers on which

The Work Culture of Steamboats

mess rooms existed, "white and black are separately [fed] and well attended to."[113] One traveler near Mobile noted seeing "a group of negroes on one side of the boat, and of the white hands, Irish or Germans, on the other, seated on piles of wood or bales of cotton, eating their bread and bacon, and drinking black coffee from an iron pan."[114] One early river historian noted that "their meals were dished up in tin pans set in rows, one side of the kitchen for the white men and the other side for the 'niggers.'"[115] Frederick Law Olmsted commented on the segregation of the deck crew on his southern steamer. The officers assigned Irish roustabouts to one task and African American roustabouts to another. "So far as convenient," he commented, the slaves "were kept at work separately from the white hands."[116] He noted, for instance, that in loading bales of cotton, African American hands hoisted them from the top of the bank and Irish hands received them on the gangway and rolled them into place on deck.[117]

Though segregation and persistent racial tension created divisions among workers, all members of the deck crew shared a rough-and-tumble brand of masculinity. Fighting, drinking, gambling, and petty stealing were all common practices among deck crew workers, white and black. Working-class people in western cities were famous for such conduct, but, on the riverboat decks, it was especially intense and visible. During the long journeys and in the confined spaces of riverboats, boatmen placed an emphasis on male values that accorded with their predominately homosocial world. Early riverman Timothy Flint defined the antebellum riverman's code when he remarked, "A riverman can get drunk, lie, fight, cheat or steal and do about as he pleases, but, if he shows a lack of manhood, he is nowhere. All are watching him to get some rub on him and if a man 'plays out,' it is terrible."[118] In his study of Galena, Illinois, police records, Timothy Mahoney found that arrests went up during the peak months of river traffic in the late spring. Mahoney found that during this period, arrests for "drunk and disorderly conduct," "quarreling, fighting, and disturbing the peace and quiet of Main street," or simply "fighting in the streets" were common.[119] The culture of river work caused similar problems for city authorities all along western rivers.[120] On July 16, 1857, after reporting a fight among a group of black boatmen, the *Cairo Times and Delta* commented, "How does it happen that so many colored blackguards are permitted to remain in Cairo? Where are these impudent niggers imported from, Cincinnati or Shawneetown? We suggest that the officers move them on."[121]

Alcohol fueled many of these disturbances. As river historian George Merrick noted, "In the old days on the river, whiskey was not classed as one of the luxuries. It was regarded as one of the prime necessities of life. To say that everyone drank would not be putting much strain on the truth, for the exceptions were so few as scarcely to be worth counting."[122] Even though it was illegal, many officers freely gave their slave workers alcohol as an incentive to work.[123] The practice of paying workers in western city saloons also suggests officers' general tolerance of the habit.[124] So prevalent was drinking among steamboat workers that one slave owner worried that his slave "would have a chance to indulge himself" with alcohol as long as he worked on a steamboat.[125] In some cases, African American workers bought alcohol directly from cabin barkeepers. When they could not buy liquor, African Americans opened kegs of whiskey being shipped.[126] Fighting and drinking were not much fun without gambling, so payday led to marathon gambling sessions that cabin passengers watched with great amusement. One Kentucky slave, who ran away from his master to work on the river, recalled, "I got me a job and worked as a roustabout on a boat where I learned to gamble wid dice. I fought and gambled all up and down de Mississippi River."[127]

Part of this masculine expression was a secular streak that continually appalled riverside evangelicals. The American Seaman's Friend Society was particularly focused on trying to bring boatmen back to the faith. The Reverend William Andrews reported in 1859 that he had the most success with the river families in portside communities.[128] Once on their boats, river workers were apparently more difficult to convert. Despite circulating over 60,000 pages of religious tracks and spending time on the docks on a weekly basis, one Pittsburgh chaplain reported only "one striking instance of conversion."[129] Pious residents of St. Louis formed special societies that constructed and maintained "boatmen's churches" aimed at providing a moral influence on the unruly occupation. But these efforts were largely unsuccessful. By the end of the antebellum period, chapels built for boatmen were gradually turned to other purposes due to lack of use.[130] One group of boatmen turned away preachers, declaring, "We cannot be religious while we are boatmen."[131] Nineteenth-century river historian John Habermehl, who had extensive experience working on steamboats, remembered African Americans as more religious than other boat workers but claimed that, in general, they, too, actively resisted religion.[132] Alex Mackay, a traveler on the lower Mississippi, overheard two black firemen mocking the hypocrisy of Christianity. They felt Protestantism conspired to deny them worldly pleasures while allowing elites to indulge.[133] Such sentiments were not universal, nor did they prevent African American river hands from singing their traditional spirituals, but they do indicate the western river workers continued a skepticism of organized religion that had deep roots in maritime culture.[134]

One of the most important ways that African Americans in the deck crew expressed their culture was through music. Whereas the cabin crew was restricted to playing music desired by a paying white public, on deck, slaves and free blacks were free to sing the traditional songs forged in the cotton and sugar plantations of the South. African American firemen, roustabouts, and deckhands sang during both work and leisure. As in other parts of the slave economy, African Americans structured their singing with call and response. Charles Latrobe observed that "their ordinary song might strictly be said to be divided into a rapid alternation of recitative and chorus—the solo singer uttering his part with great volubility and alertness, while the mass instantly fell in with the burden, which consisted of a few words and notes in strictly harmonious unison."[135] Firemen sang as they loaded wood into the furnaces, and roustabouts sang while they loaded freight. "The labor . . . is generally performed amid bursts of boisterous merriment, jests, and songs," Latrobe noted.[136] "The loud and plaintive singing of the negroes," traveler Charles Lanman commented, "gives animation and cheerfulness to all whose lot it is to toil."[137] Mrs. Trollope concurred, writing, "We were much pleased by the chant with which the Negro boatmen regulate and beguile their labour on the river."[138] Fredrika Bremer noted that firemen timed their singing to the cadence of their work heaving logs into the furnace of her steamer.[139] Roustabouts sang songs as they moved up and down the staging loading freight.[140] One former slave recalled that "de work went ahead easier when we was singin'."[141] Singing created a collective consciousness among African Americans, helping to restore their humanity amid the indignities and monotony of their labors.[142]

Dancing was another way that African Americans expressed their culture. Traveling on the Alabama River, Barbara Bodichon noted a common sight in her diary: "Last night the negro sailors danced while one played on the violin. It was the drollest sight in the world. They enjoyed it so intensely and moved with such extraordinary agility—so fast and then so slow, now all on their heels then all on their toes."[143] Dancing was a way for blacks to reclaim their bodies from the oppression of both slave and wage labor.[144]

While some travelers took singing, dancing, and music playing as evidence of the "happiness" of slaves with their status, in reality, these cultural practices reflected slave and free black resistance to the domination of white culture. Martin Delany described river workers' "apparently cheerful" songs as "wailing lamentations" that "gushed out in insuppressible jets from the agitated fountains of their souls, as if in unison with the restless current of the great river upon which they were compelled to toil."[145] African American boat workers used their lyrics to challenge and mock the white culture pressing upon them.[146] As one former slave put it, "If they liked or disliked a boat their song expressed their feelings."[147] In some songs, river workers lamented loved ones lost or left behind.[148] In others, slaves mocked particular officers or celebrated their own propensity to steal.[149] One song about stealing contained the stanza, "master had a bran' new coat, He hung it on the wall, Nigger stole his master's coat, An' wore it to the ball."[150] Still other songs played with the fears of whites about miscegenation. One song, for instance, contained the lyrics "I never kissed a white girl and I hope I never will, For I is afraid I'd never get my fill."[151] Another song imagined "white trash" doing the labors of the world.[152] Still another quietly bargained for better conditions. Through song, slaves told officers that good victuals and decent treatment could be the difference between hard work and a work slowdown:

> De Cap'n am a white man,
> De mate he treat us right,
> De cook he feeds a plenty,
> Dat why we works day and night.[153]

Fredrika Bremer noted similar subtle bargaining. She heard slave workers incorporate into their song "a hint that the singing would become doubly merry, and the singers would sing twice as well, if they could have a little brandy when they reached Louisville, and that they could buy brandy if they could have a little money, and so on."[154] While some songs bargained for better treatment others simply expressed steamboat workers' exploited condition. In his journey to New Orleans Frederick Law Olmsted recorded a roustabout lament:

> Oh, work and talk and holler,
>   Oh, John, &c.
> Massa guv me a dollar,
>   Oh, John, &c.
> Don't cry your eyes out, honey,
>   Oh, John, &c.
> I'm gwine to get some money,
>   Oh, John, &c.

But I'll come back to-morrow,
   Oh, John, &c.
So work and talk and holler,
   Oh, John, &c.
Work all day and Sunday,
   Oh, John, &c.
Massa get de money,
   Oh, John, &c.[155]

Through song, roustabouts expressed their unity and continued strength while also telling travelers and officers how they felt about slavery.

SLAVE AND FREE BLACK river hands worked in one of the most unique environments in antebellum America. Steamboats were products of the industrial revolution, yet the organization of their work crews owed much to basic divisions of labor that were inherited from Atlantic maritime culture. Maritime capitalists had long ago decided that the mass movement of materials demanded rigid discipline and hierarchical management. Thus the disparity in power between the mostly native white officers and the motley mix of European immigrants, African Americans, and native whites in the deck and cabin crews reproduced enduring conflicts. But while steamboats at once looked backward to the age of sail, they also reflected contemporary trends in the organization of labor. For many Americans, in a world where plantations were thriving and the factory system was starting to take root, steamboats were a visible expression of the increasing divisions between rich and poor. The small-scale farmer who floated his crop to market on a flatboat, the craftsman who produced goods for his neighbors, and the slave who labored shoulder to shoulder with a frontier farmer were all being transformed by the capitalist ethos that defined the era.

Slaves and free blacks experienced these transformations with the threat of death all around them. They knew they could well end up laboring to their demise on a plantation in the deep South or be killed in an instant if a steamboat engineer valued speed over safety. But what filled their day-to-day experience was backbreaking work. Their vision of the river was not from the pilothouse window or the couches of the cabin but from the lower decks, where few had the time to watch the grand scenery of the passing landscape. Their work engaged the full range of the African American community, including men and women, skilled and unskilled workers. United by constant toil, this diverse workforce ensured that there was no one African American experience on steamboats. Deck crews were male and more likely than cabin crews to be comprised of slaves; they demonstrated a more rough-and-tumble form of masculinity. Cabin crews were more heavily staffed by free blacks and were defined at once by femininity and a respectable brand of masculinity. This variation is what distinguished the African American experience on steamboats within the broader economy.

The struggle against slavery occupied African Americans no matter what their position was on board and no matter how poorly officers, masters, and passengers treated them. Regardless of the degree to which individual workers suffered under tyrannical captains or the dangerous work conditions associated with steamboats, there was widespread willingness to challenge the institution of slavery. Slave and free black workers knew they were in a strategic position in the economy. Behind the bales of Kentucky tobacco and Tennessee cotton and the sacks of grain from the Ohio Valley, in the empty chambers of staterooms, and in bustling kitchens, they could talk and plan with horizons before them that were unimaginable from the vantage point of plantation cabins. There were secrets and dreams on the slave Mississippi. There was a world that masters, officers, and well-heeled passengers could not control.

chapter three

Living Blood for Gold

African American Families and the Mississippi River

WILLIAM WELLS BROWN knew well the dual impact of Mississippi River steamboats on African American families. Brown's job as a waiter and steward put him in close contact with the lively trade in human flesh that fueled the expansion of the plantation South. "A drove of slaves on a southern steamboat," Brown commented, "is an occurrence so common, that no one, not even the passengers, appears to notice it, even though their chains clank at every step."[1] Brown's knowledge of the slave trade became even more intimate when he was hired out by Mr. Walker, a "soul driver," who had seen him working on a Mississippi steamer. Journeying from St. Louis to New Orleans, Brown spent a full year overseeing the commodification of slave bodies and the destruction of slave families. He described three separate trips from Missouri to the lower Mississippi markets during his year of service. In the Missouri component of this commerce, he helped gather slaves from as far west as Jefferson City and helped store them in St. Louis jails while they waited for steamboat transport south. He described the separation of a mother from her infant and the tortured visits of a woman to the St. Louis jail where she was "several times . . . refused admittance" to see her sold husband.[2] Brown was "heart sick at seeing his fellow creatures bought and sold."[3]

Brown's own family ties fueled his empathy. Each trip back to St. Louis reunited him with his mother, his two brothers, and his sister—a family whom he cared for deeply. After his visits, he returned "to the boat" and his "bunk" in time for the next downriver trip.[4] When his sister suggested that he escape since "on a steamboat" there was "some chance . . . to escape to the land of liberty," Brown felt the conflict that was common among so many slaves. He longed for liberty but swore to himself that he would never "leave them [his family] in the hand of the oppressor."[5] Family ties bound him to a job that fostered loneliness and suffering.

Like all slaves, Brown worried that he would eventually be sold away from his kin. Cabin workers like Brown had valuable skills that drew high prices in deep South markets. At the same time, however, steamboat slaves were partially insulated from the market by their independent culture. Buyers were afraid of river hands' worldliness and knew that the mobile river culture bred a recalcitrance that could well make for poor investments. The famous Mississippi slave trader R. C. Ballard knew well the reputation of steamboat hands. When he received a river slave in payment for a debt, he advised a business associate to sell him quickly "as he is a steamboat slave" rather than bring him onto Ballard's plantation.[6] Slaveholders knew that men like Brown were useful but that they also threatened plantation discipline.

Brown's life indicates the paradoxical nature of the relationship of slave families to the Mississippi. Steamboats were the sites of the most extreme suffering and the most devastating violence to familial relationships. Many slaves sold South would never hear from loved ones again. At the same time, the river industry was also a resource that bound slave family members emotionally and materially. Steamboat slaves like Brown were not only able to keep in touch with family in the home port; they were also part of an industry that encouraged a variety of moneymaking activities that sustained family members. More dramatically, slave and free black river workers were sometimes able to use their mobility to make connections with family members who were the victims of the internal slave trade. In such cases, African American steamboat workers acted as part of the hidden slave communication network that operated out of the sight of slave masters and steamboat officers. These networks expanded the slave community by linking local neighborhoods to distant peoples and ideas. Thus while river capitalists and slave masters united to use Mississippi steamboats to destroy the families of slaves living in the western region of the South, African American steamboat workers labored just as hard to maintain the fragile bonds of affection that made life meaningful.

The expansion of the antebellum economy westward provided the economic framework for the slave Mississippi. The congressional ban on slave importation in 1808 forced planters to look to internal trading to meet the need for more workers in expanding areas of the economy. In the 1820s and 1830s, pioneer slaveholders moved from the eastern seaboard to new territories along the Ohio and Mississippi rivers. During these years, western planters in both the upper and lower South imported more slaves from the east than they exported. This situation changed during the later antebellum period as slaveholders in Missouri, Kentucky, and eventually Tennessee began to find it more profitable to sell slaves to the Southwest, where fertile soils and longer growing seasons made slaves especially valuable. These western states joined eastern states such as Virginia and Maryland as the largest exporters of slaves. During these years, the likelihood of being "sold downriver" increased dramatically.

The destructive impact of this forced migration on slave families cannot be overestimated. Planters sold hundreds of thousands of slaves to the cotton and sugar economies of the Southwest during the antebellum period. Slave children faced a 30 percent chance of being sold south during their lifetimes.[7] The particularities of the slave market worked to ensure that most of these victims were not sold in family groups but as individuals. Few buyers were looking to purchase a whole family. Sugar planters, for instance, wanted males, who were considered more suitable than women for the notoriously physically demanding tasks of planting, harvesting, and refining sugar. The separation of slave families was exacerbated by the age selectivity of the trade. Slave traders were mostly interested in dealing in young adults, where the largest profits were to be found. Traders faced a range of fixed costs in the purchasing, transporting, and sale of slaves that encouraged them to deal in high-value workers. For slaves, this meant that the very young and very old were likely to watch as traders carried away their young adult family members.[8] In these ways slave families became victims of the new geography of slavery.

There is no way of knowing how many slave traders shipped their chattel on western steamboats. Nor is it possible to calculate from existing evidence what percentage of all slaves sold in the antebellum years were shipped by steamboat. Anecdotal evidence, however, indicates the centrality of the river to the labor economy. New Orleans trader C. M. Rutherford wrote R. C. Ballard that his slave Amanda had "landed safe" in the Crescent City but he was sorry she was not shipped "six weeks earlier . . . since I could have gotten a better price."[9] In another case, Rutherford wrote that he had "thirteen Negroes" on board his Mississippi steamer and that he planned to "get off at Natchez" where he thought he would have a "chance to sell them."[10] From his rented slave auction house in Natchez, trader James R. Franklin noted that

The Last Sale of Slaves on the Courthouse Steps, 1860. Oil on canvas
by Thomas Satterwhite Noble, ca. 1871. Courtesy of the
Missouri Historical Society, St. Louis.

"the Negroes are coming down the river very fast" and that he was worried
that the market would not be able to "sustain present prices."[11]

Steamboats helped traders extend the reach of the market to all areas of
the upper South. They facilitated trading at remote landings and jails where
nefarious deals settled the fate of unfortunate slaves. While many rural slaves
were shipped directly south from the country, upper South cities were often a
first stopping point. Virginia slaves were driven overland to Wheeling, where
a lively trade in human flesh developed. Just miles from free soil, slaves began
a several-week journey that would carry them to the heart of the slave economy. By midcentury there were at least a dozen interstate traders in Louisville, some of whom handled hundreds of slaves at a time in their yards. They
paid as little as three dollars to ship their chattel as deck passengers to New
Orleans.[12] C. M. Rutherford, desperate for slaves for his New Orleans slave
pen, sent his agent to Louisville in 1849 with the instructions to "buy all the
good Negroes he can lay his hands on." He urged his agent to "make some
arrangements through the banks of Louisville" in order to finance a massive
buying venture.[13] While Louisville had a vigorous trade by the late antebellum years, Lexington contained Kentucky's largest slave market. Here, Lewis

Families and the Mississippi

Lynch's slave market, 104 Locust Street. Daguerreotype by Thomas Easterly, ca. 1852. Courtesy of the Missouri Historical Society, St. Louis.

C. Robards was a prominent dealer. Robards's business transporting slaves downriver was so large that he found it profitable to sell some of his slaves to smaller dealers rather than manage the shipment of all his purchases himself. His Negro jail was a converted old theater where octoroons and mulattos in the "fancy girl" trade were stripped and displayed for eager buyers in the lavish upper chambers. Less valuable slaves were confined in the basement or "dungeon," where they waited in darkness for their voyage away from their home.[14] In Missouri, the St. Louis trade centered on the steps of the courthouse, the building where Dred Scott petitioned for his freedom. Memorialized by one proslavery city newspaperman as a building "dedicated to the true spirit of freedom," the courthouse was the site of hundreds of family separations in the final years of slavery.[15] Firms like Blakey and McAfee, at 93 Olive Street, were willing to "visit persons wanting to sell from any part of the state."[16] Like other major traders, they were in the business of bringing large numbers of slaves south in a single voyage, so their business demanded a size and scale that rivaled the city's most prosperous mercantile establishments. As the antebellum period progressed, even cotton ports in the mid–South like

Memphis became drawn into the trade with the Southwest. River traveler Charles Mackay captured the horror of the slave trade in a poem he penned from the decks of his downriver steamer. He wrote:

Three days on the river,—nights and mornings three,
Ere we stopped at Memphis, the port of Tennessee
And wondered why they gave it such a name of old renown—
A dreary, dingy, muddy, melancholy town,
But rich in bales of cotton, o'er the landing spread,
And bound for merry England, to earn the people's bread;—
And here—oh! shame to freedom, that boasts with tongue and pen!—
We took on board a 'cargo' of miserable men;
A freight of human creatures, bartered, bought and sold
Like hogs, or sheep, or poultry—the living blood for gold.[17]

The conditions Mackay's "miserable men" found on board steamboats were extremely harrowing. Historian Ira Berlin has called the antebellum internal slave migration a "second middle passage," an assessment that accurately conveys slaves' experiences on steamboats.[18] Traders treated slaves much as livestock: they were unprotected from the elements, given rudimentary provisions, and vulnerable to sale at any time. Like cattle and horses they were left to stand in their own excrement. Unlike farm animals, however, slaves had to be chained. William Wells Brown described a room on the lower deck "where men and women" were "promiscuously . . . chained together. It was impossible to keep that part of the boat clean."[19] In 1834, abolitionist Adam Lowry described the "unpleasant" conditions he witnessed on the *Uncle Sam* at the docks in Ripley, Ohio. He saw "two long chains, extending from the forward to the rear of the steerage deck. The ends were bolted to the sides of the boat about four feet above the deck floor. To these chains, at about equal distances apart, were attached twenty-five shorter chains with a handcuff attached to the loose end. The handcuff was attached to the right arm of each slave."[20] With their range of motion severely restricted, Lowry commented, the slaves awkwardly postured themselves on the hard deck floor.

Boat officers who did not adhere to such cruelties faced the possibility that slaves would run away or commit suicide. Slaveholder J. J. Boyd urged a shipper who apparently did not always bind slaves on his boat to make sure that his slave girl was closely watched. Particular caution was in order "when the boat stopped at Natchez," where escape was possible during the loading and unloading of freight.[21] William Wells Brown witnessed the results of slave resistance. "We lost one woman who had been taken from her husband and children," Brown recalled, "and having no desire to live without them, in the agony of her soul jumped overboard, and drowned herself."[22]

The squalor of steamboat decks and the swirling diversity of humanity that crowded in tightly confined spaces made disease a constant threat to the lives of slaves. New Orleans trader Samuel Browning told partners that "great complaint of the cholera in New Orleans and on steamboats has put a damper on the trade." He worried that he soon would not "be able to sell a Negro at any price."[23] Another Mississippi River trader told his partner that "he had nothing of importance" to report except that he arrived at the Natchez market with "all of the Negroes . . . except three men who died of cholera . . . two of which belong to your concern."[24] Downriver traders sometimes sent sickly slaves back upriver hoping to get refunds on their purchases.[25]

In addition to being exposed to disease and the general hardships of the voyage, slave women were often fondled and raped. Traders and passengers took advantage of the vulnerability of slave women during shipment. Adam Lowry watched as a trader sold one "beautiful" young slave who was "as white as any of my acquaintances" to a southern planter. To encourage the sale the trader "ordered the young woman to unfasten the front of her dress. She declined, but a stroke on the shoulder brought a reluctant obedience; a second expedited the work." The trader then "exposed her bosom to view and induced the young man to feel of her breast, then of her thighs." Suitably aroused, the young planter then paid the $2,500 asking price and led her upstairs to his private stateroom. Lowry could not see what happened to the young slave in the cabin, but there is little doubt that the brutality continued. The privacy of second-floor cabins allowed for masters to sexually assault their slaves away from the prying eyes of fellow passengers. Just as slave and free black chambermaids risked assault in the domestic hideaways of the cabin, women in the slave trade were similarly vulnerable to attack. Traveling slaveholders, separated from wives, mothers, and daughters, found on steamboats the perfect setting for debauchery. William Wells Brown recorded the horrible experience of Cynthia, a quadroon slave from St. Louis. Mr. Walker, a slave trader, directed Brown to "put her in a stateroom . . . apart from the other slaves." Soon thereafter, confined and isolated, Cynthia was sexually coerced and threatened. Brown listened as Walker promised her a chance to return to her St. Louis home as Walker's mistress if she would give in to his "vile proposals."

Walker succeeded in his sexual conquest and lived up to his promise for a time. He brought Cynthia back to St. Louis, but then he sold her several years later.[26]

The brutality of the Second Middle Passage continued once slaves were unloaded in the South. On the docks of the commercial hubs of the South, the contradictions of Mississippi River life were never more apparent. As slave and free black steamboat hands streamed into urban environments pressing the limits of liberty, traders drove coffles of slaves down the gangways of steamers and into city streets. Whereas river hands were bound for grog shops, families, and homes, slaves in the market were destined for slave auction houses and new degradations. At markets in Natchez's Forks of the Road and at hotels and from pens in New Orleans's French Quarter, slaves were sold, or resold, to masters who traveled from miles around to inspect the new arrivals.[27] Prospective buyers thoroughly questioned slaves about their skills and experiences, and this process provided slaves an opportunity to make themselves appealing to masters whom they thought would keep them near loved ones or near the freedoms of the city.[28] Most were sold to plantations far away from kin, however. After their sale, slaves began a new stage of their passage. Buyers marched their slaves back to the river and prepared for the journey to their slaves' new "home." By the 1850s, many were headed up the Red River to the plantation districts forever memorialized in Harriet Beecher Stowe's *Uncle Tom's Cabin*. As was the case with Uncle Tom, most slaves would never be reunited with their loved ones.

The pan-Mississippi world did not have such a destructive impact on all families, however. Demonstrating their creativity and vitality, African Americans worked hard to use the river industry to create alternative traditions to counteract the suffering of the slave trade. Riverside African Americans joined with mobile river workers to establish a variety of social networks that defied the isolation and commodification of the slave market.

African American steamboat workers helped create this alternative tradition by maintaining relationships with their own family members. Laboring as fathers, sons, brothers, mothers, sisters, and daughters, river workers did not forget these bonds when they began to follow the river. Married river hands had particularly strong ties to shore. According to the Pittsburgh population census of 1850, which probably exaggerates the number of married river workers, 58 percent of the city's free black river population left behind a spouse when they went to work.[29] Blood ties were just as important to slaves. According to the records of his master, "Big George," a leased slave from Kentucky, left behind two younger brothers, John and Fred, and the fifty-eight-year-old "Old George," who was likely his father. Twenty-four-year-old "Little Charley," who had the same owner as "Big George," left behind his forty-two-year-old mother, Harriet, his twenty-one-year-old brother, William, and a five-year-old sister, Josieway.[30] In another case, a slave chambermaid left her husband behind in Alabama and bore their child on the decks of a steamer on Mobile Bay.[31]

The separation of river families was intensely painful. The slave chambermaid Judy Taylor left her children in the care of her master when she worked on the Mississippi.[32] Kentucky bondsmen Lee Hobby watched as his father was sold to a steamboat owner, not knowing if he would ever see him again.[33] African Americans announced their comings and goings to family through song. Frederick Law Olmsted wrote that as his boat left New Orleans, "a dozen of the negro deck hands, standing on the freight, piled up on the low forecastle, began to sing, waving hats and handkerchiefs, and shirts lashed to poles, towards the people who stood on the sterns of steamboats at the levee."[34] Another observer recalled, "When a boat would arrive in port; one [African American deckhand] would stand on the capstan with a flag in one hand, to motion off the time of the song, like the leader of a band."[35] Once roustabouts were on their journeys, their songs took on a mournful quality. "Die night is dark, de day is long. And we are far from home. Weep, my brudders, weep!" went the lyrics of one song.[36]

A traveler recorded the following song of homesickness from slave boatmen in 1823:

Way down upon the Mobile Bay,
Close to the Mobile Bay,
There's where my thoughts is running ever,
All through the live long day,
There I've got a good and fond old mother,
Tho she is a slave,
There I've got a sister and a brother,
Lying in their peaceful grave,
O' could I somehow a'nother,
Drive these tears away,
When I think about my poor old mother,
Down upon Mobile Bay.[37]

Despite sometimes long separations, African American steamboat workers kept in contact with riverside families and communities. Steamboat work al-

"The Parting Song." From *Harper's New Monthly Magazine*, 1870. Courtesy of the Library of Congress.

ways offered the hope of return. William Wells Brown was not alone in returning to his St. Louis family in between steamboat voyages. The chambermaid Celeste, for example, reportedly "did not live with her master but with her mother, a free colored woman, living in St. Louis."[38] Slave workers were able to use the anonymity of the urban environment to reconnect with family and community. In some cases, masters permitted their slaves to live separately from them, in others masters were frustrated by their slaves' propensity to disappear for months between steamboat trips into the urban landscape.[39] In St. Louis, the slave Madison Henderson spent considerable time between river trips living at Leah's, a black boardinghouse where he knew most of the boarders.[40] A slave steamboat barber from Louisville reported that "it was just as though [he] was free" when he stopped off to live with his free friends and family.[41]

This sustained contact allowed free blacks and slaves to contribute economically to their communities. Through negotiations with officers and owners over regular, weekday wages and extra Sunday wages and with passengers over tips, slaves and free blacks earned money to support friends and family.

Families and the Mississippi

While some of their cash invariably was lost gambling or drunk away during the course of a voyage, enough was generally left over for steamboating to be an important source of financial support for slave and free black communities in the Mississippi Valley. This meant that male workers fulfilled a crucial component of the era's ideal of what adult manhood should entail: providing for a family. As was the case with free black sailors on the Atlantic seaboard, supporting family and community was crucial to the occupational and gender identities of steamboat hands.[42]

While precise comparison is impossible with existing data, steamboat workers' wages were likely equal to or higher than those of riverside laborers engaged in similar work. With room and board provided during work periods, free blacks could make more money than workers outside the industry. A free black shipping out on a steamboat was generally guaranteed at least two weeks of work and frequently more. Steamboat work thus represented a considerable opportunity for free blacks struggling to find a living wage in western cities.[43] Wage levels varied by occupation on board. In the cabin, stewards and first cooks often bargained for wages that were three or four times those waiters, porters, second cooks, or chambermaids earned. It was not uncommon at midcentury, for instance, for waiters to earn twenty dollars a month and for first cooks and stewards to earn fifty dollars a month or more. On deck, there was less variation in wage levels. As a group, deckhands generally made more in wages than lower-paid members of the cabin crew but not as much as stewards and skilled cooks did. Firemen earned about thirty-five dollars a month at midcentury. Roustabouts and deckhands generally contracted for about thirty dollars a month.[44] These wages were at their highest levels in the 1840s and 1850s and in the immediate postwar period, during the industry's peak period of growth.[45]

In most cases, vigilant riverside masters prevented their slaves from keeping these wages. Evidence suggests that most masters, whether they were officers, boat owners, or riverside leasers, collected their slaves' full wages. In the 1850s, Richard Rudd meticulously recorded the wages paid him by various boat clerks for each of his leased steamboat slaves.[46] James Lackland, who frequently leased slaves to steamers, received a letter from his agent stating, "I have collected from the SB *Tobacco Plant* $10.00 being Abe's wages from 14 to 26 May."[47] A traveler near St. Louis reported that masters "called every Saturday evening upon the clerk of the vessel to obtain their wages, amounting to the sum of one dollar per day for the services of each."[48]

Some masters trusted their slaves to collect their own wages before turning them over to their owners. One New Orleans master wrote a steamboat captain requesting that he "pay the boy George the amount due him."[49] In another case, a slave allegedly presented a pass to boat officers from his master allowing him to "hire himself and draw wages" from Mississippi steamers.[50] The Kentucky steamboat slave Washington Thomas commented in his American Freedmen's Inquiry Commission interview, "What I made I paid my boss, I paid my boss $160 a year."[51] A captain in a Missouri case who was being sued for allegedly allowing a slave fireman to escape defended himself in court by claiming that the slave's owner "permitted the said negro to receive pay and compensation for such services . . . as if the said negro was a free man and capable of making contracts."[52] In another instance, a slave named Felix allegedly received wages at a public tavern in St. Louis.[53] The slave Judy Taylor claimed in 1863 that for ten years she "collected her own wages and paid her mistress when she had the money." The casual nature of their economic relationship was evident in Taylor's claim that her "mistress never asks for the money."[54] In other instances, slaves kept a portion of their wages. Louis Hughes, a slave who worked near Memphis, commented that "it was common for slaves to be permitted to hire themselves out for wages that they were required to return, in whole or in part to their masters."[55]

To whatever extent slaves were able to keep regular wages, they were more often able to collect Sunday wages. Just as slaves in other industries bargained for compensation for Sunday work, river workers extracted money for work on their customary day of rest. Steamboat slaves received Sunday wages either from boat officers during the voyage or from their masters after the boat returned. In an example of the former practice, Frederick Law Olmsted witnessed officers paying slaves a dollar each time they worked on Sunday on board.[56] In contrast, James Rudd preferred to pay his slaves a lump sum when they returned to port. During the 1850s, for instance, he paid his slaves as much as ten dollars apiece for Sunday wages when they returned to Louisville following extended periods of steamboat work.[57] Slaves had to continually pressure boat officers, agents, and owners to get paid. An observer on St. Louis's levee wrote, "The *Gov. Collier*, a gov. Tow Boat, arrived yesterday, from N.O. and bro[ugh]t Ann's man Fred, who is chief cook on board, at 20$ per month —and discontented at that—he says he must have 25$—and that 3$ must be his, for 'Sunday wages' as they are called."[58] In 1846, James Lackland wrote his uncle from St. Louis about their steamboat slaves: "You authorized the Capt. to pay Lewis his Sunday wages, wages he paid him as per $2.00. His Sunday

Families and the Mississippi

wages according to custom for the time at the rate he has been employed are $3.50. I have therefore paid him the balance of one &50/100$."[59]

Tipping was a practice well established on antebellum steamboats. For free black waiters, chambermaids, and porters—the lowest paid free workers on board—tips were crucial to earning a living wage. Tips offered both slaves and free blacks the chance to earn money beyond the oversight of officers and owners. Travelers did not customarily tip slaves, but it was difficult to distinguish between slaves and free workers, so money often ended up in the pockets of bondsmen and -women, despite the disapproval of masters and officers.[60]

Passengers paid workers tips for regular service as well as for special tasks. In his narrative, slave Moses Grandy mentions passengers giving him from twenty-five cents to a dollar for good service at the end of a trip.[61] The free black boatman James Thomas wrote that "at the end of the trip the steward, the waiter, and all who attended the passengers were compensated. The Ladies looked after the chambermaid." Before leaving the boat, Thomas continued, gentlemen "would call up the steward, press a piece of currency or a gold piece in his hand, call for the cook and do the same. In like manner the boys who had waited on him and his family at the table."[62] One traveler recalled the "universal panacea of a dollar" in effecting good service.[63] Frederick Law Olmsted wrote that when he was traveling in a crowded boat, he secured a cabin room cot by tipping. "A waiter, whose good will I had purchased at the supper-table," he recalled, "gave me a hint to secure one of them [a cot] for myself, as soon as they were erected, by putting my hat in it."[64] Waiters also received money for shining shoes.[65] Chambermaids were known to get tips for extras like helping women lace their corsets or washing passengers' clothing.[66] One free black chambermaid recalled, "I made six dollars or seven dollars in tips [for each trip between New Orleans and Natchez]. Sometimes ladies wanted me to do a little washin', and they paid me liberally."[67] Stewards were in a particularly good position to earn tips. Food distributors wanting to sell produce to steamboats needed to line the pockets of the steward in order to make a sale. In many cases, these tips were formalized into special stewards' "fees." Not all passengers were pleased with the custom of tipping, though. One passenger was incensed that a free black woman charged her $1.50 for washing her bed and table linens during her Ohio River voyage.[68]

Steamboat work also provided both slaves and free blacks the opportunity to earn money through trading.[69] Following an ancient maritime custom, officers routinely allowed boat workers to transport a limited amount of their own produce without paying shipping fees. African American river workers thus created extensive networks of trade that linked deep South plantation slaves with urban markets. African American boat workers shipping from ports throughout the West traded with plantation slaves in Louisiana, Mississippi, and Alabama, as well as with urban hucksters and dealers. An ex-slave named Cox, whose master had leased him to a steamboat, recalled that "trade was very good on the river before the war commenced."[70] Ex-slave Sella Martin remembered trading on a steamboat plying Lake Pontchartrain between New Orleans and Mobile.[71] Northern free blacks were heavily involved in these exchanges. In addition to earning "their ordinary wages, which are good," Rev. Charles B. Ray noted in 1839 Cincinnati, black steamboat workers had plentiful "opportunities for trading . . . [in] the lower country."[72]

River trading required resources and a range of skills. Most important, slaves needed a pass from their masters allowing them to trade. Milton Clarke, for example, negotiated with his Kentucky master for special papers that gave him the right "to pass up and down the river as [he] pleased, and to transact any business as though [he] was free."[73] In another case, a slave steward bargained for a pass that allowed him to trade for six or seven years on the Mississippi River.[74] Traders also needed the requisite capital and trading contacts to get started. Knowing people, particularly commodity producers, was key. Rivermen Charles Brown and Peter Charleville decided to sell goods up the Missouri River because Charleville knew so many people that there "was no doubt of success."[75] Another skill was having a sense of the seasonal demand for different products. Sella Martin testified that it took skill, intelligence, and experience to succeed as a trader.[76]

The steady supply of slave-raised produce made bartering, buying, and selling merchandise lucrative.[77] The money steamboat workers earned through trade was theirs alone to spend. Sella Martin recalled that his master paid him wages but the money he earned trading "made the situation pay."[78] Madison Henderson felt that he could make a "handsome sum" and that "a man could make it right smart" at trading.[79] Cincinnati's free blacks reportedly made "great profits" trading in the deep South.

Altogether, wages, tips, and trading money provided river workers the resources to buy their own clothes, shoes, food, and liquor, as well as to take care of their loved ones' living expenses.[80] Cyprian Clamorgan's *Colored Aristocracy of St. Louis* illustrates the importance of steamboat wages to the wealthy free blacks in that city. James Nash supported his wife, Ellen, and three children, Laura, Kate, and Nancy, with money he earned as a steward. His house

Families and the Mississippi

at 233 South Third Street was valued at $350 dollars, and the family had other holdings worth $500 more.[81] A good job on the river could make a man an attractive marriage candidate. In 1852, for instance, the unmarried free black St. Louis resident James Holmes had to borrow $500 from a white commission merchant for a license just to reside in St. Louis. By 1858, however, Holmes, judged a "hard-working" man by Clamorgan, was worth $10,000 after he worked as a steward for several years on the steamboat *Morton*. Two years later, he married Louisa Johnson.[82] River work could also help free blacks from small black communities meet a wider range of potential marriage partners. James W. Thompson, steward of the *Moses McClelland*, "a tall, gentile looking man," became involved in the radical circles of Pittsburgh when he shipped out on the Ohio River. On one of these voyages, he met Catherine M. Vashon, daughter of John B. Vashon, Pittsburgh's leading crusader for African American rights and mentor to the young Martin Delany. Thompson charmed Catherine Vashon and took her back to St. Louis to be his wife.[83] Slave river workers' earnings also enabled them to strengthen family relationships. One slave bought his freedom and then bought the freedom of his nephews. He later sent one of them to college.[84] In another instance, although the slave named Cox complained that working on the river made his master "charge him a lot," he was able to buy his freedom and the liberty of his family. In a less dramatic case but one that was more typical of the ways in which the river nurtured slave family life, two slave women, a mother and daughter, pooled their steamboat money to support themselves independently of the meddling of their master.[85] Slaves did not have to run away to benefit from the freedoms of the river.

The ways in which the river nurtured African American family life is nowhere more evident than in the narrative of Catherine and Charlotte Grandy. Like James W. Thompson, the St. Louis steward who found a wife in Pittsburgh, the Grandys used both the economic opportunity and the mobility of the river to support their family ties. Catherine Grandy, anxious to purchase her freedom, hired herself out to a steamboat at "$30 a month," which was "the usual salary."[86] She arranged to pay her master four dollars a week, with the rest going toward the price of her emancipation, a value her master placed at $1,200. After saving enough to purchase herself, a process that Catherine expedited by earning tips and selling fruit to passengers, she set out on the river to find her sister Charlotte, a plantation slave who had been sold away years before. After some looking, Catherine found her on a Louisiana sugar plantation and then persuaded Charlotte's master to lease her to a steamboat. The two women worked together on various steamers and together gradually saved enough to pool their money and buy Charlotte's freedom.[87]

This story illustrates the creative ways in which slave families that were ripped apart by the slave trade fought to reclaim their most personal relationships. While studies of the Reconstruction era have noted the ways in which freedmen and -women sought to reclaim family ties, historians of the slave family have not devoted adequate attention to the ways that separated family members maintained contact within the institution of slavery.[88] The Second Middle Passage did not irrevocably separate families to the extent that the African slave trade did. The social, cultural, and economic linkages between the Cotton Belt and the upper South and the North were much stronger than colonial ties between Africa and North America. Most southwestern masters had economic ties to the East and North, and steamboats closed the distance between these regions of the country. When western traveler Anthony Trollope noted that "a river here is not a natural barrier, but a connecting street," he was describing more than he realized.[89] African Americans exploited the possibilities the river provided whenever they could.

Slaves tried to glean information about their families from whites, including masters, traders, and travelers, but, because such information was often severely censored, they had to rely on their own networks of communication. The docks, slave pens, jails, and food markets of the antebellum South were filled with the chatter of black voices. Wherever goods were traded, sold, or transported in the South, African American networks flourished. Blocked from modern forms of communication such as the mail and the telegraph service, African Americans resisted isolation and the accompanying parochial mindset that worked to the benefit of their masters through the slave grapevine.[90]

African American river laborers were creative in their efforts to maintain family ties. For instance, in 1852, near Cairo, Illinois, Francis and Theresa Pulszky chatted with a chambermaid who "spoke English, French, and German with equal facility" and "was rented out by her master." The chambermaid's master resided in St. Louis, but her husband lived in New Orleans. Each trip downriver, therefore, meant a chance to reunite with her husband, who had apparently been sold away. Remarkably, the chambermaid managed to mother her children, too. Through negotiations with her master and with steamboat officers, the children were permitted to travel with her, up and down the Mississippi.[91] Other slaves managed their own sales so that they would have access to the river communication network. A New Orleans slave named

Randal likely convinced his master to sell him to a riverman. "I have sold Randal to Capt. Nelson of the *Streck* for 650$ [which was] somewhat less than his value," his master wrote, "but I preferred selling him thus to sending him away from his family."[92]

Slaves like Milton Clarke got work on steamboats with the intention of finding relatives previously sold away. Until Clarke described his steamboat lease, his narrative focused on his Lexington, Kentucky, master's cruel treatment and on his relentless toil in a local tannery. Central to the Clarke's description of these early years was his poignant recollection of the loss of his sister Dela, who was sold downriver to New Orleans by their master in the early 1830s. Her transport, during which she was "chained to a gang of a hundred and sixty slaves," punctuated a series of cruelties inflicted on Clarke's family by his master.[93] Clarke's reunion with Dela was made possible by his 1838 lease to a steamboat that ran between Louisville and New Orleans. Knowing she had been sent to New Orleans, he searched the city during his time off at the end of each downriver trip. His efforts were not immediately successful. He recalled that he "was at New Orleans three or four times" before he got any information.[94] When he did get news it was through an "old acquaintance" who knew Dela and gave Milton her address.[95] The reunion, which took place hundreds of miles away from their childhood slave experiences, was no doubt typical of many such joyous events. Milton recalled, "I went to the house, but I was so changed by the growth of seven or eight years, that she did not know me."[96] Milton's sister made him prove his identity by having him identify a piece of clothing she had kept from her Kentucky days. Soon, however, they were anxiously talking about family news and rapidly catching up with each other's lives.[97]

Boat workers like Clarke came to steamboat work with hopes of finding their own loved ones, but in other cases riverside African Americans approached black river hands to carry written, as well as oral, news to loved ones who were sold away. Riverside slaves had good reason to look to them rather than native and ethnic white boat hands. The racial antipathy of many native and ethnic white river workers made them poor candidates to carry messages for riverside slaves. In contrast, African American boat workers' personal experience with the slave trade and the breaking apart of families made them sympathetic to pleas for help from other slaves and free blacks. They had not only the geographic knowledge but also the motivation to help. They were the underground mail service of the slave economy.

The narrative of Aunt Sally provides a wonderful example of how boat workers used their mobility to reconnect separated families.[98] Her narrative, written by an anonymous northern abolitionist, is constructed around the dramatic moments of slave family separation and then, years later, family reconnection. In her narrative, African American boat workers along the Alabama River were portrayed as heroic carriers of information who helped bring Aunt Sally's family a glorious and triumphant reunion.[99]

Much of Aunt Sally's narrative conveyed the impact of the internal slave trade on her North Carolina family in the early decades of the nineteenth century. Sally recalled her mother being sold to another North Carolina plantation, her husband, who lived on a neighboring plantation, being sold away for gambling, and a cousin being sold to Mobile. Her three boys also were sold away: Lewis to Alabama, Daniel to the North Carolina upcountry, and Isaac to a local planter who later resold him to Mississippi. After she watched her closest kin sold away, she married a local Fayetteville free black. But this marriage proved to be no protection from the traders who eventually came for her. Her master sold her to a plantation on the Alabama River hundreds of miles away, where she was subsequently resold locally.[100] Sally's life reflected the worst horrors of the internal slave trade. She was largely cut off from her North Carolina relatives, and for twenty years she lived what amounted to a second life in Alabama. The only word she received about her family, from helpful whites, was that her second husband had died. She heard nothing, however, of her children, mother, cousins, or first husband.

This familial isolation ended with a chance encounter with a boatman at a local wedding. Her mistress rarely allowed her off the plantation, but in this instance her mistress relented to Sally's protestations and allowed her to attend. At the dance following the wedding she saw a man "sitting apart from the rest, a forlorn looking man, in torn rough clothes, to whom no one seemed to pay any attention."[101] Moved by his outsider status, she asked who he was and where he was from. When it turned out he was from the "Carolina rice fields" her interest peaked. She asked if he knew her family and then received the information that changed her life: "Why, sartain I do," the boatmen said, "Dere's one of 'em, Mary Ann Williams, dat lives in Mobile. I knows her right well."[102] The boatman then agreed to carry "a little bundle" to Mary's Mobile cousin as soon as his damaged boat was repaired. Sally had another slave write a letter for her, and she gave it to the boatman; then she waited until his boat, the *Magnolia*, came upriver again.[103] One night, two weeks later, she heard a knock on the door of her quarters. It was Daniel, the boatman, with a letter from Mary Ann. Thus began a correspondence that reconnected Sally not only with Mary Ann but also with her son Isaac, who by chance had met Mary Ann some years before in Mobile. Isaac, who had since bought his freedom and was living in Detroit, subsequently purchased his long lost mother out of slavery and brought her to the North.

Sally's happy ending, which allowed her story to be told, was undoubtedly not the typical result of encounters with boat workers. A slave's contact with far-flung kin rarely would have led to her being bought out of slavery. Nonetheless, Sally's story is likely but one of many other examples of family networking leading to a reunion. With the slave trade booming, boat workers would have been inundated by questions like Sally's wherever they went. While the connections they established may not always have led to immediate reunions, they may well have made the ordeal of bondage easier to endure.

Historian James Oliver Horton provides several examples of river workers shuttling information between northern fugitives and their families left behind in bondage.[104] In one case, a Cincinnati resident maintained contact with her mother, a Mississippi slave, for more than three decades through a river network. Black boatmen regularly traveled between her home in Cincinnati and her mother's slave quarters. During this long separation, the daughter corresponded with her slave mother about whom to marry and later about childbirth. By 1843, she was writing her mother to tell her that one of her grandchildren was attending Oberlin College. This news cheered the proud grandmother. In her letter, the old slave woman said that the news found her bound in body but free in spirit.[105]

Black river workers helped Henry Williams secure a divorce from his New Orleans slave wife. In the 1830s, Williams had escaped from New Orleans to Cincinnati, where he found work. Soon after, he married a local woman. This angered his fellow Union Baptist Church members who knew that he had another wife in New Orleans. Charging him with bigamy, the church leaders demanded his first wife's written consent to a divorce before they would sanction Williams's new union. A local boatman who regularly traveled to New Orleans carried the crucial document to Henry's first wife, who agreed to the divorce in writing. The church recognized the new marriage.[106]

Sadly, the underground networks that brought some families together could not link all families torn apart by the slave trade. William Wells Brown lost his sister and mother to the slave trade and never heard from them again. When he was forced to say goodbye first to his sister in the St. Louis County jail and then to his mother, who was chained to sixty other slaves on the deck of a steamboat bound for Natchez, his dreams of someday living in freedom with his loved ones were forever shattered. He did not contemplate a desperate attempt to find them but instead thought more and more of an escape to the North. The benefits of steamboat work became increasingly meaningless for Brown. He was not willing to toil on, hoping to hear news of them, while waiting for the day when he, too, would be sold to the cotton and sugar plantations. With the blessings of his family in his heart, he decided to take action of a different sort. He decided to escape slavery for good.

chapter four

Boats against the Current

Slave Escapes on the Western Rivers

WILLIAM WELLS BROWN was ready to make a bold strike toward freedom. His closest loved ones, his mother and sister, had been sold away. Meanwhile, his river employment made him yearn for liberty. "Passing from place to place and seeing new faces everyday," Brown recalled, made him "several times think of leaving the boat." Fueling such thoughts was the image of Canada—a place he had "heard much about" during his travels.[1] Brown's chance came when his master took him to Cincinnati's levee. He acted quickly. Picking up a trunk, he posed as a porter and then walked down the gangway. He was soon mixing in with the crowd on the levee.[2]

Brown's escape via the river was not unusual on the antebellum Mississippi. While the precise number of river runaways is impossible to gauge, evidence suggests that thousands of fugitives rode the decks of steamboats to freedom in the region.[3] The busy docks and urban levees of western cities created opportunities not only for river slaves but also for plantation hands and urban bondsmen to abscond. Slaves throughout the western region flocked to steamboats hoping to "cross the river Jordan" to freedom by passing as a boat worker or passenger. Most were young men, the demographic profile of most fugitives seeking escape to the North, and thus were well suited to blend into the masculine world of steamboating.[4]

William Wells Brown escaped using his own wits and daring, but runaways often relied on accomplices. Free black and slave boat workers were willing to risk the loss of their own freedom to help fugitives. Their contacts in both the

North and the South allowed them various opportunities to resist the designs of slaveholders. These river networks sometimes involved whites, but more often the bonds of color helped runaways. In both the lower and the upper South, African American boat workers provided a safe passage for fugitives escaping from southern river cities and rural plantations. Through chance encounters and mutual associates in the levee districts of western cities boat workers provided a crucial link between steamboats and other networks of fugitive aid.

These contacts were part of the underground circulation of information that followed the river trade. The intersection of the commercial working class of the river with both plantations and urban environments of the South made the Mississippi a fertile site of slave protest. At the same time that divisions between slave and free workers and racism within the river working class limited collective action in the form of industrywide strikes, river networks regularly helped free runaways. River workers knew boat schedules and which boat officers were more concerned with filling positions in the crew than scrutinizing passes. They also had contacts upriver that were key to successful escapes. Talking with a river hand was often a crucial step in running away.

This communication contributed to the river-oriented mentality of slaves in the western region. One traveler reported being told that "such is the nice and critical ear of the negroes living on the banks of the Mississippi, that they can distinguish the boats regularly plying on the river long before they come in sight, by what might be called their cannonading."[5] Lafcadio Hearn, in his remarkable interviews with members of Cincinnati's post–Civil War African American community, talked with old stevedores who had "wonderingly watched in their slave childhood the great white vessels panting on the river's breast."[6] The former slave John P. Parker recalled, "I want to say right now, there was something proud and majestic the way a large river steamer swam the waters. They were a sight never to be forgotten."[7]

Inevitably, such wonderment turned to thoughts of escape. In the context of beatings, the breakup of families, and the mental anguish of the day-to-day life of slavery, the river provided hope. Before running away, Henry Bibb recalled standing "upon the lofty banks of the Ohio River, gazing upon the splendid steamboats, wafting with all their magnificence up and down the river" and thinking that he "might soar away to where there is no slavery."[8] John P. Parker recalled, "[The] Mississippi River attracted me like a magnet, for as soon as I was free to move in my own selected direction I made straight for the river."[9]

Slaveholders' own mentality was shaped by the possibility of losing their chattel to the river economy. Jefferson Davis felt "exposed" because of the opportunities his slaves had to escape on the river.[10] Less prominent slaveholders voiced their concerns in newspaper runaway advertisements. These notices often concluded with the statement: "Steamboat captains are cautioned not to harbor or employ him."[11] The Missouri Supreme Court echoed such concerns. "The facility of escaping on the boats navigating our waters," the court reported in an 1846 decision, "will induce many slaves to leave the service of their masters. Their ingenuity will be exerted to invent means of eluding the vigilance of Captains, and many ways will be employed to get off unnoticed. One escape by such means, will stimulate others to make the attempt."[12]

Such concerns led to the passing of laws in Missouri, Kentucky, Tennessee, and Louisiana that made steamboat owners financially responsible for the loss of fugitive slaves.[13] Officers were prohibited from allowing slaves to stow away, book passage, or obtain work on steamboats unless they had their master's consent. These laws were difficult to enforce, given the tumultuous environment of the western rivers. In cases in which officers leased slaves from riverside masters, liability laws were particularly ineffectual. When officers used what western courts called "due diligence" to prevent escape, western courts generally found boat owners innocent for the loss of the slaves of riverside masters.[14] "Where a slave is hired as a boat hand," the Missouri Supreme Court declared, "we must presume that the owner is fully aware, that every facility for escape is afforded by the very nature of service. He is apprised, that the boat will touch and be detained at the wharves of populous towns; that it passes near the banks, and will stop at the landings of States where slavery is not tolerated; and that his slave will be associated with free negroes, and others who will not be unlikely to leave him in ignorance of the various opportunities which present themselves for escape."[15]

Contact with free land gave slave steamboat workers more reason to flee brutal conditions. One officer, who testified in a case in which a leased slave absconded from a Mississippi steamer, recalled, "The slave disappeared because I intended to whip him for some cause."[16] The rebelliousness associated with river culture made boat workers particularly intolerant of physical abuse. By traveling between societies dependent on slavery, those that had just a few slaves, and those based on free labor, river work made slaves constantly aware of their unfree status. William Wells Brown, for instance, was motivated to escape in part by the free laborers that he encountered on northern rivers.[17]

Martin Delany similarly thought that boatmen's mobility caused their discontent. He wrote in his novel *Blake; or, The Huts of America* that steamboat workers' jobs allowed them to see the pleasures of freedom, thereby "augmenting their own wretchedness."[18] For many slaves even the monetary rewards of steamboat labor were not always sufficient compensation for the knowledge that a true masterless existence was within their reach. Seeing the most brutal forms of slavery could also transform the consciousness of slaves who had experienced relative freedom. Traveling through the deep South changed the slave Isaac Throgmorton's view of bondage. After a trip to the "coasts," he recalled, "there was no comfort for me. I found no pleasure in anything."[19]

The consequences of river slaves' discontent fill the documentary record. While the problem of legally leased slaves running away was never devastating to the industry, it was a constant irritant to slaveholders and steamboat owners. The advertisement a St. Louis master posted in October 1847 announcing a $100 reward for his "negro boy called Harry" who "ran away from the steamer St. Paul yesterday afternoon" was typical.[20] In another typical notice, a master offered $25 to anyone finding a slave Peter who "strayed away from the steamboat Opelousas."[21] Lawsuits filed by masters against boat owners for the loss of their leased slaves contain testimony that illustrate the frustration of masters. A leased steamboat slave named Wesley became a "fugitive from labor," in the words of one irate witness, when he ran away from the *Trabue*, a packet that ran in the Louisville-to–New Orleans trade.[22]

As was the case with William Wells Brown, slave steamboat workers sometimes took advantage of sudden opportunities, or momentary lapses in officers' supervision, to escape. One slave escaped under the cover of a steamboat explosion that officers believed had killed him.[23] Since many masters were reluctant to lease their chattel to steamers that traveled along free land, slaves had to be ready to spring into action when the opportunity arose. In December of 1850, two slaves, one from New Orleans, the other from Missouri, took advantage of an unexpected trip to Cincinnati's levee. Because boat officers failed to follow the custom of temporarily jailing their slaves in Kentucky, the two ran into the streets of the city.[24] In another case of good fortune, Sella Martin took advantage of ice on the Ohio River and an emergency stop on free soil to leave his steamboat berth at Cairo, Illinois.[25] Allen Sydney's unusual lease to Pittsburgh allowed him to orchestrate his escape.[26]

Rural slaves who were not leased to steamboats faced a long and difficult journey getting to them. But reach them they did. Fugitives traveled from the sugarcane districts of Louisiana and the region's vast cotton belt, as well as small border state farms. River workers memorialized this exodus when they sang:

I's gwine from de cotton fields. I's gwine from de cane,
I's gwine from de ol' hut that stans down in the lane;
De boat am in de river, dat comes to take me off,
An I's gwine to join the exodus an' strike out fo' de no'f[27]

These lyrics must have been very hard for slaveholders to hear, especially because they were accurate. Slaves escaped from rural places in Louisiana such as Bayou Sara and Pointe Coupee Parish. They left the small towns of New Madrid and Glasgow, Missouri; Napoleon, Arkansas; and Warrenton, Mississippi.[28] In journeys that varied in length, slaves fled overland to places where they could most easily board a steamboat. Henry Bibb, for example, after escaping from his Arkansas master, ran overland to Jefferson City, Missouri, where he went to the docks seeking passage to St. Louis.[29] In another case, runaways Harry and Nelson, rather than trek across central Missouri, instead fled the few short miles to the Glasgow landing, where they came upon the steamer *Leavenworth* headed to St. Louis.[30] Farther south, a slave named Williamson walked forty miles through an Arkansas swamp to reach the Mississippi and steamboat service north.[31] And a captured Louisiana fugitive reported to his overseer that a fellow runaway named Bob was "amin for the Red River."[32] Before his eventual escape, the Alabama slave Sella Martin had expressed his desire to get to New Orleans so "that [he] might conceal [him]-self on some steamboat, and come up the Mississippi River to the Ohio River, and so reach Ohio, a free state."[33] In Kentucky, escapes down the Cumberland and Tennessee rivers were a continual annoyance to slaveholders.[34] In this region, fugitives commonly ran to the banks of the Ohio River, took a skiff or ferry to the Indiana or Ohio side, and then got on a steamboat upriver.[35]

In order to circumvent rural patrols and pursuing masters, fugitives turned to various people for aid. In the deep South, maroon colonies dotted the swamps of Louisiana and provided support for runaways. In Arkansas and Texas, slaves fled frequently to Native American communities. In the upper South, people in mountainous upcountry areas supported groups of runaway slaves. Along the rivers, free black farmers and lumbermen cutting wood for steamboats also aided fugitives.[36]

Rural networks often helped fugitives reach southern cities from which steamboat escapes were more easily accomplished. While rural slaves sometimes fled on steamboats directly to free territory, often they first traveled to major cities such as New Orleans, Louisville, Nashville, or Memphis.[37] Some rural fugitives negotiated the difficult overland trek to these cities, while others used steamboats to escape from peripheral areas to southern cities. In the latter case, fugitives' escape routes followed patterns of commerce. Just as southern commodities frequently required reshipment in a major city to reach emerging national markets, steamboat fugitives often needed several berths to reach their destinations.

In cities, rural fugitives took advantage of the anonymity of the urban environment. The New Orleans mayor complained in 1834 that runaways "came in great numbers, crowd in the city, hide, and make our city a den."[38] Border-state cities Louisville and St. Louis similarly attracted fugitives, including some who fled enslavement thinly veiled as indentured servitude in southern Illinois.[39] Some slaves fled to cities and immediately headed for the docks, but others hid from authorities in the urban landscape and gathered their resources. The slave John Warren, for example, escaped overland to Memphis, where he worked for a period of time earning money to further his river escape.[40]

The city served as a springboard to freedom for urban slaves as well. During both work and leisure, the loose master-slave relations of the urban environment gave slaves opportunities to wander along levees.[41] Throughout southern cities, slaves left jobs as cooks, coopers, waiters, levee workers, and draymen to attempt river escape. On September 3, 1842, William Johnson, the famous free black barber from Natchez, remarked that "Wellington [a barber] left this place to night on The *Maid of Arkensaw* [*sic*] for New Orleans intending to run on the boat."[42] In another case, a New Orleans slave who was thought to be a "good house slave and cook" absconded on the steamer *New York*.[43] In the same city, a slave named Jack, who was "openly and publiclly [*sic*] employed" loading and unloading steamboat goods, used his job to escape.[44] In Louisville, several slaves who had been employed carrying meat from a wholesale butcher to steamboats used their connections to run away.[45] John P. Parker left his apprenticeship to a plasterer in Mobile and headed straight for the landing where steamboats bound for New Orleans docked.[46]

Urban slaves may have had the advantage of living near crowded dock areas, but all fugitives faced similar obstacles in getting on a steamboat that would carry them to freedom. Riverside authorities and steamboat captains worked together to prevent river fugitives from escaping. In addition to runaway slave advertisements that were posted in dock areas, city patrols who commonly looked for runaways hanging about the levee helped stop potential escapees. Captains posted watches on gangways and instructed stewards, engineers, and mates to carefully check the papers that free blacks were required to carry. Captains also instructed clerks to hold on to the free papers of all free people of color on board.[47] Captains' desires to expedite hiring workers and booking passengers compromised such procedures, but they still presented formidable obstacles to fugitives.

Despite these risks, many fugitives were undeterred in their quest. Mixing in with the African American draymen, stevedores, peddlers, and boat workers, fugitives risked recapture for a chance at liberty. Some fugitives looked for boats heading downriver, hoping to reship at New Orleans either back upriver or onto the decks of an Atlantic ship. Going downriver was less suspicious, and by the time fugitives changed course northward, they were far away from their masters' homes. Despite the advantages of initially heading away from free soil, most fugitives felt that the dangers of remaining in the South longer than necessary were too great. Thus the majority of runaways sought out levee landings where steamboats departed for Cincinnati or Pittsburgh. At St. Louis's levee, Henry Bibb looked for the "first boat which was destined for Cincinnati."[48] A Memphis runaway reportedly saw a sign for Cincinnati on a steamboat and went aboard.[49] In Louisville, a slave headed toward "a Pittsburgh boat going to Cincinnati."[50] John P. Parker recalled of his escape, "As I sauntered along the dock, I came on a steamer which was being loaded with freight. Looking up, I saw a large sign: 'for Memphis and upriver points.'"[51]

Many fugitives used forged passes to deceive boat officers and to negotiate the difficult transition from land to river. One of the most prevalent tactics involved buying or manufacturing forged free papers. The fugitives who could not obtain free papers often resorted to buying, forging, or stealing the more easily duplicated passes allowing self-hire to steamboats.[52] The underworld of southern river cities nurtured a flourishing trade in all such articles. On October 17, 1854, the *New Orleans Picayune* expressed concern about "the number of negroes with forged passes" and guessed that "a manufactory must exist somewhere in the city, as most of them bear a stamp of common origin."[53] In grog shops, the homes of free blacks, and rivermen's boardinghouses, all located just minutes from river levees, fugitives bought or bartered for illegal passes. The free black James Thomas, who worked for a time on a steamboat, commented on the large number of slaves who used forged passes to gain a berth. "Colored men and . . . women," he said, could always buy a pass "if they [could] afford to part with twenty-five dollars."[54] When a Tennessee slave named Tom found he could not afford the going price, he simply slipped into Memphis at night and copied a slave's steamboat lease.[55]

Such passes were often crucial to escape plans. In Tom's case, he showed his forged pass to a captain at Memphis who reportedly "did not hesitate" to hire him on board.[56] Another slave, John Warren, who escaped from a Tennessee plantation to the Memphis levee, similarly had no trouble getting a captain on a White River steamboat to hire him with his forged pass.[57] In another case, a "copper colored, heavy built" slave named Sam escaped from his Warrenton, Mississippi, master by using a forged pass. His master advertised that he was last seen in Natchez "with a pass from some person unknown to me, giving him permission to hire his own time, and receive the wages therefore, on any boats running on the rivers and lakes."[58] Another slave, James Fisher, wrote himself a pass in a Nashville tavern for a slave "Jones," which allowed him to hire his own time to steamboats. In his case, captains repeatedly denied him a berth, telling him he needed a white man to vouch for his freedom. Undeterred, Fisher convinced a white man in his boardinghouse to recommend him. Telling Fisher, "I reckon you can't be a runaway, or you wouldn't be staying here so bold," the man helped get him a berth. He was soon off toward Louisville.[59]

Slaves who worked on steamboats were at an advantage in the struggle to reach freedom. They could rely on their existing knowledge of the river system to pass into trades from which their master had barred them and from which escape was more easily accomplished. Some passed into northern trades as free workers, but most simply pretended to have their master's authority to work on northbound steamers.[60] Given the prevalence of self-hire among steamboat slaves, convincing boat officers of a master's consent was often easy to do. For example, in New Orleans during the spring of 1830, John Scott, a slave whose master had apparently allowed him to hire himself out on southern steamers, used his previous freedoms to negotiate a berth on an Ohio River steamer. He subsequently escaped, and the court found the steamboat owner liable.[61] In September 1855, a slave chambermaid, Celeste, apparently frustrated at the difficulty of saving her boat earnings to purchase her freedom, used a similar strategy to get work on the *Reindeer*, which plied the upper Mississippi trade. Celeste's master allowed her to make her own bargains for steamboat work, but only on "boats running in the New Orleans or Missouri River trade."[62] Boat officers on the *Reindeer* who had observed her loose relationship with her master believed she had a pass "to go where she might choose," so they hired her. Her hire turned out to be an expensive mistake, for they were sued for her escape.[63] Slaves bargained with their trustworthy reputations, which they carefully planted in officers' minds.[64]

Fugitives who had neither work experience on riverboats nor a pass resorted to a variety of strategies to board steamboats. On the Missouri River, Henry Bibb bought a large trunk and pretended to be the servant of a group of passengers boarding a steamer. He recalled, "I acted as if the trunk was full of clothes, but I had not a stitch of clothes in it. The passengers went up into the cabin and I followed them with the trunk. I suppose this made the captain think that I was their slave."[65] In another case, two fugitives boarded the *Hercules* at Natchez's landing, where they mixed in with the boat's workers.[66] Similarly, a New Orleans slave employed variously as a house servant, cook, and drayman adopted the alias "Ned" and mixed in with a northern free black crew as they discharged on the levee. An engineer on the nearby *New York* signed him on as a fireman without even asking for his papers.[67] Others passed as free passengers, such as one group of fugitives who pretended to be a troupe of musicians.[68] One particularly desperate Memphis slave reportedly attempted to ship himself in a wooden box to Cincinnati with the help of a local free black.[69] Harriet Tubman credited divine intervention with providing her steamboat passage north. Just when it seemed boat officers on her Mississippi River steamer would discover that she had boarded the boat with fugitive slaves, the clerk suddenly handed her tickets for her whole party.[70]

As several of the previous examples indicate, the process of escape required that runaways act with a confidence and assertiveness that signified they were free. Runaways attempting to pass as free men also had to dress the part. Therefore, respectable clothing was of utmost importance. One fugitive stole from his master a linen shirt, cashmere pants, an overcoat, and a black silk hat.[71] Another wore a cloth coat and pantaloons, and, according to observers, he was generally "well dressed."[72] Two others wore "new suits of . . . clothing and new wool hats."[73] John Parker recalled, "My good clothes [were] my open sesame, for I was not even noticed as I strolled by steamer after steamer."[74]

Fine clothes and an air of superiority allowed some fugitives to pass as white, the ultimate badge of freedom. One light-skinned New Orleans fugitive used clothing and confidence to book first-class passage in the all-white cabin. Reveling in his newly found power, he reportedly ate at the first table and usually sat near the ladies.[75] Slaves took advantage of their ability to pass as white to get jobs as well. The steward of the *Missouri* hired a slave, Felix, a New Orleans cooper and store clerk, without asking for a pass.[76] He hired him because, in the words of the captain, "the boy he is so white that you can't tell if he is a white man or a slave."[77]

No matter what strategies runaways used to deceive officers and passengers, they all took advantage of the public nature of steamboating and the anonymity of the West's bustling commercial world. In the *Confidence-Man*, Herman Melville captures the underlying social changes taking place in the mid-nineteenth century that runaways exploited. Melville's story, one of the first modern novels in its themes and narrative structure, illustrates the problems that modernization posed to a western society accustomed to determining trustworthiness and discerning personal character from appearances. On steamboats, where passengers came and went as quickly as the landscape passed, people could never be sure of other people's identities. On the steamboat *Fidele*, the setting of Melville's novel, passengers' appearances are often deceiving and their motives are often hidden. The racial implications of this uncertainty are frightening to many of the white passengers on Melville's mythical steamer. When passengers encounter a fellow traveler who calls himself "Black Guinea," they are immediately suspicious. They demand to see his free papers, and when the "negro" states, "No, dis poor ole darkie haint noneo' dem waloable [valuable] papers," they insist that he produce a person who knows he is free.[78] The "negro" says he has references on the steamer, but the matter, like many of the questions regarding people's motives and identities in the novel, is never satisfactorily resolved. "Black Guinea" melts into the crowd; the Confidence-Man's masquerade has begun.

For slaves who were unable or unwilling to carry on a public masquerade, stowing away was a favorite escape strategy. The Mississippi slave Louis Hughes tried twice to stow away on steamers leaving Memphis. On the first attempt, after escaping to the city, he went to the levee and climbed aboard the *Statesman*, hiding himself behind four hogsheads of sugar. After being caught and returned to his master, he escaped again, this time in the hull of the *John Lirozey*, a Cincinnati mail packet.[79] The slave John P. Parker walked out on the New Orleans levee after dark to the *Magnolia* to make his escape attempt. Hiding from the flickering lights of boat lanterns that threatened to expose him, he "watched and watched and wondered and wondered how [he] was to get on board my steamer." Avoiding the main gangway, he decided to run for a small plank at the boat's bow. "When the light in the fire box faded out," he recalled, "I made a run for it, dropped into the hold, just as my enemy the fire box lighted even the hold where I was lying panting with fear. But then I was unseen, safely aboard my steamer bound north. This episode I believe gave me confidence in myself, in my ability to meet any and all situations that might arise to confront me."[80]

Stowaways knew their best chances of escape were from upper South cities.

The attraction of freedom proved irresistible for an eighty-year-old Louis-ville slave who reportedly "secreted himself" in the hold of the Cincinnati-bound *Wisconsin*.[81] J. D. Green left the same city stowed away on the *Pike No. 3*. After passing as a porter to gain access to the boat's hold, he hauled a pas-senger's trunk on board. He was paid six cents, and then he jumped in the hold "among the cotton bags."[82] He was off to Cincinnati.

In many cases, clandestine networks that linked levees to steamboats helped fugitives. Free passengers, both white and black, bought tickets for fugitives, sometimes pretending that the runaways were their slaves.[83] Despite the vir-ulent racism that plagued the industry, abolitionist-minded Irish, German, and native white boat workers were known on occasion to aid fugitives.[84] North-ern captains with abolitionist sympathies were sometimes known to help, but in most cases captains' commercial interests prevented them from taking ac-tion.[85] Solomon Northrup, who was enslaved on a Louisiana plantation, begged a northern captain to let him stow away. The captain replied that he "pitied him" but that it would be "impossible" for him to avoid customhouse officers in New Orleans. He said he was scared that he would be imprisoned and that his vessel would be attached.[86]

These networks sometimes involved white steamboat workers, but more often African Americans were involved. The bonds of race made slave and free black boat workers natural allies for fugitives looking to negotiate their way on board steamboats. African American stewards and cooks, who hired their own assistants in the cabin, would sometimes risk hiring slave fugitives, especially if they were friends or family members. Boat clerks and captains who were busy with other duties and sometimes failed to check passes in the frequently changing cabin crew made this method of escape feasible.[87]

African American workers also aided stowaways. Stewards and chamber-maids used their access to staterooms to smuggle fugitives. Henry Bibb, look-ing for passage from St. Louis, found a steward "who was a colored man with whom I was acquainted."[88] The black steward "very kindly aided [him]" in getting "into the land of freedom."[89] He soon found himself on "that lovely stream" the Ohio River and then on free soil.[90] In another case, the *Magno-lia* stowaway John P. Parker, who was foraging on deck for food and water, re-ceived help from a deckhand, who was likely African American.[91] When the deckhand noticed Parker peering from below deck, Parker recalled, the man "never said a word but took the plate of food of the man next to him, emptied it into his own, gave me his cup of coffee, and motioned me to go back into the hold."[92]

The story of a Louisiana fugitive named Tom illustrates the spontaneous help that African Americans provided to fugitives. Tom escaped from his master's plantation with two other hands. After stealing their master's skiff, the men set out downriver but were soon captured by a local lumberman in a desolate place known by rivermen as Island No. 95. After nearly a month of forced toil, during which time they chopped wood the lumberman then sold to passing steamboats, Tom stole the skiff for a second time, this time alone and armed with a new plan. Pulling up alongside a large flatboat, which he probably reasoned was from western Pennsylvania because of its coal cargo, he asked the captain for a berth. He told the captain that he was a free black cook from Pittsburgh, put off the *Sultana* onto the island after he fought with the boat's steward. All appeared lost when the officer told him that he "could not take darkies on the boat."[93] At this moment of despair, the boat's free black crew interceded, providing the sort of informal support fugitives came to expect from the region's African American river workers: they pretended to recognize him. The captain hired him. From this moment, Tom's fortunes changed. He worked his way to New Orleans and then fooled another captain when he mixed in with his helpful fellow workers as they booked passage as free men on the northbound *Empress*. He rode past his master's plantation and made it to Cairo, Illinois, where he left the boat. His master never saw him again.

Such stories of unsolicited help were common and appear throughout the written record. Advertisements for runaways repeatedly refer to networks of underground aid. A typical advertisement, placed in New Orleans newspapers, sought a slave Eliza, noting that she likely "was decoyed away by a free colored man, well known on several steamboats, now in the city."[94] Another advertisement warned captains of a "black boy Griffen" who might try to escape upriver, "as he is acquainted with some stewards of steamboats."[95] In July of 1841, an article in the *New Orleans Picayune* reported that a slave stowed away on the *Empress Mail* at Vicksburg and it was "presumed that he was aided by some free negroes on the boat."[96] Philo Tower, a traveler who toured the South in the mid-1850s and published a book about his journey, reported meeting a slave named Margaret who had escaped her Mississippi plantation with the help of an African American chambermaid. According to Tower, Margaret stole her mistress's clothes, "metamorphosed herself into a lady of quality, left the mansion, passed through a crowd, thickly veiled, to the levee, [and] entered an up bound Cincinnati boat." On board she "was secreted by the colored chambermaid in her room to this city."[97] In another case, a myste-

rious black boatman reportedly helped a pregnant house servant named An-
geline to elude the mate, who sat "at the edge of the staging," and to slip aboard
the *El Paso* during the boat's four-day stay near Lexington, Kentucky. The
boatmen then hid her on board. The captain of the *El Paso*, who apparently
"had seen . . . much trouble about them [runaways] on the lower Mississippi,"
testified in court that he had been vigilant in his efforts to prevent fugitives
from coming aboard.[98] He was forced to concede nevertheless, "Where there
is a negro crew on board of a boat, I think it is possible that a negro might be
concealed without the knowledge of the officers."[99] While some accounts of
fugitives receiving unsolicited help were no doubt fiction, their prevalence suggests that many were true.[100]

Slaveholders were well aware of the threat African American boatmen posed
to their hopes of controlling their chattel. They were particularly concerned
about northern free black boat workers. In a May 14, 1844, article titled "Caution to Ship and Steamboat Masters," the editors of the *New Orleans Picayune*
denounced free black boat workers who were part of the "continual stream"
of free blacks who moved in and out of New Orleans in open defiance of the
city's residency laws. These boatmen and -women, the editors warned, came
"with no other view than to entice away our laboring population, and to assist
in concealing and harboring them here, and then facilitating their flight to Ohio
—which is our Canada." The editors charged, "Colored stewards, or cooks,
or hands on the boats use their cunning and the means peculiar to their position to conceal slaves on board boats till they reach safe places for landing."
The editors encouraged boat captains, whose efforts, they claimed, had been
"repeatedly eluded" in recent weeks, to "double their watchfulness."[101] In another article, the newspaper declared that free blacks were "fomenters of disturbance" and that "not a few of them are actively engaged in instigating and
aiding slaves to escape."[102]

Once on board a steamer, fugitives experienced an upriver passage to freedom that mirrored the horrible downriver passage to the auction block that
less fortunate slaves endured. The nature of these journeys to freedom varied
according to the strategies and plans of individual runaways. Fugitives who
passed as workers, for instance, were often content to work for weeks, even
months, in the western river world. Like most slave runaways, slaves who escaped via steamboat were often fleeing their masters temporarily and were not
intending to abscond north. By working on a steamboat, fugitives could evade
tyrannical masters, earn cash, and stay in touch with loved ones in the South.
Although most temporary deserters in the South were female slaves who did

not want to abandon their families but sought respite from plantation life, the presence of escaped male slaves on riverboats illustrates that men sought temporary freedom as well. The slave who worked without his master's permission on a steamboat "for several weeks" between St. Louis and Galena; the Louisiana slave named Peter who "passed" as the free black "Jim" for some ten months aboard the New Orleans–based steamer *Tiger*;[103] and the deep South fugitive named Jacko who worked for seven months on the river steamer *H. M. Wright* before his master recaptured him are just a few examples.[104]

A large number of runaways, however, sought permanent freedom in the North. For these men and women, steamboat passage tested their will and stoked their fears. Whether fugitives were from the city or countryside, whether they had worked on steamboats prior to their escape or had never seen one before in their lives, whether they had help from the crew or not, the danger of recapture loomed large. Each upriver landing presented new danger for fugitives. Elite slaveholders had their own river networks that threatened to expose slave runaways at every stop. In contrast to Atlantic fugitives, whose passage to freedom was often unhindered by interruptions along the way, riverboat runaways were never far from land and the coercion of the law. Steamboats' close proximity to land allowed pursuing masters to telegraph ahead and to alert local constables. In addition to these worries, runaways traveling incognito as free workers or passengers worried about meeting someone who knew them as slaves. The constant comings and goings associated with the steamboat world were such that help from black workers could easily be countered by exposure at the hands of travelers and officers. The journey was one of constant anxiety.

Runaways also risked being exposed by African American crew members.[105] Consequently, African American boat workers had much to gain by courting the favor of captains and other officers. In one case, an engineer began to suspect that one of his firemen was a runaway when he "discovered from the boys cording at wood piles, and other acts, that he was probably a slave."[106] On the steamboat *Doswell*, an African American boatmen betrayed a runaway named Toney to boat officers.[107] In another case, a fugitive reported, "The steamer had hardly gotten under way when the Negro who had hid me brought a white mate to my hiding place." It was "the only time," he said, "I was ever betrayed by one of my own color."[108] Sometimes African American workers betrayed not only fugitives but also the laborers who aided them. In a Missouri case, an African American steward charged an African American porter with hiding a slave on a boat to St. Louis.[109] According to a witness in the case, "There was

Slave Escapes on the Western Rivers

a dispute between the negroes on the El Paso, one negro charging the other with secreting this girl and attempting to run her off."[110]

Because of these dangers, runaways had to constantly guard against revealing their personal histories. The narrative of John Lindsey, a slave who escaped by steamboat from a west Tennessee town, illustrates the lengths to which fugitives had to go to hide their identities while on board. When a "very black" cook approached Lindsay and asked if he was free, he responded with a curt: "I heard of a man in Maryland who got rich by minding his own business" and that it was "in his own interest to mind his own affairs."[111] While such acerbic wit was probably not the norm in such situations, Lindsey's reaction reflects the distrust that operated alongside incidents of racial solidarity during the process of river escape.

The horrors of the passage to freedom varied somewhat according to the means of escape. Stowaways, especially those not having help from a crew member, faced perhaps the most difficult journeys. Louis Hughes's multiple attempts at stowing away reveal the perils of this strategy. In his first attempt he was so near the boat's engineers that they were in constant sight.[112] Lack of food and water soon forced him from his hiding place. Hughes "crept out" at night from his hiding place and "found the table where the deck hands had been eating." On one such occasion, a mate caught him, and Hughes was sent back to his master's plantation. In his second attempt, Hughes hid himself in a hold that was "dark as a dungeon" and filled with hides and cotton bales. After two days without food and water, he was "so weak and faint that [he] could not stand it any longer." At this point, he began "howling and screaming" in a desperate attempt to end his sufferings.[113]

Another stowaway named Willis slipped on board the *Swallow* at a country landing near Bayou Sara and began the long journey upriver.[114] His master missed him and sounded the alarm. A slave catcher, who stood to collect a tidy sum for returning Willis, presumed that Willis took "the first boat up," so he went to Natchez, where he checked all boats for "runaway yellow boys."[115] After the bounty hunter searched the *Swallow* and found nothing, the captain asked him if he was satisfied. "I am not," he replied. The search continued. The slave catcher reported that the men went through "the forepart of the cabin and then the after part." The captain then began "uncovering the heads of the negroes who were lying all over the cabin floor." Still the slave catcher was not convinced. He announced that he "would not leave the boat" until he "was satisfied that he [Willis] was not there."[116] At this moment the men saw Willis "rise up" from under some blankets and they immediately captured him.

John P. Parker had a similarly grim story to tell. "All I could see then was starvation ahead of me," he remembered, "because the latches would not be taken off until Memphis, which meant several days." "Festered with thirst more than hunger," he recalled, "I tried to drink the bilgewater, but it made me deathly sick. Then I took to wandering aimlessly around in the darkness hoping to find something, I did not know what." He grew increasingly desperate. "Weaving around in the darkness," he recalled, "I suddenly found a drop of moisture strike my hand. I stopped [and] held my breath, lest the least movement of mine would take me away from this precious gift. I waited when again there came that slow drop. Holding my hand steady, I moved my body until it had taken the position of my hand, then stood with my mouth wide open to receive that welcome drop. It never came again."[117]

Fugitive passengers faced their own challenges. The slave Charles encountered numerous obstacles in his passage to freedom down the Missouri River from Boonville, Missouri, on the *Wappello*. The word of his escape had spread, and the boat's cook became convinced that he was a fugitive. Soon a series of interrogations ensued involving Charles's papers and his claimed free status. Was he the free man represented in the papers he carried or was he the local escaped slave? Charles was actually posing as Pompey Taylor, a five-foot, eight-inch twenty-two-year-old man with straight hair and a broken right hand. But the fact that Charles was a few years older, stood a few inches taller, and had a bald "seard" head did not deter the fugitive. With the help of a hat and a faked injury (he pretended to not be able to bend one of his fingers), he won the captain's confidence and managed to land in St. Louis. He was last seen boarding a northbound steamer.[118]

Sella Martin faced similar trials during his own passage to freedom. After he managed to board a steamer headed north from New Orleans, his passage was still far from secure. He recalled, "My papers described a man thirty-two years of age, and I was ten years younger at the time."[119] This discrepancy aroused the suspicions of the clerk, who repeatedly questioned him about his background. Finally the clerk announced, "These papers are not satisfactory alone, and unless you can get some responsible person aboard to vouch for your being free, I shall have to put you in irons."[120] At this point, a free black pantryman, whom Martin had recently met in a New Orleans boardinghouse and who was in the clerk's office to vouch for another African American worker, told the clerk "that he knew [Martin] to be a free man." Because the man was a longtime employee of the boat and a man of some property, the clerk "took his word at once" and the matter was settled.[121]

Henry Bibb faced his own difficulties in two separate voyages to freedom. In his first trip, after finding a conveyance across the Ohio River to the village of Madison, Indiana, he boarded a steamer coming from the South in order to get farther upriver. He recalled praying for God's protection and then stepping "boldly on the deck of this splendid swift-running Steamer, bound for the city of Cincinnati." Anxiety and worry consumed his voyage. "This being the first voyage that I had ever taken on board of a Steamboat, I was filled with fear and excitement," he remembered. These feelings also stemmed from the knowledge that he "was surrounded by the vilest enemies of God and man, liable to be seized and bound hand and foot, by any white man, and taken back into captivity." He hid amid the deck passengers, hiding from the light and hoping to be mistaken for white. "Every time during the night that the mate came round with a light," he said, "I was afraid he would see that I was a colored man, and take me up; hence I kept from the light as much as possible."[122] To further shield himself from passing officers, he later paid a deckhand twenty-five cents for the use of his hammock. Bibb also worried about mechanical failure. He stayed awake all night for fear of explosions, which he "had often heard of." Every time the engines blew off steam, he feared that "the boilers had bursted" and that he would be killed. By morning, he was thankful to have lived "through all the dangers" of his voyage.[123]

Bibb did reach freedom, but he returned to the South to help his family escape and was recaptured. He escaped again and then faced another steamboat voyage—this time on board a Missouri River steamer. After sneaking on board, he mixed with the deck passengers and waited fearfully for the clerk to come by and collect his fare. Knowing that the officer would almost certainly demand his papers and that he would be sent back again to his master, he "insinuated himself among" a large group of Irish passengers "so as," he explained, "to get their good graces, believing that if I should get into difficulty they would stand by me."[124] With money he had taken from his master, he brought a "crowd" of them up to the bar and "treated" them to drinks. His generosity had the desired effect, for, Bibb recalled, drinking together "brought us into a kind of union."[125] When the porter came around telling everyone who had not purchased passage to go to the clerk's office, Bibb asked some of his newfound friends to buy him a ticket. Filled with liquor and entertained by a few "yarns" from Bibb, they gladly agreed. When the boat reached St. Louis, his ticket was taken with the rest, no questions asked.

Another fugitive passenger, Edward Hicks, "did not sleep for four of five nights at all" but instead "dozed a little in [the] daytime."[126] Fearing that a boat following his own was pursuing him, he joined the firemen heaving wood into the boat's furnace, hoping that his efforts would induce more speed. He also worried about the clerk, who could at any time check his papers. Luckily his fears were unrealized and he continued safely upriver to Pittsburgh.

Fugitives passing as workers faced similar threats. In one case, two fugitives, Peter and Paul, faced the harrowing trial of having to pass by their master's woodyard on their voyage up the Mississippi.[127] They successfully passed only by virtue of an unusually abbreviated stop for fuel that did not allow their master time to thoroughly search the boat. Harry and Nelson, two fugitives who had recently passed as workers to gain passage on a steamboat at Glasgow's landing, were similarly anxious to avoid being seen in their master's community as the boat pulled out and headed downriver. A suspicious watchman recalled that "the . . . negroes kept on the side of the boat off from shore, they continued on that side until the boat turned in the mouth of [the] Chariton to go down the [Missouri] river." When the boat came about and headed downriver, the witness testified, "He again noticed that said negroes changed sides and got on to the side of the boat off from the Glasgow shore and there stayed until the boat had passed Glasgow."[128]

The fugitive New Orleans slave Shadrack, who passed as the free black Jim Thorton, faced what Harry and Nelson only feared: he met someone who knew that he was a runaway. When the passenger Henry Peterson boarded the *Wave* on the lower Ohio River, he immediately saw the man he knew as Shadrack. He reportedly "spoke to him and knew him well" and told the captain that he should be arrested.[129] Luckily for Thorton, who was working as a waiter on the *Wave*, the captain stood by his worker and disregarded Henry Peterson's charges.[130] Not waiting for a change of heart from his captain, Thorton disappeared one night when ice blocked the *Wave*'s progress upriver.

Regardless of how fugitives shipped on board steamboats, all faced the possibility of detection when getting off them. Fugitives needing to change boats within the South in the process of escape faced questioning by levee police. John P. Parker fooled New Orleans police by mixing in with workers on his new boat.[131] Fugitives were at just as great a risk of being caught on levees in free states. One slave boatman recalled in the 1850s that "though Cairo was free in name, it was one of the most active depots of the Negro catchers" who "made quite a large income by returning [slaves] to their masters under the sanction of the Fugitive Slave Law."[132] As threatening as bounty hunters could be, vigilant boat officers posed a bigger danger. After his steamer docked at Cincinnati's levee, Henry Bibb recalled waiting "until after most of the

Slave Escapes on the Western Rivers

passengers had gone off of the boat" before he "walked gracefully up the street as if [he] was not running away."[133] At the same levee J. D. Green "waited until the passengers had left the boat."[134] Seeing no officers, he went ashore, walked up the embankment, and proceeded into the city.

By leaving the *Pike No. 3* in Cincinnati, J. D. Green escaped to a city that attracted a large number of river fugitives. In a case involving a slave worker who ran away into the Queen City, the Kentucky Supreme Court commented: "It may be, and we believe it is true, that it is more hazardous [for steamboats] to land with slaves at Cincinnati, than at other points in free territory on the Ohio River."[135] Cincinnati was the closest major free river city to the South and one of the most vibrant commercial cities in the growing western economy, and hundreds of boats each month traveled to the city's levee. It was the gateway to Canada and the beginning of freedom.

The city's small but vibrant African American community helped fugitives considerably. Many were former fugitives themselves or had migrated from the South and were active in a range of political organizations, including the Ohio Anti-Slavery Society and the Anti-Slavery Sewing Society, which supplied fugitives with needed clothing. Runaways could find shelter at the African Methodist Episcopal Church, where they could be treated to sermons denouncing slavery. The church made sure it was a friendly audience by denying slaveholders membership in their fellowship.[136] The city's abolitionists also took direct action to prevent the recapture of fugitives. Cincinnati was home to the most active antislavery population in the West.[137]

Composing nearly a quarter of the city's employed male population, free black boat workers provided a crucial link to this community. One fugitive, who had already escaped to the city, claimed that when runaways got to Cincinnati's levee, "the colored men in the boats" whispered to them "where to find the abolitionists."[138] The free black barber John Hatfield helped fugitives in a variety of ways. In one case, he warned a fugitive in Cincinnati that bounty hunters were coming to recapture her. While he was at work on a steamboat, he recalled, "it came to [his] ear" that the woman's pursuers were closing in on her.[139] After warning her, he "never felt so pleased with any thing [he] ever did in [his] life."[140] Hatfield also claimed to have repeatedly sheltered runaways in his Cincinnati home.[141]

Cincinnati was an especially favorite destination for runaways, but fugitives fled to nearly every port city and country landing that was on free soil. On the upper Mississippi, Alton, Galena, Nauwoo, Davenport, and St. Paul all attracted runaways. Along the Ohio, Evansville, Jeffersonville, New Al-

"Meeting in the African Church, Cincinnati, Ohio." From the
Collection of the Public Library of Cincinnati and Hamilton County.

bany, and Marietta were a few of the destinations. At Ripley, Ohio, just beyond Cincinnati, runaways knew to look for the lantern of abolitionist John
Rankin, who had a reputation among slaves for helping runaways. Rankin col-
laborated extensively with the town's free black community and aided countless river fugitives.[142] In Pittsburgh, men like Martin Delany and ordinary
hotel workers with links to the river all were ready to help runaways. Delany's
Philanthropic Society helped 269 fugitives pass northward in one year.[143]

When fugitives reached free soil, the rivers that helped them gain freedom
became a reminder of how close the world of slavery remained. Runaways
knew that steamboats collapsed time and space for masters and slave catchers just as they had for them. Thus many fugitives chose to keep moving. Using
informal networks of aid, river runaways took advantage of every available
form of transport to get farther north. Those with access to northern rivers
often continued with steamboat travel. Illinois River steamers, in particular,
were a gateway to Chicago and Canadian ports for many fugitives. Others
simply traveled overland. Allen Sydney, Henry Bibb, and William Wells Brown
all followed roads in their journeys from Cincinnati to northern Ohio. Others,

like Sella Martin, who escaped a steamer at Cairo, booked passage on north-bound trains to Chicago.[144]

Such stories illustrate an important component of the hidden history of the slave Mississippi in the antebellum West. The slaveholding class was determined to control the mobility of labor in the western region, but the technologies that underlay their capital accumulation made it impossible for them to consistently control the movements of their workers. The southern economy necessarily relied on a close relationship among rural, riverfront plantations, where slavery was most cruel, the relative freedoms of southern cities, and the even greater freedoms of the river. Bounty hunters, riverfront slaveholders, levee police, and slave patrols could not prevent the freedoms of the river from creating a cosmopolitan mentality among the broader slave population and the creation of networks that denied slaveholders' mastery.

The Mississippi River escape vignettes are testimony to the remarkable creativity that slaves were able to muster in order to flee their proscribed status. In many cases, slaves were able to manipulate categories of race and labor in order to create the appearance of freedom. They used their knowledge of the social conventions of southern society to create new personas that furthered their escapes. These were defiant acts that challenged southern beliefs that rigid boundaries divided white and black, slave and free. The creativity of slaves was also evident in their ability to form the connections between river and land that so often facilitated escapes. The oral culture of the river was able to link faraway places. It provided western slaves with both the mental image of freedom and the social networks that helped hatch escape plans.

Runaways' efforts were a part of a broader fight against slavery. River fugitives challenged southern ideas of loyal slaves, provided hope to those still in bondage, and supplied a steady stream of abolitionist activists to the North. After making his way north from the Ohio, William Wells Brown began working on a Lake Erie steamboat, a job that allowed him to help others gain the freedom that he so enjoyed. Each time his boat arrived in Cleveland, he "never failed to have a delegation" of runaways that he helped transport to Canada.[145] His efforts, and the narrative that inspired thousands more, became one of the many ripples of the slave Mississippi.

chapter five

Rascals on the Antebellum Mississippi

The Madison Henderson Gang

THE YEAR 1841 was a momentous one for two steamboat slaves, William Wells Brown and Madison Henderson. Henderson made his mark on history through violence. In April, with the help of three free black rivermen, he killed two St. Louis bank clerks in a robbery the men hoped would make them rich. It did not. By July he was swinging from the city's gallows with his fellow conspirators. Three-quarters of the city's population turned out to see the execution.[1] It was later that fall when William Wells Brown escaped up the Ohio River bound for freedom.

Madison Henderson and William Wells Brown were both products of the same slave Mississippi world. Both worked on steamboats and lived in St. Louis and New Orleans. Both knew the lash and had personal experience with the horrors of the internal slave trade. But history has been far more kind to William Wells Brown. Brown's life story was heralded by the antislavery establishment of his time and has become part of the canon of slave life in our own. In contrast, Henderson's confessions, and those of his friends, have languished in obscurity. Slaveholding whites shuddered for some time about the "robbers" and "murderers" who made a practice of "having agencies sleeping" but most reformers preferred to forget the incident.[2] Even Brown, who probably knew Henderson, chose not to include him or his spectacular crimes in his life story. He apparently did not think Henderson's story would advance a respectable case for abolition. Historians of slavery have echoed Brown's uneasiness over Henderson's tale of murder and death. Despite the contem-

FOR SAINT LOUIS!

The Regular Steam Packet

EAGLE!

THE undersigned, having chartered the above Steam-boat, for the purpose of accommodating all the citizens of **ALTON**, and the vicinity, who may wish to see the

Four Negroes Executed,

At St. Louis, on *FRIDAY NEXT*, would inform the public that the Boat will leave this place at **SEVEN** o'clock, A. M., and St. Louis at a-bout **FOUR**, P. M., so as to reach home the same evening.

The Boat will be repaired and fitted up for the occasion; and every attention will be paid to the comfort of Passengers.

FARE FOR THE TRIP TO ST. LOUIS & BACK
ONLY $1 50 !!!

The Negroes are to be hung on the point of *Duncan's Island,* just below St. Louis. The Boat will drop alongside, so that **ALL CAN SEE WITHOUT DIFFICULTY.**

For Passage, apply to

W. A. Wentworth,
P. M. Pinckard.

ALTON, JULY 7, 1841

A broadside advertising the *Eagle*'s excursion to view the execution
of Madison Henderson, Charles Brown, James Seward, and
Amos Warrick, July 7, 1841. Courtesy of the Missouri
Historical Society, St. Louis.

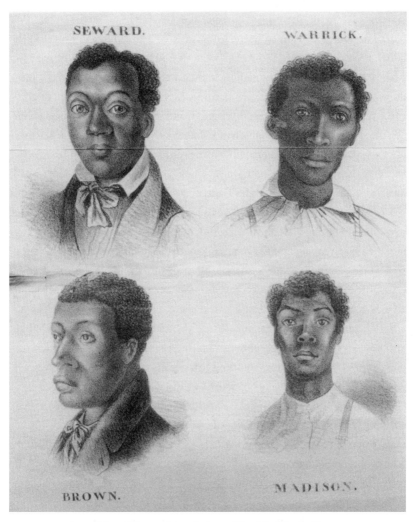

An etching of James Seward, Amos Warrick, Charles Brown,
and Madison Henderson. From *Trials and Confessions of Madison
Henderson*. Courtesy of Cornell University Law Library.

porary sensation over the men's rascality, historians have not viewed the four
men hanged on Duncan Island as worthy of more than passing comment. There
has been excellent work done on slave crime and its meanings, particularly in
the context of plantation labor struggles, but public, larger scale lawbreaking
has been neglected.[3]

The men's stories reveal an important rascal tradition that flourished alongside, and at times in conjunction with, more romanticized forms of African
American resistance. While their deaths symbolized the strength of the South's

systems of control, their lives illustrate the weaknesses inherent to that system. The four men hanged in St. Louis created a world of their own on the docks, levees, plantation landings, city quays, and steamboat decks of the Mississippi River economy. Although these men were not above occasionally swindling other working-class people, for the most part their actions were directed at the region's elites. They lied to, cheated, and stole from bankers, shopkeepers, plantation owners, and merchants. Indeed, their countinghouse heist was not an isolated incident. The men's confessions reveal lives spent roving the western rivers in pursuit of money. Their accounts depict a widespread, loosely organized, lawless underworld that connected the levee districts of western river cities. Their multifaceted activities, which included helping slaves to escape, theft, illegal trade, forgery, and, eventually, murder, suggest the ways in which lawbreaking and the river culture could be a powerful combination. In a world founded on the wholesale theft of human life and structured by economic exploitation, the men roved the western rivers in pursuit of spendable cash, a quest that frustrated boat owners, urban authorities, and southern slaveholders in the bargain. When the *Louisville Journal* called them "desperate rascals, thieves, robbers, cut-throats, and blacklegs," the newspaper's editors conveyed long-standing worries about working-class criminality in both the slave and free economies of the western rivers.[4]

The stories of most river workers are lost to history, but the *Louisville Journal*'s "desperate rascals" had their life stories preserved by an opportunistic newspaperman, Adam B. Chambers, and an accomplice jailer, George Melody. The men worked together to profit from the men's sensational crimes and the widespread interest in the condemned men. Chambers transcribed the confessions, and Melody apparently demanded coauthorship and probably a share of the profits, in exchange for granting Chambers access to the four men. The *Trials and Confessions of Madison Henderson, alias Blanchard, Alfred Amos Warrick, James W. Seward, and Charles Brown* is composed of four sections, each one the story of a single man's life.[5] Chambers's self-proclaimed "rascally yellow covered book" was sold at the hanging and carried by riverboat to a wider national audience.[6]

Trials and Confessions has the same problems of reliability as do other similar types of slave narratives. The confessions of Nat Turner, the trials of Denmark Vesey, and other black criminal narratives all were shaped in no small measure by the prejudices of elite white male authors and the buying public for whom they were intended.[7] Chambers was selling his narrative to a southern white community who firmly believed in the dangers that free blacks, and loosely supervised slaves like Henderson, posed to society. Ira Berlin writes that whites in the upper South believed free blacks to be "inveterate idlers and potential incendiaries."[8] This context undoubtedly influenced *Trials and Confessions*, but how, and in what ways, is difficult to fully unravel. Certainly the fact that Chambers was the writer and that the men were condemned to die gave him overwhelming power. The mechanical, structured pleas for forgiveness that open and close each story suggest that Chambers knew the popular genre of confessional narratives and was seeking to emulate a generic formula. What is less certain is the extent to which Chambers created or manipulated the facts of the stories. While he claimed, "My object was to get from each a true narrative, regardless of the effect it might have on the sale of the book," he also said that he saw his mission as collecting details that would help communities guard from such criminals in the future.[9] He wanted to hear a lurid story that would rouse slaveholders to action, and that is certainly what he recorded. In Madison Henderson's story, for instance, Henderson boasted about his ability to date white women in New Orleans, thus confirming whites' worst fears of the aspirations of black men. His testimony was never challenged in the New Orleans press, but Chambers may have written it in an attempt, consciously or unconsciously, to create a criminal image that would elicit public outcry. This kind of testimony raises doubts about its authenticity, but a close reading of the narratives suggests that the men's voices were not silenced, despite their decidedly subordinate position in the creation of the stories. Chambers was a well-known professional journalist, and he had respect for his craft. He put in a lot of effort over a five-week period between the men's sentencing and execution, interviewing the men and writing their stories. He took notes in the presence of others, wrote their formal stories in the evenings, and then read the confessions back to the men, who he claimed were given a chance to make corrections.[10]

The condemned men apparently used the opportunity Chambers gave them to shape the facts of their lives to suit their own objectives, and their objectives were not always different than those of their interviewer. Chambers's desire to tell a detailed tale of the lawless underworld of the western rivers was apparently shared by men who had nothing to lose by augmenting their already notorious reputations. While in some instances, the men may have honestly conveyed their autobiographies, in others, the four may have had an interest in collaborating with Chambers in hyping the more sensational passages of their confessions. In his confession to Chambers, for instance, Charles Brown said that he had attended the abolitionist hotbed Oberlin College and that he was paid by the Ohio Anti-Slavery Society to help slaves escape. However, citing a desire to clear his conscious of any misrepresentations, he later modified his story. He claimed in a last-minute confession to a local pastor that he invented aspects of his story in order to shock southern whites.[11] In the days before his hanging, he affirmed that he had helped runaway slaves but said that he had never been to Oberlin and that he had never been a member of any abolitionist organization. While Chambers held to the veracity of his own account of Brown's life, records from Oberlin College reveal no student with Brown's name and thus support the pastor's version of Brown's story.[12] Modern scholars' portrayals of the Underground Railroad as a loosely organized network rather than a highly structured, well-funded organization suggest that Brown's second confession was far more plausible.[13]

While both Chambers and the four men brought their own interests to the crafting of the account, there is little doubt that the men's stories had a core of truth. Contemporary commentary from both the abolitionist and the southern press suggests that significant portions of the men's stories were based on verifiable fact. Newspaper coverage quickly seized on the debate over the veracity of Charles Brown's abolitionism, but no contemporary questioned either the men's guilt or the substance of their stories. The *Boston Liberator* complained about the speediness of the men's trials, and the inequity between punishments given to white and black murder defendants in St. Louis, but it did not dispute the credibility of their confessions.[14] The *St. Louis Daily New Era*, a rival of Chambers's *Missouri Republican*, took a balanced view as to the narrative's reliability. "That parts of the revelations may be untrue," the paper asserted, "we think highly probable: that other parts are correct, we think equally certain: that the whole has been compiled with a view to strict accuracy as to the disclosures, on the part of the editor, we have every right to believe."[15] The *New Orleans Picayune* felt that "while there may be some exaggerations," there were not enough to "render the story undeserving of confidence."[16]

The vitality of the men's confessions is especially evident in the apparent struggle between prisoner and interviewer over the meaning of the men's lives. Tensions within the text suggest that Chambers differed from the men over how their lawbreaking was best interpreted. Although in some cases, Chambers and the men may have had common interests, the stories indicate a struggle over themes and tone. Chambers's newspaper editorials about the narratives suggest that he interpreted the men's stories as a descent into sin and a lesson about the need to control people of color.[17] He felt that, left to their own devices, people of African descent were bound for moral corruption and would succumb to the disease of vice. If Africans were given too much freedom, their inherently rascal natures would emerge. He believed whites could do more to prevent black criminality from manifesting itself, but the ultimate source of lawlessness was the inherent wayward tendencies of the black race.

Chambers's use of the word "rascal" was not original. The ruling class had for a long time used "rascal" to describe the rebellious rabble. The word originated with the Old French word *rascaille*, and its early-modern English derivatives, "rascality," "rascaldom," and "rascalism." Rascals were associated with lawlessness, dishonesty, and fraud.[18] On Herman Melville's *Fidele*, white passengers immediately labeled a downtrodden old black beggar a rascal.[19] By the mid-nineteenth century the word had also taken on new "scientific" meanings among southern slaveholders. Samuel Cartwright, a New Orleans doctor and proslavery essayist, defined rascality as a disease of the mind "peculiar to the negroes," caused by idleness.[20] Inactivity, according to Cartwright, led to overly carbonized blood, which in turn led to "slothfulness, torpor, and disinclination."[21] Black liberty always fostered the disease. Free blacks "who lived in clusters by themselves" were especially vulnerable, since they had no masters present to encourage the vigorous exercise on plantation crops necessary to thwart the onset of the malady.[22] Once in the throes of rascality, according to Cartwright, blacks "break, waste and destroy everything they handle . . . and pay no attention to the rights of property."[23] Cartwright developed his theories a decade after the men's hanging, but Chambers shared his belief that black freedom inevitably led to mischief.

While the introduction and conclusion of each narrative is filled with the men's misgivings and remorse for their lawlessness, the main texts of their stories convey a much different understanding of the word "rascal." The men used the term matter-of-factly when referring to any of a number of illegal acts that allowed them to create a life on their own terms. Henderson, for instance, referred to friends who were "adept at rascality" and others who were "great rascals."[24] They associated the term with a variety of positive attributes. Rascality demanded intelligence, a quality all the men had in abundance and took pride in. Henderson's intelligence manifested itself in the great cunning and cleverness of his schemes. His three free black accomplices used their intelligence to acquire literacy. New York abolitionist Gerrit Smith recalled that James Seward displayed "uncommonly good mental powers" when he attended his school.[25] The men's rascality also conveyed their embrace of masculine virtues such as toughness, courage, cleverness, dexterity, and flamboyance.[26]

The appeal of rascality stemmed from their experience with exploitation and racism. In the stories, Chambers's proslavery beliefs no doubt prompted him to present the conditions of slaves and free blacks as less dire than they actually were, but all four men conveyed their oppression. Each man told a coming-of-age story that revolved around a gradual, but growing, disgust with slavery, with abusive supervision, and with a society that denied them opportunity. Each story portrayed a violent world, a world in which physical abuse was a constant threat and one in which slave traders and masters threatened to disrupt their family lives at any moment.

The men's critique of their world shared many themes with the trickster tales that flourished in the oral tradition of African American slave communities. Trickster tales were pragmatic stories that educated slaves in how to negotiate the overwhelming power of the master. They sometimes involved stories of people, but more often they utilized animal heroes that allowed for more symbolic meanings. The central theme running through these tales celebrated the efforts of the weak to manipulate the strong. Using their wits, and their intimate knowledge of the ways of the powerful, heroic spiders, hares, tortoises, and the ubiquitous Brer Rabbit deceived powerful wolves, foxes, and alligators in order to achieve their desires. While most plantation slaves emulated tricksters in their effort to accumulate food for survival, the stories indicate yearnings that went far beyond struggles over provisions. The tales feature heroes that seek wealth, success, prestige, and sexual conquest. They imagine a world where the weak are able to overpower the physically strong, a world where the rabbit vanquishes the wolf.[27] The four St. Louis rascals shared both the intelligence and the individualistic fantasies of the trickster heroes. They probably crafted their stories knowing that these themes would resonate well with their friends, to whom they addressed their confessions.

In some ways, however, the men did not resemble tricksters so much as they foreshadowed another figure in African American folk tales: the turn-of-the-century Badman. Unlike tricksters, and like Madison Henderson and his free black friends, Badmen were willing to use violence to assert their power. In addition, whereas slave tricksters challenged plantation rules and customs, Badmen challenged the public law. Badmen were bandits like Railroad Bill, a real person whose stories were told for many decades into the twentieth century. In 1893, Railroad Bill, or Morris Slater, killed an Alabama policeman who demanded he surrender his gun. He then fled to begin a career of eluding the law by riding the rails through the state. Railroad Bill stole food from trains, often using threats of violence to make away with his dinner. He continued in this manner for three years until two bounty hunters shot him to death.[28] He became a symbol of how individual black men could assert their power within an immoral social, economic, and legal system. Heroic men of violence were difficult to celebrate within earshot of antebellum masters, so we will never know how the slave community remembered Madison Henderson and his friends. But these men's lives suggest that Badman figures predated their folk celebration in the Jim Crow South.

MADISON HENDERSON portrayed his life as a rascal as beginning with his sale to the West. Born in a Virginia plantation county, he was in his early teens when he was sold by his master to a trader and was forced to move away from his family. He then spent six weeks in a Virginia jail waiting for the trader to amass enough slaves so that they could proceed to Richmond. After another week in a Richmond jail, the trader loaded his slaves on board an Atlantic ship bound for New Orleans. That Henderson's narrative begins with this series of horrible events indicates their centrality to his consciousness.[29] While his separation from his family was formative, he also blamed slavery for his inability to realize his talents. A man of many skills, he felt there were few opportunities to exercise his talents while he remained a faithful, law-abiding slave. In contrast, his remarkable ingenuity, courage, mental acumen, and physical dexterity were all useful in leading a life outside the law. When an early master, who was a slave trader, introduced him to various cons, he quickly became interested in an opportunity to "manifest" his "talents."[30] Soon Henderson had little compunction about robbery and swindling. Indeed, he claimed that obtaining money "by any means" was "fair and right."[31]

Amos Warrick's life story is also told in the context of the horrors of slavery. Like many other free blacks in both the North and the South, he was kidnapped into servitude. Warrick grew up the free son of a North Carolina barber, but when he ran away from home in his early teenage years he ended up in jail for a minor offense. A trader then took him from jail and sold him to a barber in New Orleans. Encounters that reveal the brutality of slavery punctuate the rest of his tale.[32]

Like Henderson, Warrick became an outlaw in part because what the men called "honest" labor was so unfulfilling. He recoiled against the tight discipline and the lack of opportunity for slaves and free blacks. When he ran away from an abusive New Orleans master and passed his way onto the deck of an Atlantic brig as a free black, he found that free black sailors worked very much like slaves. When he was denied wages from the *Elizabeth Jane*, a ship that ran between New York and New Orleans, he fought the captain. Because Warrick "worsted" the old man, he ended up back in New Orleans's Calaboose for two months.[33] Back on the forecastle again after his release from jail, he had another wage dispute; he fought back this time by deserting with several other hands.[34] Later, on the *Florida* near Liverpool, England, another altercation started when Warrick's captain criticized him for not doing his duties. Warrick, who apparently felt unjustly accused, challenged him to a "fair fight" on deck. He so decisively won the bout that he proved himself "so good a man"; his captain, on the other hand, was reduced to "a boy."[35] When his New Orleans master recaptured him, Warrick was sent to a sugar plantation that he "did not like" because his "arms got sore." He didn't like the food either. The slaves were given no meat, a situation Warrick rectified by stealing "a lot of hams" in the manner of the trickster folk heroes. He soon ran away and headed for New Orleans, where he began working as a free hand on steamboats.[36] Here his struggle with authority continued. In one case, he quit an upper Mississippi steamer after having a falling out with the steward.[37] Warrick eventually saved enough money to open a St. Louis barbershop, but he remained resentful of his limited opportunities. While Chambers no doubt viewed his rebelliousness as evidence of poor character, Warrick's narrative stresses that his rascality took place in a violent world of racism and class struggle.

In a different part of the country, James Seward's early decision to live outside the law similarly involved an intense dislike and distrust of honest labor. Growing up in upstate New York, Seward was influenced early in his life by the radical ideas that flourished in this reform-minded region. He traveled through Ithaca, Geneva, Seneca Falls, Rochester, and Buffalo at the peak of the Second Great Awakening and the leveling spirit it bred. Contact with the region's abolitionists and his extensive reading made him even more conscious of the depth of American racism. He soon believed that his chances of advancement and fulfillment were minimal if he labored within the law. Opportunities for free blacks in New York were certainly better than they were for slaves in the South, but, for Seward, they were not nearly enough. Early in his adolescence he "became adverse to labor."[38] In his late teenage years, he took a job teaching school, worked in a wool factory, did farm work, and even held a position as an apprentice shoemaker. He found all these jobs unsatisfactory.[39] At this point in his life he became greatly influenced by a relative who believed that "the world was dishonest and that it was the right of every man to live without labor if he could make a living any other way. All men practiced in their trading and intercourse with each other greater or lesser fraud, and it was perfectly fair and right. It was only the weak minded and ignorant who depend on gaining property and wealth through the drudgery of labor."[40] He soon became restless "under any restraint."[41] From this time on, Seward determined to "cheat the world as much as possible" and to "support myself in an easy life."[42] In the *Boston Liberator*, Gerrit Smith recalled Seward's view on racism: "I well remember that, in poor James' opinion, nothing but the possession of riches could turn aside the daily shafts of this prejudice." According to Smith, Seward had left his school to "recover . . . his humanity in spite of his dark skin."[43] There were limits, though, to Seward's lawless philosophy: he preferred what he called "fashionable rascality."[44] Seward told Chambers that he wanted to "cheat the world as much as possible" but sought not to commit any "heinous offense."[45] He thought that gambling, counterfeiting, and other "cheating in trade" was permissible but that break-ins, with their possibility of violence, were beyond the pale of morally conscionable rascal activities. By making this distinction, Seward attempted to distance himself from Henderson and Brown, both of whom he considered more hardened rascals. In Seward's mind he was an unlucky accomplice to these ringleaders.

In contrast to Seward, Charles Brown interpreted rascality very broadly. Born free in South Carolina, he became interested early in his life in the cause of abolition. "Before leaving Charleston," Brown said, "I heard and studied considerably about the abolition of slavery, and had imbibed a strong passion to engage in the cause."[46] He probably read David Walker's *Appeal to the Coloured Citizens of the World*, a pamphlet that northern free black sailors distributed through Charleston's slave and free black communities during Brown's years in the city.[47] Unlike most abolitionists, Walker encouraged slaves to use violence to overthrow bondage. Walker's *Appeal* was the most radical denunciation of slavery in the nineteenth century, and its influence on Brown was likely immense. Brown carried Walker's ideas first to New Orleans, where he worked as a pastry cook, and then to Cincinnati, where his belief in direct action took root within the city's black abolitionist community. Unlike the city's respectable abolitionists, however, Brown had little respect for property laws of any kind. He helped fugitive slaves run away, but his thieving was not limited to human property.[48]

Brown's willingness to break the law in order to acquire wealth apparently strained his religious principles. In Cincinnati, he was a "punctual" member of the "Methodist church" (perhaps the African Methodist Episcopal Church).

He "made no profession of religion," however, during his rascal operations outside the city.[49] In this respect, his lukewarm Christianity resembled Seward's beliefs. After an early interest in religion Seward "learned that my religion was not real."[50]

All four men, in fact, defined themselves not through religion but by their ability to consume. Having the power to purchase material goods, and to advertise it publicly in front of both slaveholders and slaves, was a way of transgressing the bounds of their proscribed status. When Madison Henderson's schemes were successful and he was flush with cash, he acted as if he was a New Orleans Creole dandy. He treated his friends, dressed in the finest of garments, and escorted Crescent City ladies on carriage rides through the streets of the French Quarter.[51] "I always dressed fine," he recalled, "and took any other indulgence I desired."[52] He said, "It would be impossible to tell all the money I spent with women."[53] Seward remembered discovering early in his life that "the things of this world . . . were not abhorrent to [his] feelings." He sought out a "whirl of sensual passions and enjoyments" and looked forward to "a long life of iniquitous pleasure."[54] For all but Brown, liquor was central to this pursuit. Henderson was the light drinker of the three. He claimed that he never got drunk but had a "usual number of glasses," which he consumed "morning, noon, and night."[55] Unlike tricksters and Badmen, who were nearly always self-centered in their designs, by engaging in drinking and other consumptive habits, these men acted collectively. The men sometimes cheated each other out of money, but they were also generous with their cash. Madison Henderson was well known around New Orleans, the base of his operations, as a free spender. Warrick reported that he "always had plenty of money and was very free with it. Any little thing any of us wanted he could manage to get for us, and was a general favorite."[56] Even as city authorities continued to jail and beat Henderson for theft, Warrick "never heard anything disreputable of him" in the circles in which they traveled.[57] Henderson's generosity helped build his folk hero status within New Orleans's diverse working class.

The men's rascality was intimately linked to their mobility through the pan-Mississippi region. All of the men moved into river employment in the last years of their lives, a period that began in the late 1830s and lasted until their deaths in 1841. During these final years, they moved on and off boats and in and out of ports, learning the social landscape of the Mississippi world. Madison Henderson's contact with the river world was less constrained than that of most river slaves; he controlled his own time, lived apart from his master, made his own bargains with boats, and apparently kept some of his wages.[58] He shipped out from New Orleans and St. Louis and was frequently on free soil. Brown, Seward, and Warrick traveled even more widely. Because of their contacts in both free territory and the slave South, they were the most feared of free black river workers among whites. Brown moved between Cincinnati, where his wife lived, and New Orleans, where much of his life story took place. Seward worked in Ohio River trades and thus moved with ease between the lower North and the upper South. Warrick, after working for years as a sailor on Atlantic ships, began shipping out of New Orleans, and later St. Louis, journeying up the Yazoo River, up the Missouri River, and to upper Mississippi River cities, among other places.[59] Their movement through the slave economy no doubt broadened their understanding of the evils of slavery and may have helped inform their graduation from subtle trickery to brutal killing as a way to satisfy their hunger for material goods.

Since the men sought wealth and status, it is not surprising that they tended to work in cabin positions on western steamboats. Warrick variously shipped as a second steward and a fireman, and later, after working as a barber in a St. Louis shop, he began cutting hair on steamboats. Drawing on earlier experiences with hotel work, Seward often shipped as a waiter, but he also worked as a fireman and a second cook. Henderson recalled shipping as a waiter on one occasion, but he likely filled other positions as well on his many journeys up and down the Mississippi. Brown apparently worked as a barber but may have also worked as a cook.[60]

Working in the river culture gave new support to their rascality. Steamboat workers were more likely to end up in jail than other occupational groups and this propensity to live outside the law may have influenced the men.[61] Poverty, transience, youth, and the occupation's rough masculine deck culture all encouraged crime. Most of these crimes were misdemeanors, but violent assaults and even killings were not uncommon in the levee districts of western cities.[62] Warrick, Seward, Henderson, and Brown may have worked in respectable cabin positions but they were more like deckhands in their general contempt for authority. Southern newspapers certainly were quick to connect the four men's actions with their participation in a criminal river culture. The *Louisville Journal* reported that the men's St. Louis crimes were part of the yearly escalation in lawbreaking that came with the spring thaw and the accompanying increase in river commerce. In an article titled "Robberies, Robbers, and Blackleg, and etc.," the editors wrote that "the season is at hand when the whole hordes of desperate rascals, thieves, robbers, cut-throats, and blacklegs who have been during the winter congregated at New Orleans, usually disperse in bands through the more northern towns on the western rivers. . . . The terrible affair at St. Louis, which we published yesterday, shows that they are already there, and that they have begun their operations with a bold hand."[63] The *Memphis Enquirer* also reported on the association between the river and crime that people were making in the wake of the St. Louis killings. In an attempt to stop the spread of violence to their city, editors warned river hands that Memphis citizens were an "ugly set of customers" to deal with.[64]

The connection between the river and criminality that southern newspapers were so quick to make stemmed in part from the broad communication networks that river mobility fostered. Henderson, Brown, Seward, and Warrick cultivated friendships during their travels that spanned the varied topography of their world. Many of these connections were made during work on steamboats. Madison Henderson remembered that it was on the steamboat *Agnes*, on the upper Mississippi, that he first met James Seward and another man named Prime Bruce.[65] Henderson's job as cabin boy facilitated this meeting. By carrying food to passengers, he moved in and out of the kitchen in which Seward and Bruce worked. The levee was another place where the men made contacts. In New Orleans, Henderson and Brown met after hearing about each other. As Brown recalled, "I had frequently heard of Madison, before I became acquainted with him, as a man of extraordinary talents and great daring. The boys about Orleans both loved and feared him. I first saw him on the *Tuskarora* steamboat, where he was pointed out to me."[66] The men also fraternized in city jails. Seward and Warrick met in New Orleans's Calaboose, where each was trying to prove his free status to city authorities. Warrick met Henderson in the same prison. Warrick remembered, "It was during my stay in jail that I first got acquainted with Madison the man who is condemned with me. He was in jail three or four times and once was flogged."[67] The four men frequented places that catered to transient workers. Leah's black boardinghouse in St. Louis was one such place. Run by a local free black washerwoman and her free black riverman husband, Peter Charleville, Leah's was a center of off-the-boat social life. During meals at Leah's all four men met Ennis, the man who eventually turned them in. It was also here that Brown met Warrick and Seward. The boardinghouse, and Warrick's barbershop, became meeting places for plotting the group's final series of St. Louis burglaries. The men's rascal activities predated their river employment, but the slave Mississippi allowed them to forge new friendships and created new opportunities to strive for their freedom.[68]

Like other river workers, the men had a variety of family connections in port cities. Warrick and Seward made little mention of their personal lives in their stories of Mississippi River life and were apparently single, but Brown and Henderson both reported having family ties. Brown said, "I leave many friends—many associates, companions, relatives—and, hardest of all, I separate from a dear wife and child."[69] Brown begged the community of Cincinnati not to harm them because "of the offenses of the husband and father."[70] Madison Henderson reported having a variety of affairs in New Orleans and claimed to have fathered children with both a white woman of French descent and a local slave. His relationship with a slave named Serena lasted five or six years and exemplifies the freedoms that were possible within the institution of slavery. Henderson used money from his various schemes to hire her time and rent a house for them to live in. When she got pregnant, he paid for servants to attend her. Henderson's money, however, could not protect his family in the end. When Serena's liberal master died, his children inherited her and the child. They, in turn, put Serena in jail to prevent her from living with Henderson.[71] These events may well have precipitated Henderson's increasingly aggressive rascality.

This rascality was very much facilitated by the river trade. Henderson articulated the importance of the river to his fortunes when a former New Orleans master told him of his impending sale. Madison recalled hoping to be sold to an "indulgent" master, noting that he "preferred being sold to a boatmen, so that [he] might be kept on the river." He continued, "Next to that, I wished to be sold to some merchant who did business with ships and boats. I thought myself sufficiently smart to make my way through the world, and get what money I needed if I staid [sic] on the river, but if sold to the country, I knew that I would not have so much opportunity for the exercise of my talents and might have to run off, in which event I would get into trouble and to no profit."[72] Henderson got his wish. He was sold to Blanchard, a local merchant with interests in river commerce. Henderson did not take long to make some plans. Subsequent to this sale, he met several local thieves and "sat up nearly the whole night talking about what might be done in the way of rascality in New Orleans and on the river."[73]

Counterfeiting was an important component of the men's activities. Henderson's initial New Orleans heists, before he moved on to break-ins, involved forging merchant orders, a practice that swindled local elites at the weak points of their commercial networks. Such activities required literacy and intimate knowledge of the flow of commodities between the levee and city neighborhoods. His network of friends made such operations successful. While his accomplices forged orders from local merchants, he picked up goods, paid off draymen, and fenced the merchandise in the city's black market. In one case, Henderson sold twenty boxes of candles that were procured in this way to a man heading north on a steamboat.[74] Whereas Henderson forged orders in New Orleans, Seward spent much of his youth learning the trade of counterfeiting paper money. Passing counterfeit bills required moving broadly and quickly, so steamboats were a natural attraction for the young Seward. Most of his operations were in New York, but, in one instance, Seward made counterfeit money in Akron, Ohio, and then distributed the currency throughout the Ohio Valley. He traveled through Cincinnati, Louisville, Frankfort, Lexington, and Nashville, all the while passing phony bills.[75]

Helping fugitive slaves escape their masters was another of the men's rascal activities, though they did not always have runaways' interests at heart. Charles Brown's connections to northern abolitionist organizations were a matter of public controversy after the publication of *Trials and Confessions*, but there is little doubt that he was an important participant in networks of fugitive aid. During his leisure time in New Orleans and during longer stints in the city between voyages, Brown used his connections to help slaves obtain free papers. He then either booked them on steamboats or helped them obtain work on the river. The *New Orleans Picayune* verified that many of the slaves he mentioned in *Trials and Confessions* had indeed escaped from their masters.[76] While Brown was committed to helping slaves, Madison Henderson was in it for the money. Henderson claimed that he helped entice slaves to escape before helping his master to resell them in the slave market.[77]

Trading was another activity that tied the men to the river. The river was a key center of both legal and illegal trade that linked urban communities in both the North and the South with cotton and sugar belt plantation slaves. The Mississippi enabled Brown to steal goods, trade the stolen merchandise, and leave town before the authorities caught on. He recalled, "A large share of the time I spent on the river trading. I purchased a great many stolen articles from slaves which I carried on the river and sold out as opportunity offered."[78] He made money in a variety of other ways, but his "principal business" was "to purchase articles from slaves and sell them on the river."[79] While these networks generally involved foodstuffs, Brown sometimes dealt in more valuable merchandise. He remembered, "I bought at different times large amounts of silver spoons and jewelry from slaves and others. They were stolen articles and when not marked were easily disposed of at large profit on the river. When

"The Levee.—The Cotton Thieves." African Americans were active participants in a culture of appropriation that had deep roots in antebellum levee districts. From *Scribner's Magazine*, 1873–74. Courtesy of the Library of Congress.

spoons were marked I had them run up into bars."[80] Brown's trading helped leave his family "a competence" after his death.[81] Henderson organized an elaborate plan to "purchase fruits, oysters, segars [*sic*], &c, in New Orleans and ship them to St. Louis to sell them."[82] He thought, "By purchasing from smugglers . . . and [in St. Louis] investing the proceeds in fresh butter, eggs, &c, we could soon realize a handsome sum."[83]

Before the Pettus Bank robbery, Brown and Henderson had extensive experience breaking in to New Orleans shops, and these schemes escalated in late 1840 when they relocated to St. Louis. It was on a boat out of this city, the *Agnes*, that Henderson, Seward, and a third free black hand named Prime Bruce, first used the mobility of steamboats to aid their thievery. Docked in Galena for several days, the men decided one night to rob a local merchant. Going ashore, the men drank and played cards until ten o'clock. After this, they walked to a store, went in through a window, and stole $1,260—a huge sum. The men divided up the loot and returned to the *Agnes*. As Seward, who recalled his first robbery with great detail, remembered, "The next morning there was great excitement, and the boat and all hands were searched. I had my money on my person, but they did not find it after two searches. I felt very uncomfortable and uneasy about it. I had never been engaged in any thing of the kind before. Madison came to me and talked to me about my appearance, told me my looks were enough to condemn me."[84] On the way back downriver from St. Peters, Seward gave his money to the cool, unflappable Henderson to hold. When the boat docked at Galena, the boat hands were again searched and Henderson was able to hide the money from local constables. The men returned to St. Louis, where they split up. Seward left on a steamboat for Pittsburgh, where he spent three weeks laying low in the city's Hill District.[85]

At the spring thaw some months later, after a series of local robberies around St. Louis, Henderson led a group of men to Galena in the hopes of repeating his previous luck. This time things did not go so smoothly. On the appointed day, Warrick, who up until this time had not engaged in break-ins, backed out at the last minute. Seward was too hung over and had to wait an additional day before booking passage to join the others. Henderson could not get the captain of the *Agnes* to ship a slave from St. Louis without a master's pass, so he and Brown crossed the Mississippi to Alton. Here he was able to buy a ticket because on the Illinois side of the river, steamboat captains bore no risk of being sued for helping a slave to escape. The men's slow start to their journey was a bad omen. Once they were assembled in Galena, things went no better. After several days of planning the men robbed a local bank but made off with very little cash because they were unable to open the safe. Disappointed but not dispirited, the men left town on the *Iona*. They left that steamboat for the *Illinois* when the captain refused to allow them to take meals with the rest of the cabin passengers.[86]

After the Galena episode, the men escalated their scheming. Chambers no doubt understood this development as the natural progression of rascality, but the men's stories suggest alternative readings. Henderson told Seward that he "wanted to make one good haul and then quit entirely."[87] Brown "contemplated a time when [he] would retire and live with my family in peace and security."[88] He thought that if the Pettus Bank job succeeded that "they would get enough to last us."[89] As did Brer Rabbit, Henderson and Brown imagined that rascality could lead to a resolution where wealth and power for the weak was assured. With the failure of their recent plans they felt compelled to make a large robbery.

These dreams were important motivators for Brown and Henderson as they led the effort to rob the St. Louis bank. Ennis, who had been boarding at

The Madison Henderson Gang

Plan of St. Louis, ca. 1848. Henderson, Brown, Seward, and Warrick were executed on Duncan Island in the Mississippi River. Engraving by James M. Kershaw. Courtesy of the Missouri Historical Society, St. Louis.

Leah's with several of the men, first suggested the robbery because of rumors he had heard of the vast amounts of silver held in the shop. He also heard that the silver was often not confined to a safe on Saturday nights—it was left in the storefront's easily opened counter cases. Henderson and Brown quickly seized on the plan and apparently contemplated the possibility of murdering the clerks who lived in the store—a point both Seward and Warrick made in their attempt to distance themselves from the heart of the conspiracy. Seward blamed Brown in particular. "He was the worst of our party," Seward said, "for he was willing to go further than any of us, not hesitating to kill if necessary."[90] The plan moved forward. When Henderson, who was working on the *Missouri* at the time, heard that the boat was delivering a large shipment of silver to the bank, he told the others. The men then decided the time was right.[91]

The robbery was bloody and unsuccessful. Henderson went in first, presented a bank bill and asked the clerk, a man named Jesse Baker, if it was good. As Baker examined the bill, Henderson struck him with a crow bar and knocked him to the floor. The others, except Ennis, who had to work that night at a local barbershop, then came in. Once inside, Brown and Henderson reportedly vigorously pummeled Baker until he emitted nothing but "gurgling" sounds from his mashed skull. The men searched the place for money. At this point, Seward, who was watching the front of the countinghouse, alerted the others that a second man—another clerk later identified as Jacob Weaver— was approaching the store. Brown took the lead. Coming behind the door, he slugged Weaver, knocked him to the floor and then beat him until he was dead. Meanwhile, the search for money continued. But it was to no avail. Ennis's information proved incorrect. All the silver was locked in an impenetrable safe. After repeated attempts to pry open the vault door, the men gave up, set the place on fire in a futile attempt to cover their tracks, and left. The men fled to Warrick's barbershop, where they divided their meager plunder, a few hundred dollars in bills.[92]

The citizens of St. Louis became outraged as news of the killings quickly spread through the city. An intense manhunt ensued. The day after the failed heist, the *Missouri Argus* called the city's men to arms to defend the town from the murderers.[93] The *St. Louis Daily New Era* reported that it was "impossible to convey the excitement that pervades the city."[94] On the following Monday, the paper asserted that "the safety of the city demands that the fiends be brought to punishment," that the city should be "ransacked," and that "every suspicious person be made to give account of himself."[95] The intensity of the search continued for the rest of the month. In the days after the killings, St. Louis's mayor offered a $5,000 reward for information leading to the fugitives' capture. On April 30, the *Missouri Republican* reported, "Nothing will be left undone to secure every avenue of escape."[96] As reports of the crimes were carried via steamboat to other western cities, the entire region became riveted on the spectacular St. Louis events.[97]

With public pressure mounting, the men decided to leave the city. They scattered in all directions, using the river, as they had so often before, as their means of escape. Brown and Seward left for Cincinnati, Henderson for New Orleans, and Warrick shipped out up the Missouri River.[98] But their escape attempts were futile. This time the vast, fluid world of the western rivers was unable to shield the men from their pursuers. Soon after they left St. Louis, authorities caught Ennis, who was turned in by a confidant. In an attempt to save himself from prosecution, he then told authorities what he knew of the heist and the destinations of the four men. St. Louis newspapers published Ennis's account, and police in western river cities scanned levee districts for the fugitives.[99] Mounting pressure was eventually successful. Seward was intercepted at Cairo by St. Louis constables searching passing boats. He had previously left Cincinnati on the *Atalanta* and was bound for New Orleans when the police apprehended him. Authorities caught Warrick on the Missouri River as the *Omega* made its return trip to St. Louis.[100] Brown was next. With Peter Charleville in tow to help identify him, St. Louis authorities traveled to Cincinnati and scanned the city. After a lengthy search, and with the help of some city residents, they finally apprehended Brown on the levee, where he was seeking a berth.[101] Evidently, Brown's Cincinnati friends planned to rescue him from the city's jail, but he was sent downriver before these plans could materialize.[102] Henderson was the last of the men to be captured. He had quickly grown restless in New Orleans, especially when he realized that he faced trial in a separate theft case in that city. To avoid prosecution in the Crescent City, he shipped back upriver toward St. Louis. Police apprehended him at Cairo.[103]

The Missouri justice system gave the men little chance to mount a defense. Brown, Warrick, and Seward all "confessed" to St. Louis constables, who provided testimony at their trials. These confessions, which may yet be found in the voluminous court records from the period, were made under severe duress. During Seward's incarceration on board a steamboat back to St. Louis, police told him that unless he confessed he "would be burnt when he got to St. Louis."[104] Warrick was similarly told that "the people at St. Louis would burn him" if he did not confess.[105] The men knew that these were not idle threats since a free black steamboat hand from Pittsburgh had been burned at the stake in the city just four years earlier. Police tactics may have included physical abuse as well, for Warrick said, "It would be some satisfaction if I could feel that the facts were obtained from me in the manner the world supposes."[106] The men most likely were treated like the innocent New Orleans steamboat slave who was captured during the hysteria. The *National Anti-Slavery Standard* reported that New Orleans police believed he was Madison Henderson and "threatened and whipped" him until he confessed.[107] Police carried him all the way to St. Louis before he was able to prove his innocence. Fortunately for the slave, a steamboat captain testified that the bondsman was at work on his steamboat on the night of the murder. The real Madison Henderson, however, was able to withstand whatever abuse he suffered. He maintained his innocence throughout his trial.[108]

The trials of the men gave them little hope for acquittal. The all-white jury, the *Missouri Republican* reported, "included some of the oldest and most highly respectable citizens of this city."[109] Prosecutors used Ennis's testimony, Brown, Seward, and Warrick's confessions to police, and Grand Jury testimony to fashion a case against each of the men. None of the men was allowed to testify on his own behalf, which was standard practice for African American defendants in the nineteenth century.[110] The jury heard only their confessions to police officers and their statements to the Grand Jury. These procedures particularly hurt whatever chance Warrick and Seward had of receiving a lesser sentence for being only accessories to murder. Under these circumstances, appointed defense attorneys for each man could do little to prevent the guilty verdicts that jurors in each trial returned in just minutes.[111] When the judge summoned the men together for sentencing, their fate was not in doubt.

During the men's trial, sentencing, and incarceration, they exhibited the toughness, resilience, and independence with which they led their lives. All the men were composed at the proceedings. Henderson wore fine hats to his trial and acted with "a rigidity of countenance" that was "truly astonishing" to one St. Louis reporter.[112] The *Missouri Republican* reported, "The only evidence he gave of interest, was an occasional expression of denial of parts of the testimony."[113] That the men's spirit had not been damaged was evident in their escape attempt just days before their execution. Even as Chambers was transcribing their stories laced with remorse, they were sawing at their shackles with a knife and planning for their liberation. The men prided themselves on their ability to escape the prisons of the Mississippi world and thus to the bitter end believed that they would again see freedom. When Chambers came to record their stories one afternoon in their crowded jail cell, they ran past him and their jailers, escaping momentarily to the streets of St. Louis. As the *Missouri Republican* put it, "There was probably never a more daring attempt made by men."[114]

Jail conditions apparently worsened for the men after they were caught. James Seward, the most literate of the men, was allowed to send a letter to abolitionist Gerrit Smith through Chambers. In it he described his cell in his final hours. "I am in a Spanish cell, 8 feet underground. The cell is 8 by 12,—no light but through a loophole in the iron door," Seward wrote. "I have heavy handcuffs on each hand fastened in the center. Heavy irons are on my feet, and fastened to a ring in the floor by a chain three inches long. My fare is coarse bread and water. In this cell are six other persons. The heat is so intense that the prisoners are to strip naked upon entering, and remain so while they stay."[115]

The men entered the daylight for a final walk to the gallows two days later. At one o'clock in the afternoon of July 9 the four men mounted the scaffolding on Duncan Island, just outside the city. Minutes later, in the words of one observer, they were "launched into eternity together."[116] When, after several minutes of agony, Charles Brown finally succumbed to a weak knot the crowd dispersed, having seen stern justice done. The show was not over though. In the days after the hanging, the men's heads were displayed in the window of a local store. The meaning of the severed heads was unmistakable: the city would not stand for rebellion from its slave and free black population—particularly its river workers.[117]

St. Louis papers put the event in the context of the continued problems of managing the city's slave and free black populations. Their shrill reactions reveal the seriousness of the gang's challenge to the authority of the city. City papers portrayed an out-of-control free black population. They also railed against the prevalence of self-hire among the city's slave population and drew attention to the dangers that African American steamboat workers posed to the city. Abolitionist "madmen" were somehow behind it all.[118] The editorials began as soon as it became clear that free "negroes" were responsible for the crime. On May 1, 1841, the *St. Louis Daily New Era* wrote that "three of the fellows implicated are free negroes—the fourth may be justly regarded as one, as no-one seems to have any control over him."[119] The newspaper railed, "It remains to be seen whether the officers and courts will do their duty, and enforce the law,—not only that law which prohibits a free negro from taking up residence here, but that one which prohibits masters from permitting slaves to hire their own time. If masters are not acquainted with the law upon this subject, the sooner they are made to know the better. The suffering of the city requires the prompt execution of all the laws in connection with *free negroes* and *slaves*."[120] The *Missouri Republican* concurred with this initial assessment, stating on May 5, 1841, that "the recent crimes in our city" make clear that "the subordination of our black population both slave and free is dangerously loose."[121] These kinds of comments continued through the summer. In an article titled "Our Free Blacks," the *St. Louis Daily New Era* commented that the city's free black residents were tools of the abolitionists and that their lives alternated between indolence and crime. On these bases, the paper urged the police to enforce the laws and to send the free blacks "back to their sympathizers." The *Missouri Argus* called the city's slaves "not more than half governed" and argued that a crackdown on free blacks was necessary.[122] Such calls were echoed in other cities, especially in New Orleans, where interest in the St. Louis events was particularly keen.[123]

Much of the hysteria centered on the danger of free black boat workers. The *St. Louis Gazette* encouraged the "disuse, on board steamboats navigating the western waters, of all free negroes" because they "caused excitement and discontent among the slaves of the states through which they pass."[124] In New Orleans, where worry about African American boatmen had been building for years, the outcry was particularly vociferous. After the hanging, the *New Orleans Picayune* reported that free black steamboat workers were "prowling about the cities of the South." According to the newspaper, they were a "dangerous body of incendiaries" that were "fomenters of disturbance."[125]

According to the *New Orleans Bee*, there "was no evil . . . more dangerous to the institutions of the South" than "the employment of free blacks on steamboats whereby the free negro and the slave are brought frequently together."[126]

Not surprisingly, a crackdown soon followed. A year and a half after Brown, Warrick, and Seward came and went from St. Louis with ease and without legal restriction, the Missouri legislature passed a law prohibiting free blacks from leaving their boats and entering the city.[127] Farther south, reaction came even more swiftly. The news of a gang of black riverboat thieves was most threatening to whites in the heart of the plantation South. The thought of roving bands of lawbreakers was threatening to elites everywhere, but particularly in the deep South, where men like Henderson also posed the specter of insurrection. In Louisiana, Charles Brown's testimony reinforced long-held fears of boat worker abolitionists. Lawmakers reacted immediately. The men's robbery and murder in St. Louis coincided with the passage of a law requiring the incarceration of free black boatmen entering the state.[128] In the days following the St. Louis executions, the *New Orleans Bee* called for strict enforcement of the recently passed law. The paper's editors hoped that the "dangerous class" of free black boat workers would be prevented from practicing their "insolent" behavior.[129] In Mississippi, reaction was similarly quick. Soon after the men's execution, the state legislature considered a petition prohibiting free black boatmen from coming into the state.[130] It passed six months later.[131] Individual river communities did not wait for state lawmakers. In Natchez, city authorities who were consumed with the thought of free blacks coming into their city to burn, steal, and take their slaves away launched intensive campaigns to rid the city of unlicensed free blacks. "All Sort of Tryals Going On," the free black Natchez barber William Johnson noted in mid-August 1841. "The different Offices have been full all day and they continue to arrest."[132] These campaigns marked the beginning of a long-term decline in the free black population of that city.[133]

THE STORIES OF Madison Henderson, Charles Brown, Amos Warrick, and James Seward reveal how one group of African Americans responded to oppression in the Mississippi River economy. These men sought to live outside the formal economy in a black river world where talents were rewarded and material gain was possible. There was a tragic logic to the way they pursued their advancement. Slavery was theft and it was maintained by brutality. Since planters pursued their material desires through violence, why shouldn't they?

Like tricksters and Badmen, these river rascals both resisted and reflected the will of the powerful. The river rascals often acted with community interests in mind, but their main goal was achieving individual wealth and power. Theirs was an important form of African American resistance, nonetheless, and one that historians of slavery should be encouraged to explore in contexts beyond the antebellum Mississippi. The *Colored American*, an African American newspaper published in New York, was the sole sympathetic voice for the men in the wake of the killings. It summarized the significance of the men's actions in words worth remembering: "So long as the people of that state [Missouri] sanction by law all manner of depredations upon the colored people, even murder, so long . . . may they expect to have among them a gang, with habits for murder."[134]

chapter six

Emancipation and Steamboat Culture

THE COUNTERCURRENTS of the fiercely independent antebellum river culture reverberated throughout the Civil War and Reconstruction years. Skills learned surviving and resisting slavery on antebellum boats were transmitted to the era of freedom. William Wells Brown became a leading abolitionist agitator and a groundbreaking African American novelist and historian. P. B. S. Pinchback, who worked as a free black steward during the late antebellum period, became a state senator in Louisiana and then the first African American governor in the nation's history. As a politician he fought for the basic civil rights of African Americans, including equal access to public conveyances like steamboats. These remarkable men owed much to the fight for freedom aboard antebellum steamers.[1]

Most antebellum river workers did not achieve such fame during the emancipation process, but they were just as important as these leading figures. The story of emancipation is one of how ordinary people took advantage of extraordinary times to fight for new rights, risking their lives and livelihood to extend their liberties and the freedoms of their sons, daughters, and friends. This spirit was inherited from slavery-era struggles and rekindled and redirected in countless ways during the Civil War and Reconstruction. During the war years, the trickle of slaves who used the river to escape became a flood. African American river workers had always been a crucial link in resistance networks, but now increasingly slaves saw new potential river allies: white men in Union blue. Many of these sailors shipped from midwestern ports, the most racist part of the North, yet slaves used persistence and guile to turn the western flotilla into a navy of liberation, pushing policy changes in Washington as they went.[2] White river workers may not have liked these changes, but they wanted to win the war and knew that every runaway behind their lines took labor power away from the Confederacy.

African American steamboat workers remained at the center of this great drama. The tradition of African American maritime work and the persistent shortage of maritime workers made it impossible for racist whites to create an all-white navy.[3] African Americans took advantage of this situation and used navy service on the Mississippi during the war as a new way to combat slavery, this time in a public and violent way.[4] Long before African Americans were permitted to serve in segregated army regiments, they were fighting next to whites in the heat of combat, loading guns, firing at the enemy, and doing the maintenance that allowed Union commanders to press the attack. African Americans helped win key battles that secured most of the western rivers for the Union by the end of 1862, a development that fatally divided the South and kept potential foreign allies wary of backing the new southern nation.

African Americans were not always fighting for the Union during the war years, however. On new ironclad gunboats and modified merchant tinclads and rams, slaves and free blacks also served in the Confederate navy. They also worked on privately owned steamers, many of which were contracted for military service. The number of African Americans who served in Civil War navies is difficult to accurately gauge, but it is clear that their numbers were higher for the Union than the Confederacy. While the Mississippi Squadron by 1864 alone had about 5,500 enlisted crew members, the Confederate navy was made up of a total of approximately 3,000 men.[5] Confederates were unwilling to draft slaves into the army until the war's closing hours, but they allowed up to 5 percent of the workforce on each newly commissioned naval vessel to be filled by blacks.[6] As for the Mississippi Squadron, historian Steven Louis Roca has suggested that African Americans may have filled over half of the crew positions.[7] Once the Civil War started, former slave George Burns recalled, "negroes were given jobs as roustabouts on nearly all the steamers. I imagine the places on the decks were left vacant because so many white boatmen enlisted for military service."[8] Having an able supply of African American recruits played an important role in Union fortunes.

Greater Union material resources, of course, played a huge role as well. Union forces controlled crucial Ohio River boat-building ports, which processed orders from the Quartermaster Department for ninety-one steamboats specifically for the war effort. The Quartermaster Department also financed the chartering of 640 other boats for specific operations, far more than the number of steamers that composed the Confederate Mississippi River Defense Fleet, the major rebel fighting force on the rivers.[9] The Confederate navy gambled its meager resources on producing four ironclad steamers in New Orleans and Memphis that they hoped would be able to dominate both federal blockaders on the Gulf Coast and the Mississippi Squadron. But General Winfield Scott's Anaconda Plan, which focused on winning the war through maritime supremacy, worked too quickly for Confederate boat builders to complete their work. Admiral David Farragut's 1862 Union victory at New Orleans, coupled with federal victories at Island No. 10, at Memphis, and at Corinth, left Confederate forces isolated on scattered mid-South rivers by the summer of 1862. The fall of Vicksburg on July 4, 1863, ended all but a few isolated Confederate river maneuvers. The Union's military successes in the region had the additional benefit of shoring up Abraham Lincoln's political fortunes. His pivotal midwestern constituencies cheered the return of commerce to the Mississippi.[10]

African Americans working on Mississippi steamboats in Confederate waters faced new levels of coercion during the war. Many now found themselves fighting for a cause they did not believe in, often under conditions made worse by the strain of severe labor shortages. The Confederate Congress passed a law allowing army personnel to impress both steamboats and the slaves necessary for their crews.[11] Slave leases that were contracted before the war sometimes turned into several year odysseys as Confederate captains—unable by 1862 to return to ports in either the deep South or the upper South—ran month after month on remote rivers in the mid-South. In such cases, in addition to being separated from family, friends, and their home ports, African Americans faced the threat of combat. Their lives were also more restricted, since they now were unable to play off the interests of riverside masters and boat officers to their own advantage. One result of this situation was that African American workers often lost wages.[12]

Through rare court testimony of newly freed slaves, federal treason cases illustrate how Confederate captains impressed African American workers.[13] Court records reveal, for example, that at the outset of the war a Captain Combs sold his Louisville hotel before buying the *Louisville* and impressing its slaves in order to aid the Confederate cause. In the process, Judy Collins, a slave chambermaid, was taken away from her children. Combs also impressed a slave passenger named Joseph Jackson. Traveling upriver with Combs to rejoin his Louisville master at the time of the Union blockade, Jackson was forced to work on his steamboat for the next two years in unpaid servitude. Jackson received no regular or Sunday wages during these years. Seven other slaves on board reported similar experiences.[14]

The experience of African Americans on Union-controlled rivers was quite diverse and always prone to change. The individual predilections of boat officers, policy changes on contrabands from Washington, and the struggles of African Americans to extend their rights whenever possible made for a revolutionary mix. Some river workers simply lost their jobs during the war's early years when river trade collapsed. A free black steamboat hand reported to federal authorities that "most of the colored people have been waiters, and run on the river, until the last year, when they have commenced working on shore. A great many have quit the river."[15] Some antebellum free blacks worried that the war would increase their chances of being reenslaved. Washington Ward took part in a crew revolt on the *Shreveport* after he had heard "the boat was going south."[16]

Washington Ward may not have wanted to go south, but many blacks were willing to take the risks in order to fight for the Union. At the same time that some established boat workers were being thrown out of work, many newcomers, most of whom were slave runaways, filled the barges towed along by the western flotilla. These contrabands, who flocked to the Union forces in the cotton belt along the Cumberland, Tennessee, and Mississippi rivers, forced the federal government to redefine its slavery policy. Well before the Emancipation Proclamation freed slaves in rebel states, the first Confiscation Act, enacted on August 6, 1861, allowed runaway slaves who had previously served at Confederate fortifications and on other war projects to remain behind Union lines. With this justification, army commanders began sending contrabands to key steamboat ports for enlistment.[17] While this act recognized and formalized the revolutionary implications of slave actions, it left the legal status of contrabands undetermined. This matter was addressed in the second Confiscation Act, passed on July 17, 1862. With this law, all runaways to Union lines were pronounced free. The Militia Act, passed along with the second Confiscation Act, formally allowed navy and army commanders to recruit slaves for the military. Together these acts ensured that it was mostly former slaves who filled the increasing demand for naval enlistments during the final years of the war.[18]

These laws reflected a gradual shift toward free labor on wartime steamboats. Union forces, for instance, freed the slaves on the *Louisville* after they captured the boat. Many of the slaves immediately shipped out from Cairo,

152   *Emancipation and Steamboat Culture*

Illinois, as free laborers.[19] Just as runaways in the antebellum years knew to escape to urban levees where help could be found, wartime rebels fled to dock areas looking for work and passage to areas where slavery had been abolished or where it survived in law only. One Memphis observer noted that after the city fell to Union gunboats in 1862, freedpeople from local plantations swarmed the city's riverfront, forming a "mass of humanity."[20] While many of these runaways were sent to contraband camps in places like Cairo, many others joined the western flotilla.

The flood of runaways to the Mississippi Squadron exacerbated the steamboat industry's already tense race relations. White navy recruits were often initially sympathetic to the refugees they encountered, but they soon became concerned about the increasing competition for their jobs and the uncomfortable reality that their labor was becoming associated with "nigger" work. Navy commanders tried to reduce the potential for conflict by enforcing rigid segregation. Whites and blacks messed separately, slept separately, and worked in "checkerboard" shifts. The close confines of steamboats limited the effectiveness of these efforts, however. The result was the most tense race relations in the Union navy and a persistent pattern of racial strife.[21]

This tension was probably made worse by the fact that slaves continued to work shoulder to shoulder with contrabands, as well as free black and white workers, throughout the war. Peter Boyd is a case in point. Union forces captured Boyd in 1862 when he was laboring as a blacksmith at an Arkansas fort. He was taken north with other prisoners on the *Die Vernon*, a St. Louis boat drafted for government service. A boat officer named Mr. Van Keuren, Boyd later reported, "wouldn't let them [federal forces] put me in prison" and "put me to work on these boats." The forced labor lasted for years. He remembered, "I worked thar all the time the war was."[22] Boyd worked on supply boats that traveled the Missouri and Cumberland rivers. Only at the end of the war was he finally released. His story illustrates that the steamboat industry's conversion from slave to contraband labor was slow and uneven.

Slaves like Boyd, and the freedmen and freedwomen who worked with them, served in positions as coal heavers, stewards, firemen, chambermaids, cabin boys, and cooks. Initially contrabands were only permitted to enlist as cabin boys, the lowest-ranking position in the navy, a job that paid only 10 dollars a month. By the end of 1862, however, the U.S. Navy liberalized its policy and allowed contrabands to advance to nonofficer positions, a decision that rankled white crew members. All of these jobs required learning skills appropriate for battle. Cabin boys, who were mostly contrabands, for instance, not only attended officers and ordinary sailors but also served on watches and carried ammunition in the heat of combat.[23] African American women served on the first hospital ship in the U.S. Navy, the USS *Red Rover*, as nurses and chambermaids.[24] The steady stream of wounded from Union boats allowed them to learn skills that broke both racial and gender barriers. Together, contrabands, free blacks, and slaves contributed considerably to the African American fight for freedom and survival on the wartime Mississippi.

When emancipation was finally won, and the Thirteenth Amendment forced the loyal border state of Kentucky to free its slaves, the victory ushered in a new era on the Mississippi River. It was no longer legal for a master to own a slave and hence to buy and sell human beings as property. But what rights would freedmen and freedwomen have in the wake of these fundamental changes? How "free" would free labor be? Freedpeople faced these questions all over the South. The struggle over work—over who would control it, how it would be organized, and how it would be compensated for—was central to the matter. Just as farm workers resisted gang labor and the vicious overseers, so too did steamboat freedpeople challenge officers' traditional disregard for the physical well-being of their workers.[25] Consequently, the lower Mississippi and its tributaries, where the African American workforce remained concentrated, became the site of continued conflict. Armed with the traditions of antebellum slaves, as well as of Union navy men and women, a new era of struggle emerged in which African Americans placed their emphasis on redefining their day-to-day working lives on steamboats. Using federal and state courts as their allies, they sought to rid steamboats of abuse and to defend their new right to wages. Drawing on their experience with labor bargaining during slavery, newly free boat workers redoubled their efforts to challenge boat owners. Through strikes and lawsuits they continued slave traditions of resistance. Their struggles were part of a wide range of strategies African Americans used to enforce new codes of conduct, and a modicum of dignity, in workplaces throughout the South.

These struggles took place in an industry that remained as firmly dependent as ever on black labor. As the river trade rebounded from wartime disruptions, freedmen and -women flocked to the decks of steamboats. While numbers are difficult to accurately estimate in a mobile occupation such as river work, as many as 5,000 African Americans labored on Reconstruction era rivers. The influx of African American labor during the Civil War and the continued vibrancy of the lower Mississippi economy ensured that African Americans could find work on postbellum levees. One Memphis observer noted in the immediate postwar years that a "swarm" of blacks, "a new kind of man power," was suddenly thrust into the river trade.[26] In the 1870s Lafcadio Hearn noted, "The calling now really belongs by right to the negroes, who are by far the best roustabouts and are unrivaled as firemen."[27] Many freedmen and -women, perhaps lured by the positive associations of the occupation within the slave community, began working on steamboats as their first paid labor following emancipation. After laboring as a slave on a sugar plantation, Primus Smith first tasted freedom on the decks of the steamboat *Robert E. Lee*, named for the most revered defender of the Old South.[28] After emancipation, Peter Corn worked on a Missouri farm and in several St. Louis iron factories and then took a job on a steamboat.[29] Another freedman, Peter Brown, came to work on the decks of Mississippi steamers after laboring on an Arkansas farm.[30]

These new workers did not view steamboat work as favorably as did their antebellum predecessors, however. In a typical comment, a freedman named Billy said, "Fo' duh war I was a slave, now I's free . . . now I's a slave to this here steamboat."[31] Freedmen and -women often spoke of unrelenting work, rigid supervision, and the general hardship of riverboat life. In part this changed opinion reflected new liberties blacks had on land. Historians have widely cited African Americans' freedom of movement as one of the key gains of emancipation.[32] By the immediate postwar years, because riverside freedpeople were able to move about without restrictions, and because steamboat travel to northern states no longer led to significantly greater freedoms, steamboats and their workers were no longer viewed as beacons of hope and liberation. Steamboat laborers' wages and tips continued to be important for the survival of African American families, but as real wages declined in an era of industry stagnation, even these benefits were eroded.

Working on a steamboat was one of the most demanding jobs in the Reconstruction economy. Primus Smith lasted only six months in the industry. "Sonny, it was the hardest work a man ever done," he recalled, "I couldn't stand any more of it."[33] Tony Piggy said simply, "They called me a rouster—that means a working man."[34] For Boston Blackwell the labor was unrelenting. "Never is no time to rest," he recalled, "Load, unload, scrub. Just do whatever you is told and you do it right now, and you'll keep outen trouble."[35] Recalling his eight tough years on a steamboat for a Works Progress Administration interviewer, George Bollinger compared the difficulty of that work with the laziness of his Depression era grandson. Pointing to his grandson sitting on the porch he said, "What do these young folks know about work? Nothin'!"[36]

The most onerous elements of this work continued to be associated with the deck crew as opposed to the cabin crew. One steamboat barber reported, "I'd go to stealin' 'fo' I'd be a rooster. Certain su' I would, 'cause dey couldn't wuk a man no harder in de penitentshuary ef he got caught dan dey do on dese boats."[37] As African Americans increasingly filled deck crew jobs, African American "roosters" became an ever-present part of the Mississippi landscape.[38] Ernst von Hesse-Wartegg found the degraded position of roustabouts excellent evidence for his passionate belief that African Americans were worse off during freedom. He thought that the conditions of roustabout labor "would sadden any humanitarian" and pronounced, "Behold the consequences of the Civil War! Look upon the Freed Man, the liberated Negro, the white man's equal at the ballot box and before the law! See what freedom has given him! . . . The roustabouts carry sack after sack into the cargo space of our bottom deck. . . . At work early this morning, they work now at midnight, as doggedly now as then—all for a dollar!"[39] So difficult was the work that some believed that only the strongest African Americans could endure the conditions. "The work is so hard, and the hours so long," one captain pronounced, "that it has driven all but the strongest off the river."[40] Postwar traveler Julian Ralph agreed with this captain's assessment. "There are nights on the *Providence*," he wrote, "when the landings ran close together, and the poor wretches got little or no sleep. They 'tote' all the freight aboard and back to land again on their heads or shoulders, and it is crushing work."[41] To Ralph these workers looked very much like the field hands of slavery times.[42] Another traveler commented, "Perhaps there are worse occupations in life than theirs, but if I had a choice in the way of manual labor, it would not be in the line of a 'rouster.'"[43]

Mates, often called "Nigger runners" among officers on Reconstruction rivers, drove workers to exhaustion.[44] One traveler reported that the mate on his steamer growled unremittingly, "Take a sack, take a sack, take a sack!" or, when the barrels of flour came in, "roll, roll, roll!"[45] Hesse-Wartegg watched as the mate on his steamer drove "the Ethiopians to their task."[46] Among themselves, freedmen frequently talked about tough mates. Boston Blackwell recalled that although he liked his captain, "the mate was sure rough."[47] The African American oral culture of the Mississippi Valley was replete with stories of men like Lew Brown, Bull-Whip Shorty, Mike Carkin, and a host of other hard-driving mates.[48]

Freedpeople resisted such characters in time-honored ways. African Americans continued to use work slowdowns as a tactic after emancipation, and captains continued to complain of the "indifference" of their workers.[49] In

The *Natchez*, ca. 1891. Mississippi steamboats continued to dominate the shipment of lower Mississippi cotton through the nineteenth century. From the collection of Thomas H. Gandy and Joan W. Gandy.

1870, one steamboat owner described his crew of freed workers as "worthless"; he replaced them with a Chinese crew.[50] Captains also complained of African Americans' drunkenness, their propensity to steal from boat supplies, and their willingness to vandalize boat property.[51] As they had been during slavery, roustabout songs continued to be an important way in which African Americans controlled the pace of their work and allowed them to comment on the abusive aspects of their labor. Freedpeople also demanded to be called their proper names.[52] For example, following the example of free blacks who objected to being called "boys" during the slavery era, Ishe Webb, who shipped out on steamboats from Little Rock after emancipation, exclaimed to one captain who never referred to him by name, "I got a name jus' like you have." He then told him that he would come when called and be "a lot more willing" if his real name was used. A radical change then occurred on deck. The captain started calling the men by names of their choosing.[53]

Freedpeople also began to demand wages commensurate with their free status. African Americans transferred labor bargaining skills learned in slavery to the new era, and quickly river workers' right to full wages became one of the most cherished gains of emancipation. The letters of John W. Tobin, who owned a line of Mississippi steamers, reveal freedpeople's insistence on

Roustabouts. From *Every Saturday*, September 2, 1871. This image captures many white observers' opinions of roustabouts: that they were shiftless and lazy. Courtesy of the University of Iowa Libraries, Special Collections.

being paid on time. The captain of the *J. Frank Pargoud*, a boat that ran between the Ouachita River and New Orleans, wrote Tobin asking for money to pay off his workers. When Tobin sent him $700, the captain thanked him, adding, "I do not know what I would have done. Freedmen are so exacting they forget all favors and must have their money regularly."[54] He later reported, probably after yet more help from Tobin, "My hands are all at work since the assistance. I can be with them *now* more cheerfully."[55] Apparently on the *J. Frank Pargoud* officers paid a price in productivity if wages were not paid on time. The threat of a work slowdown or strike was a significant bargaining tool.[56] The *New Orleans Picayune* reported that roustabouts "wait until the boat is ready to start out and then jump ashore and refuse to come on board until their demands are complied with."[57] One officer commented that "whenever they think there is a chance they will strike for wages."[58] There were even moments in which class interests could bridge the racial divide. An 1866 strike in Cincinnati, for instance, involved the combined effort of more than a hundred African American and Irish boatmen.[59]

Such moments of solidarity were short-lived; race relations remained volatile in the larger work culture. Petty theft and racial slurs among workers led to levee fights. Officers responded, and perhaps worsened the situation, by either segregating mixed-race crews or shipping crews separately by race. One mate who tried to have black and white workers on the same boat testified that "he could not get on with one black and one white watch," so he had switched to "a crew of negroes" to avoid trouble.[60] Following antebellum practices, when whites and blacks did ship together, they messed separately and were kept as separated as the confines of the work would permit.[61]

Race relations limited the possibilities for large strikes, but federal courts provided an important outlet for river workers' grievances. Emancipated river workers took advantage of their legal status as maritime workers and brought a variety of suits.[62] Maritime law strictly regulated the relationship between employers (ominously called masters) and seamen. Seamen were required to sign labor contracts that criminalized quitting (desertion) or insubordination (mutiny). At the same time, however, they gained new protections under maritime statutes that enforced payment of wages to seamen, payment of disability costs stemming from workplace injuries, and penalties for officers who whipped or beat their workers. Mariners could simply go before a federal judge and make a claim, even without a lawyer, and were expected to pay court costs only when they lost. Nineteenth-century court records indicate that steamboat workers used this extension of federal jurisdiction to go to court much more often than steamboat owners did. Their litigiousness indicates both the frequency of their complaints over workplace issues and the tenacity of their commitment to defining their freedom.

Steamboat workers who were put off boats without pay now had legal recourse. Between 1866 and 1877 common steamboat laborers filed 190 cases in the Eastern District of Louisiana federal court in New Orleans. While the race of the petitioner was not indicated in most wage disputes, the large proportion of African Americans in the river labor force suggests that many suits were filed by African American workers. "I was employed on the *Robert Semple* as a chambermaid and cook from January 1st, 1876 until the boat was seized," Annie Carter testified in a typical claim. "The Captain hired me, Captain Moore, at $35 dollars a month. My bill is made out for a month and sixteen days at that rate which amounts to $52. That amount is correct and due me. I received nothing on account. It is all due to me now, and remains unpaid."[63] Later, during cross-examination, as if to underscore the crime, she repeated that she "received no compensation" and that it was "still due and

"Outside the Court-house." African American steamboat workers went to court in an effort to expand their freedoms after emancipation. From *Scribner's Magazine*, 1873. Courtesy of the Library of Congress.

unpaid."[64] Freedman Joseph Brady sued for wages after being put off the steamboat *Carrie Converse* for not cleaning the cabin glasses well enough.[65]

Workers generally won their suits. When the court awarded wages to Annie Carter, and to the rest of the crew of the *Robert Semple*, it acted with typical support for workers' suits. Out of the 190 Louisiana suits filed by workers for wages, only four resulted in denials, and in three of those cases, the plaintiff(s) had not appeared in court. The outcome of most suits does not appear in court records, but in 48 instances the court ruled in favor of workers' claims.[66] With the law stipulating that boat owners were liable to workers for the duration of the voyage (or the length of time stipulated on shipping papers) and

Emancipation and Steamboat Culture

that workers' wages took precedence over all other boat debts, workers were in a strong position before the court. Lafcadio Hearn believed that these suits brought change to the day-to-day river work culture. "It used to be common" for some "ruffianly mate," he commented in 1876, to ship sixty or seventy river workers and then discharge them once the boat was loaded. "This can no longer be done with legal impunity."[67]

Demanding wages was only one way in which African Americans defined their freedom on steamboats. Freedpeople also fought workplace abuse. Unlike in the agricultural sector, where freedpeople generally withdrew from plantation-style management techniques, on steamboats, hierarchical, white-dominated, management structures were fixed and were a seemingly intractable component of the system of riverboat commodity distribution. In this context, freedmen and -women sought to challenge abuse within the existing organization of work.

African Americans resisted abuse in a number of ways. In some cases they quit or fought officers. George Arnold, a postwar roustabout, remembered, "The negroes had only a few years of freedom and resented cruelty. If the mate became too mean, a regular fight would follow."[68] African Americans also used the institutional resources of federal courts to put pressure on employers. They frequently sued during the Reconstruction era under admiralty statutes, passed in 1835 and 1850, that aimed at ameliorating the lives of sailors by outlawing "cruel" treatment and punishment by flogging. If a river worker won a suit, the court could either fine the offender or award damages to the plaintiff. No such suits were filed in the Eastern District of Louisiana before the Civil War.[69] Between 1867 and 1877, in contrast, the federal district court heard twenty such cases. In addition, the federal circuit court in the Eastern District of Louisiana, which normally handled appeals from the district court on maritime matters only, evidently began hearing cases involving officer abuse of steamboat hands. In this court in the 1873 to 1881 period a total of sixty-seven cases of common deckhands suing boat officers for mistreatment exist.[70]

Since personal testimony was included in many of these suits, it is clear that many of these plaintiffs were African American workers. "William Scott, a freedman of color . . . and freedman citizen" began a typical district court case.[71] Gloster Hill claimed he was a "freedman of color" who was assaulted "contrary to his rights and privileges."[72] A roustabout who worked on the lower Mississippi simply stated, "I was not born free. I am a freedman."[73] Circuit court records reveal a similar story. While less testimony is contained in these cases, a comparison of these records to the New Orleans census suggests the prevalence of African American plaintiffs. Eight out of the ten names that could be traced to the census were African American.[74] In the aftermath of the 1866 Civil Rights Act, as citizens with the right to bring lawsuits, and, as maritime workers armed with the ability to appeal to admiralty judges, African American steamboat workers worked to change the experience of labor on steamboats. Deep South steamboat workers, many of whom had worked in the brutal sugar and cotton plantation economies of the region, were particularly intolerant of abuse from officers, who were undoubtedly reminiscent of antebellum overseers.

The Louisiana petitions report brutal treatment. Complaining of lazy workers or petty theft, and sometimes with no explanation at all, mates viciously assaulted workers. One steamboat mariner testified that he was "struck upon the head and other parts of the body with an iron instrument known as a wrench."[75] Another complained of "being beaten with a heavy piece of iron."[76] An African American man named Charles Stewart stated that the mate beat him with his fists "and with an iron instrument usually known as an ice pick."[77] Another inland mariner was pistol-whipped.[78] The most frequent complaint, however, was abuse by a heavy stick. Typical was the steamboatman who recalled being "beaten with a heavy stick on the head and other parts of the body."[79] While most of these cases involved deck crew workers, cabin workers were not immune to the abuse. Martin Self, an African American who worked in the ladies' cabin of a Louisiana steamer, reported being tied with a cord, blindfolded, and severely beaten after being falsely accused of stealing a gold watch.[80]

The drama of these actions is nowhere more evident than in the case of *Mamie May v. Phillip Crooks, master and captain of the* Ozark (1871). May claimed she was "grossly assaulted, insulted, and abused by the use of opprobrious language and epithets" by Crooks and his wife. May became severely ill soon after the *Osark* began its trip up the Mississippi from New Orleans, but Crooks and his wife ordered her to work. May refused. When Mrs. Crooks upbraided her for her supposed indolence, May spat back to Mrs. Crooks, "I believe this is a free country and I am a free woman." Mrs. Crooks then struck her, saying, "Don't you have the impudence to tell me about your freedoms." Later, when May protested as she was about to be put ashore on a remote riverbank in a driving rain, Mrs. Crooks injected, "You stinking black nigger wrench how dare you speak to these white officers so." With this insult still ringing in her ears, May was marooned ashore, sick, alone, and in a strange place. Strangers nursed her back to health, but it would be several months before she could return to New Orleans.[81]

May asked for $5,000 for the damages she sustained on the *Osark*. Given the fact that such suits were new to the region in this period, May was likely hoping to effect a lasting change in the treatment of boat workers. A victory of this magnitude not only would be a victory for her but it would also have a ripple effect on labor practices throughout the industry. May no doubt knew that if boat owners had to worry about losing their boats to damage claims, officers would be instructed to take greater care in their dealings with workers. But these hopes were unrealized. The judge did side with May, but he awarded her only $74 plus court costs. He essentially ordered her wages paid for time lost due to the incident but refused to consider punitive damages.[82]

Most plaintiffs in abuse cases were not awarded even the modest settlement May received. Unlike in wage cases, where judges were given little room for discretion in deciding the outcome, allegations of abuse demanded that judges assess the nature of the abuse in each case—a process that in Louisiana nearly always favored boat owners and officers over workers. According to a study of sailors on deep-sea Atlantic whaling ships, the "cruelty" laws were often successfully prosecuted in the context of a northern, more heavily native white labor force. In Louisiana, where boat workers were predominantly African American, on the other hand, guilty verdicts were extremely rare.[83] Of the 67 abuse cases filed by steamboat workers with the federal circuit court in the Eastern District of Louisiana, the results of 51 were included in the court's records.[84] Of these, 34 resulted in not-guilty verdicts, 14 were either officially discontinued or never given a verdict, and only 3 resulted in guilty verdicts. In all three cases where guilty verdicts were returned, the defendants had pleaded guilty, giving the court no opportunity to exercise discretion. In the federal district court the situation was not much better. Plaintiffs won only three suits, and in these cases, judges awarded only wages lost due to flight from abuse and no additional damages.[85] Through this systematic refusal to implement federal law, the Louisiana federal court showed its unwillingness to protect the predominantly African American labor force.

Suits by African American steamboat workers concerning physical abuse were not limited to federal court. Chambermaid Mary Johns appealed her abuse case all the way to the Louisiana Supreme Court.[86] In fact, according to the Louisiana Supreme Court, "suits of this character were of somewhat frequent occurrence about the time this arose."[87] For Johns, and for unknown others whose stories remain buried in local courthouse records, the Recon-

Chambermaids on the *Charles Rebstock*, ca. 1883. From the
collection of Thomas H. Gandy and Joan W. Gandy.

struction era brought renewed attempts to resist not only beatings but sexual
abuse as well.

Johns's case reveals that the precarious position of African American chambermaids that existed before emancipation continued into the Reconstruction
era. Johns's testimony documents a history of abusive confrontations with
officers. In order to bolster her case against Captain Brinker, and to convince
the court of a need to set a precedent, she let the court know that sexual assault was widespread on western steamboats. To counter the prevailing stereo-
types of African American women, she made it clear that sexual advances
were unwanted. She testified, for instance, that a former captain named Kouns
repeatedly made sexual advances to her. She recalled that on one occasion he
grabbed and attempted to kiss her. She fought back, asserting, "You better go
off to your wife or somebody else: that is not my business or character! I am
not going to do it!"[88]

This attack was mild compared to what she experienced a few years later
on another Red River steamer, the *Mary Louisa*. Captain Brinker, Johns charged,
"cursed me and called me names and hit me a lick on the nose. Then he dragged

me by my dress into a little place called the laundry where the fire is and where the washing is going on. He put me down on the floor but by straining considerably I got to my feet again and ran out on the guards. I ran then and tried to see if I could get rid of him by going in the cabin. When I went in the cabin he caught me by the back of the neck and dragged me out on the guards and kicked me until he got back on the recess and pushed me into the door of the recess."[89] Put ashore at Alexandria, near her home, she went to a friend's house. In court, that friend testified that Johns "was bloody from head to toe. She looked like she had been butchered more than anything." Her breasts had been "severely assaulted," and she had a lump on her head "as big as a hen egg."[90] Johns sued the captain to recover damages for a "malicious, wanton, and inhuman assaulting and beating."[91] She lost in the state district court and appealed to the state supreme court.

Over a period of seven years, Johns sank $1,300—all the money she had—into her case. Defense lawyers implied to the court that it was unfathomable that an African American woman could have such funds without engaging in crime. Johns vigorously defended her reputation by documenting her finances. She asserted that her modest living habits allowed her to save a small inheritance from her mother, as well as money earned on steamboats. "Well, I worked for it, that is where I got it," she said. "I was getting twenty-five dollars a month [on the river] and many ladies have given me presents of five and ten dollars for nursing and so on . . . that accumulated considerably."[92] She emphasized how hard she had worked for the money during her four years on the rivers. She described working twenty hours a day washing and cleaning for officers and passengers from six in the morning until two in the morning the next day. She was the only chambermaid for 120 cabin passengers on the *Mary Louisa*.[93]

The Louisiana Supreme Court was not sympathetic to Johns. It agreed with Brinker's claim that she was a poor worker, that she drank, and that she threatened him with a lump of coal previous to his assault. It reported, "The commander of a steamboat has a right to use whatever reasonable and lawful force may be necessary to maintain a proper police of his vessel, and discipline among his employees."[94] The court also made it clear that such suits would be futile in the future:

Most of them [abuse suits] were no doubt born of the false teachings and bad advise of the hour, and we trust the occasion and the disposition for them on the part of persons of the class of the plaintiff have passed away, and that instead of cultivating an offensive spirit of insubordination toward those in authority over them, they will learn the necessity and benefits of civility to all and the obedience to the authority to which they voluntarily submit themselves, and with which custom and the law from necessity clothe the commanders of ships and steamboats. . . . We trust the plaintiff will be wiser in [the] future than to embark on such ventures.[95]

Johns's testimony, and that of her coworkers, was of little consequence. The position of the Louisiana Supreme Court mirrored the Louisiana federal courts' "cruelty" rulings: physical violence in the workplace would go unpunished in the era of freedom. In the Reconstruction South a steamboat master still had the right to discipline his servants.

Workers also struggled for compensation for on-the-job injuries on Reconstruction era steamboats. Long before workers' compensation laws were passed during the Progressive Era, maritime courts often covered hospital costs and wages lost due to injuries sustained on the job.[96] African American steamboat workers fought vigorously after emancipation for the same benefits. Between 1871 and 1877, the federal district court in New Orleans heard twenty-one cases in which workers sought compensation for workplace injuries. Workers testified to lost limbs, crushed hands, broken legs, and frostbite. They slipped on ice, were toppled by improperly stowed goods, and were dragged underwater by the boats' giant waterwheels. Steamboats loaded with cotton from deck to pilothouse were picturesque to postbellum photographers but dangerous to workers. Fireman Henry Reed was eating his dinner on a pile of cotton when a bale fell from above. He "found himself so crushed and injured as to be entirely paralyzed in all of his lower limbs."[97] Work near the engines was no less dangerous. When the engineer of the steamboat *Exporter* ordered African American fireman Robert Kyle to clean the engine while the boat was underway, Kyle lost two fingers that had gotten caught "between the rock shaft and the lever."[98]

Steamboat hands also pursued compensation for injuries in state courts. Peter Dyer's court battle reveals the tremendous odds facing African American plaintiffs in this era. Dyer sued the owners of the *Natchez* for damages in 1871 when the mate blinded him in one eye with a piece of cordwood. Angry that his workers had put a hole in a whiskey barrel during their previous trip, the mate announced in New Orleans that if it happened again "some nigger would have a broken head."[99] Later, near Baton Rouge, when the mate suspected that Dyer's coffee cup was filled with whiskey, he made good on his promise, permanently injuring Dyer. Unable to talk, and "out of his head" with pain, Dyer was put ashore at Natchez with enough money for passage home.[100] Supported by his mother, who paid for his counsel, Dyer sued boat owners for $20,000 in damages in the Fifth District Court of Louisiana.

Neither the State of Louisiana in the Dyer case nor federal courts in general were willing to support workers' claims. The verdicts of most workers' suits are not recorded in court records, but in four cases that did reach a decision, the court ruled narrowly in favor of steamboat workers. Judges were willing to award lost wages, but as was the case in abuse cases, they were not willing to award additional damages. Peter Dyer had better luck with a lower state court. The court found the defendants guilty and awarded him $5,000 in damages. The boat owners appealed the decision to the Louisiana Supreme Court, however, claiming that they were not liable since the mate was not under the captain's direct orders to throw cordwood. The owners won the appeal, leaving Dyer with no settlement. Through this decision, the court asserted that steamboat employers still had the right to discipline their employees with little worry of judicial interference. Unless captains directly ordered their lower officers to discipline workers in ways that led to injury, boat owners were not liable. After several of months of recuperation, Peter Dyer went back to work as a one-eyed roustabout.[101]

Although the results of many suits brought by Reconstruction era steamboat workers were no doubt disappointing to their litigants, the efforts of freedpeople to reform their work environment may not have been as futile as the extent of boat owners' legal victories would suggest. In 1872, the "wandering vagabond" John Morris noted the change. Traveling through Louisiana, he commented that "the formal brutal treatment of steamboat hands is no longer tolerated; such amusements became too costly to be indulged in by their officers."[102] He added, "Humanity and courtesy has made mighty strides in this part of the country over cruelty and oppression. The recklessness and brutality that once characterized steamboat officials has totally disappeared from our western waters."[103] Although courts steadfastly refused to enforce new standards, economic pressures may have served the same purpose as court protection. When a worker (or workers) sued in federal court, judges often required that owners post bonds or have their boat attached until their cases were decided. In this way the procedures of the court favored plaintiffs. Owners had to commit valuable resources to a lengthy proceeding in an increasingly competitive marketplace. By taking the time to testify in their defense, officers spent valuable time away from their business pursuits. In 1895, Julian Ralph interviewed the former pilot of the *Providence*. He recalled, "It used to be the custom for the mates to hit the lazy negroes on the head with a billet of wood." But, he added, "they do not urge the help with cord-wood now because the negroes get out warrants and delay the boat."[104] While Ralph's informant no doubt overstated the transformation of labor relations, African American river workers' efforts may have had a tangible impact on some boats.

While African American working-class river workers struggled for reform as laborers, middle-class African American travelers were fighting their own battles on Reconstruction era steamboats. During the antebellum and early Reconstruction periods, the highly decentralized nature of the steamboat industry encouraged a lack of uniformity in segregation practices. On southern rivers, however, it was common for well-to-do free black travelers to be excluded from cabin passage and relegated to deck passage with poor travelers. African Americans challenged this exclusion under the provisions of the Civil Rights Act of 1866 and especially under the provisions of the Civil Rights Act of 1875. This act guaranteed African Americans "full and equal enjoyment" of public conveyances, something that African Americans variously interpreted as meaning access to, or integration of, the steamboat cabin. In several important federal cases, African Americans fought for access to cabin travel and sometimes for integrated accommodations.[105]

Although southern courts generally found ways to avoid awarding victories to African American plaintiffs, these suits may well have helped codify segregation practices.[106] Gradually during the Reconstruction years it became common for African Americans on larger steamers to have the option to purchase a cabin ticket in the "freedmen's bureau," a segregated compartment above the main cabin and to the rear of the pilothouse and officers' quarters on the hurricane deck.[107] "Southern folk . . . insist upon a recognition of caste in every relation of life," Julian Ralph wrote during his travels in the South. "The negro passengers . . . were sent up above, to quarters far from the rest."[108] With fares as high as $25 for long-distance trips, few freedpeople could afford even the modest luxuries the freedmen's bureau provided. Nonetheless, middle-class African American travelers had significant new liberties, even though the radical provisions of the Civil Rights Act of 1875 were unrealized.

EMANCIPATION BROUGHT new opportunities for African Americans to resist exploitation and to redefine their liberty. During the war years, the river industry lived up to its antebellum image as a beacon of freedom. The downriver internal slave trade was disrupted at the same time that the river became a focus of African American activity of a different sort. Thousands of runaways flocked to the Union Mississippi Squadron, winning their freedom on the banks of the Mississippi and its tributaries. The service of thousands of free black sailors in the crucial western theater further suggests the importance of the African American river experience. By helping win the war, African American mariners worked to abolish slavery.

The nature of the fight for freedom changed dramatically again once the bullets stopped flying. African Americans streamed back to the river with the return of commerce, but with a new focus. Now that the river no longer bound together two rival social systems, African American river workers did not seek escape into the river world in the same ways they did during slavery. African American workers remained active in their workplace, however, as they launched new kinds of resistance that aimed to fundamentally transform power relations in the industry. By resisting the continued patterns of slavery-era abuse, by asserting their rights to wages, and by insisting on their rights to compensation for workplace injuries, they challenged boat owners' and officers' efforts to withhold their basic rights. Middle-class travelers added to the ferment of the period by fighting for access to better accommodations than those to which they had traditionally been confined.

Freedom had changed a lot for African American river workers. Although they still had masters of a kind on the job, and they were only modestly successful at changing the conditions of their work, when in port they could move without concern for masters and leasing agents. They took these urban journeys with wages in hand, and if boat officers denied them, they were quick to complain to the nearest federal judge. With the end of the slave trade, they also could count on their families being there when they returned from a river journey. The river industry may have lost some of its antebellum-era appeal, but there was little doubt that river laborers valued the difference that emancipation made in their working lives.

The Decline of Mississippi River Steamboating

IN THE MID-1890S, photographer Stoughton Cooley prowled the steamboats of the lower Mississippi. There had been thousands of pictures taken of steamboats since the invention of the camera at midcentury, but Cooley tried a new style that was becoming popular in the cities of the region. Instead of taking distant landscape shots that celebrated "picturesque" steamboats, he decided to portray the life of African American roustabouts. The images that resulted, now part of the Sophie Cooley Pearson Collection at Louisiana State University, reveal that in many ways working on the deck of southern steamboats had not changed much since slavery. Roustabouts still got jobs at huge levee shape-ups in New Orleans; they continued to labor under the supervision of whites; they persisted in wrestling unwieldy cargo to precarious positions on steamboat decks; and they continued to sleep and eat amid the cotton bales that they had heaped onto the decks of river steamers. Though most of the young workers photographed would never have known slavery, their lives were intimately structured by the legacy of bondage.

The heavy concentration of African Americans in the steamboat industry revealed in Cooley's photographs is supported by data on the late-nineteenth-century river labor force. According to a national sample of census data, the total number of river workers in the Mississippi River region declined from about 19,000 in 1850 to 16,500 in 1880.[1] The percentage of African Americans in the river population increased, however. While data from the St. Louis census of 1850 indicates that 18 percent of the river workforce arriving in that

"The Unwilling Ox." The steamboat workforce remained strictly racialized after emancipation. Here a white mate oversees a gang of African American roustabouts. Photograph by Stoughton Cooley, ca. 1895. Courtesy Sophie Cooley Pearson Collection, Mss. #3237, Louisiana and Lower Mississippi Valley Collection, LSU Libraries, Louisiana State University.

city were slaves or free blacks, the 1880 public-use sample, an admittedly different measure in that it reflects all steamboat workers in western river states, suggests that 26 percent of steamboat hands were African American. This percentage represents 4,300 African American workers—about the same number of African Americans who worked on antebellum riverboats at any one time. So while the total number of river workers was declining in the second half of the nineteenth century, it was white workers who were leaving the occupation. This persistence of African American participation in the labor force was quite unique compared to other maritime occupations. As African American river workers were becoming more important to the declining inland maritime economy of the Mississippi River, they had all but disappeared on Atlantic ships.[2] The continued relative scarcity of laborers in the West, the preponderance of African Americans living in key western port cities, and the sheer difficulty of river work likely explain these developments.

Just as in the antebellum period, most of these African American workers lived and worked in Mississippi River system cities. The 1880 public-use sample indicates that as many as 75 percent of African American steamboat workers lived in New Orleans, St. Louis, Louisville, Cincinnati, Memphis, and Nashville.[3] Manuscript census returns for 1880 from St. Louis and New Orleans reflect these concentrations in more detail. In St. Louis, out of a total of 1,886 steamboat workers, 700 (37 percent) were African Americans. Fewer African American river workers lived in New Orleans, but they composed a higher percentage of the labor force: out of a total of 1,024 workers, 431 (42 percent) were African Americans.[4] Meanwhile, although large numbers of river hands continued to live in cities, their importance to the overall urban labor economy was diminishing. By 1880, New Orleans's population had grown to 216,090, 57,723 of which were African Americans. The river was not a significant employer of African Americans by this date. The situation was the same throughout the region. As urbanization increased, the relative importance of steamboat work to cities of the Mississippi River system was significantly reduced.[5]

African Americans composed a high percentage of the labor force in the postwar years, but racism continued to confine them to nonmanagement positions. In New Orleans, only 2 out of 431 African Americans were officers (see Table A.4). The situation was worse in St. Louis: all 700 African Americans listed on census roles worked in either the deck or the cabin crews (see Table A.5). Just as in the antebellum period, whereas a minority of European immigrants were able to rise to officer positions, the best African Americans could hope for was to get a position on the cabin crew as a steward or a barber. Officers also formally excluded African Americans in their postwar labor organizations. St. Louis pilots, for example, wrote in their bylaws that "no person shall become a member of the Harbor who [is not] . . . a white person of 21 years of age [and] of good moral character."[6]

The age structure of the postwar steamboat labor force was similar to that in the antebellum period. Urban census rolls provide the best indication of the industry's age structure, though they likely are biased toward older, more residentially stable workers. In 1880 in St. Louis, the mean age of African American steamboat workers was 31.9 years, while the average age of white steamboat workers was 37.6.[7] In New Orleans, the census reveals a mean age of 33.0 years for African Americans and 39.1 years for whites.[8] Just as in the antebellum years, the continued dominance of whites in skilled occupations meant that their careers often lasted longer than those of African Americans. The

"Shipping a Crew at New Orleans." Attending the anonymous mass levee shape-up remained a common way to get work after emancipation. Photograph by Stoughton Cooley, ca. 1895. Courtesy Sophie Cooley Pearson Collection, Mss. #3237, Louisiana and Lower Mississippi Valley Collection, LSU Libraries, Louisiana State University.

demanding nature of unskilled labor on steamboats and the desire of employers for younger and stronger workers forced most African Americans out of the industry when they reached their late thirties.

The African American workers reflected in the 1880 census returns had fewer resources to challenge racism than did their Reconstruction era counterparts just a few years earlier. As Radical Reconstruction ended and Redemption set in, steamboats were one more place where southern whites effectively stifled African American efforts to expand their rights. I know of no cases involving African American river workers that were heard by state supreme courts during the closing years of the nineteenth century. In contrast to the large number of cases that workers filed in federal court through 1880, only a few scattered suits were brought by workers during the next two decades. The 1870s abuse and wage cases filed by African American river workers marked a short-lived period of political activism.

Steamboat workers continued to push for changes in their work environment after Reconstruction despite the more hostile legal climate. There is no way to measure the extent to which mates took advantage of the closing of legal outlets to increase the pace of work or the brutality against workers, but roustabouts surely continued to complain about being "driven and beaten."[9] One turn-of-the-century observer commented that New Orleans's roustabouts were "the lowest class of laborers in the city, and were driven like beasts by their overseers."[10] Ignored by the American Federation of Labor's focus on craft workers, common river laborers relied on spontaneous organization to counter abuse and declining real wages.[11] A New Orleans newspaper reported a typical disturbance in November of 1900. "The negro roustabouts on boats, which ply between this port and the great plantations and towns along the river," it reported, "struck for higher wages during the past week, and caused considerable delay to river packets."[12] Such efforts were often effective, but they failed to transform conditions in the long run. Although New Orleans stevedores unionized and fashioned a tradition of interracial cooperation, African American deck crew workers, and some of the less fortunate cabin workers as well, were among the most exploited laborers in the late nineteenth century.[13]

In this environment, lawbreaking continued to be associated with river workers. Postbellum steamboat workers shared the same rough culture as their antebellum forbears, the same disregard of property, and the same propensity to band together in ways many civic leaders found threatening. In Cincinnati, Lafcadio Hearn commented that "a number of the colored river men are adroit thieves" and that the "little clothing shops and shoe stores along the levee are almost daily robbed of some articles by such fellows, who excel in ingenious confidence dodges."[14] John Boland, a mate who worked in the deep South in this period, concurred with Hearn's assessment, remembering, "Not infrequently the niggers would get into trouble for stealing or some other misdemeanor."[15] During this period, a St. Louis attorney actually began to specialize in defending African American rivermen.[16] While no African American lawbreaker gained the notoriety of Madison Henderson, Charles Brown, James Seward, and Amos Warrick, the river continued to foster rascality.

With the end of slavery, river work no longer provided the only source of mobility for African Americans, nor was it essential to the African American grapevine of communication. Rivers no longer united radically different labor systems and thus river workers no longer had such a dramatic role to play in the African American community. The changing patterns of the river trade

"Roustabouts Are Sound Sleepers." Photograph by Stoughton Cooley,
ca. 1895. Courtesy Sophie Cooley Pearson Collection, Mss. #3237,
Louisiana and Lower Mississippi Valley Collection, LSU
Libraries, Louisiana State University.

also contributed to moving the industry away from the center of African
American labor activism. While the industry rebounded from its wartime
dislocation, the rise of the railroad ensured that the era of unquestioned river
dominance in the shipment of goods was over.[17] After 1870, the total number
of steamboat arrivals in western cities declined with each passing year.[18] Those
steamboats still engaged in river trade were mostly local trading packets. As
railroads became almost exclusively used for long-distance trade, steamboats
became relegated to local trades not yet served by railroads. In 1870 Pittsburgh, for example, steamboat arrivals had fallen to 1,500 a year—less than
half the number of steamboats that arrived in Pittsburgh during peak antebellum years; moreover, 1,224 of those were small packets coming up the
Monongahela River.[19] In late-nineteenth-century New Orleans, the vast majority of steamboats arrived from local trade with the sugar and cotton coasts,
not from the upper South and the North.[20] These industry changes meant

"Posing for a Group Photograph." Photograph by Stoughton Cooley,
ca. 1895. Courtesy Sophie Cooley Pearson Collection, Mss. #3237,
Louisiana and Lower Mississippi Valley Collection,
LSU Libraries, Louisiana State University.

that African American river workers were decidedly less cosmopolitan than
their antebellum predecessors. At the same time, southern African Americans were building new institutions and networks. As oral networks expanded
beyond the river, as newspapers gained new readership among African Americans, and as formal Republican politics emerged, the political significance of
the river to the African American community gradually eroded.

There were exceptions, of course. In 1879 and 1880, freedpeople calling
themselves Exodusters, a name that linked their struggles to those of the bib-
lical Jews, fled the worsening conditions in Redeemer Mississippi, Louisiana,
and Texas and migrated to the western states of Kansas, Oklahoma, and Nebraska, where they hoped to obtain their own land and a better future. During these years, the Mississippi River and the cities and landings on its banks
were once again the center of a struggle over black labor mobility. The conflict that followed on the banks of the Mississippi was reminiscent of the strug-

gle over labor mobility in the antebellum years. Landowners, worried about the loss of their labor force, pressured steamboat captains not to ship Exoduster migrants. They also pressured police to arrest migrants on a variety of trumped-up charges. The result was that thousands of African Americans were stranded for months on the banks of the Mississippi.[21] Many migrants persisted and made their way upriver to St. Louis, where they reshipped, not up the Ohio River, as they would have before the Civil War, but up the Missouri, where the promise of western lands beckoned.

But the creative linkages between workers on the river and the shore that marked African American resistance to slavery were gone forever. Symbolic of this change was the way in which steamboats became sentimentalized in this period, a sure sign that the industry was becoming economically and culturally marginal. As capitalists increasingly looked to the railroad to ship their goods, steamboat owners attempted to revitalize the industry by marketing it as a leisure institution. In exchange for a few dollars, they offered local white middle-class urban dwellers an excursion and a chance to romanticize the technologies of the past.[22] Not surprisingly, this was not a fertile setting for resistance to the economic and social discriminations of the Jim Crow South. The most notable African American to be associated with riverboats in this period was not a riverman at all but a young musician named Louis Armstrong.

Louis Armstrong played in jazz bands early in his career from 1919 to 1922 on the Streckfus line of excursion boats out of St. Louis. Americans had long been exposed to African American workers' informal musical performances on steamers, but by the 1920s, boat owners—well aware of the steamboat industry's growing irrelevance—commodified and repackaged this music as a way to sell their day trips. The Streckfus line's choice of entertainment, which was mirrored in other river cities, reflected broader changes in an industry desperate to remain economically viable. The music, according to historian David Chevan, was not very good.[23] Whereas antebellum travelers were awed by the raw power of the songs of black roustabouts, travelers in 1920 were serenaded with a variety of watered-down popular musical styles that boat owners could be sure would not offend their audiences. Louis Armstrong quit under these restrictions, but the "excursion industry" persisted for years—into the 1940s—a final, faint reflection of a lost world.

The decline of steamboating did not mean the end of river commerce. Just as flatboats successfully challenged steamboats in the transport of nonperishable produce in the nineteenth century, so, too, did diesel-engine-powered barges challenge railroads in the twentieth. The river remained, and remains, a very efficient means of transporting coal and other nonperishable raw materials to market. The social structure of the industry changed dramatically, however. The decline of steamboats and the rise of barge traffic eliminated most traditional African American river jobs. As loading and unloading became mechanized, and as passengers left the river for the railroads, river work became even more marginal to African American communities as the twentieth century progressed. River workers, including a small number of African Americans, continued to move between the North and the South, traveling to and from the Jim Crow South, but the river no longer nurtured a broadly significant African American activist culture.

The radical possibilities of African American geographic mobility remained, however. The political boundaries of oppressive social systems are always vulnerable to the movement of subordinate peoples on the fringes of power. As the means of distribution of goods evolve, so, too, do the centers of protest and resistance. Thus, in the twentieth century, it was railroad workers who became key activists. Edgar Daniel Nixon, future planner of the Montgomery bus boycott, was changed forever when he took a job as a Pullman porter. "Until I started working for the Pullman Company," Nixon said, "I'd felt that the whole world was like Montgomery. I figured if there was segregation here, there was segregation everywhere. I just didn't think about it. When I first went to St. Louis, I remember I could hardly believe it. St. Louis was a Jim Crow town, yet in the station black and white people sat down together. . . . I came back here and started thinking about things."[24] Nixon was not alone. While the river influenced nineteenth-century black leaders such as William Wells Brown, Milton Clarke, and P. B. S. Pinchback, the railroad spawned twentieth-century civil rights pioneers such as Thurgood Marshall, Harry Haywood, Claude McKay, and Langston Hughes.[25] With the rise of A. Philip Randolph and the Brotherhood of Sleeping Car Porters in the 1920s, the railroad industry became an important center of African American labor activism in the early civil rights movement.

Unionization, though, is not the only measure of effective collective action. This book has illustrated the power that African Americans claimed in an era when public organization was impossible. At a time when planters and merchants were most interested in getting their goods downriver to market in order to make their fortunes, African Americans created countercurrents that contested this larger story of expropriation at every turn. The power and creativity of African Americans was on display with every secret escape, every swindle, and every human relationship rescued from the travesty of a system that placed no value on slave families. The efforts of roustabouts, cooks, waiters, stewards, barbers, and chambermaids were not always successful, but they suggest the presence of alternative traditions within one of the most romanticized industries in American history.

appendix

TABLE A.1. Crews of Ninety-three St. Louis Steamboats, Racial/Ethnic Composition, 1850

	Total Number	Native White	Irish	German	Other[a]	Free Black	Slave
River workers	3,627 (100%)	1,584 (43%)	866 (24%)	400 (11%)	106 (3%)	230 (6%)	441 (12%)

Source: Manuscript Seventh Population Census of the United States, Free Schedule, St. Louis, Ward Four, 1850, Reel 417, and Slave Schedule, St. Louis, Ward Four, 1850, Reel 424, National Archives, Washington, D.C.

[a] Includes but is not confined to people born in Scotland, France, England, Spain, Portugal, Italy, and China.

TABLE A.2. Crews of Ninety-three St. Louis Steamboats, Race and Ethnicity by Occupational Rank, 1850

	Free Black	Native White	Irish	German	Other[e]	Total
Cabin crew[a]	199 (87%)	343 (22%)	41 (5%)	40 (10%)	13 (12%)	636 (20%)
Deck crew[b]	24 (10%)	592 (37%)	784 (91%)	330 (82%)	71 (67%)	1,801 (57%)
Officer[c]	3 (1%)	618 (39%)	31 (3%)	26 (7%)	21 (20%)	699 (22%)
Other[d]	4 (2%)	31 (2%)	10 (1%)	4 (1%)	1 (1%)	50 (1%)
Total	230 (100%)	1,584 (100%)	866 (100%)	400 (100%)	106 (100%)	3,186 (100%)

Source: Manuscript Seventh Census of the United States, Free Schedule, St. Louis, Ward Four, 1850, Reel 417, National Archives, Washington, D.C.

Note: A portion of the crew would not have been on board when the enumeration took place. Some occupational groups were more likely to be off the boat than others. The category "other" in the occupational variable, for instance, is likely severely under-represented. Barbers and barkeepers, who were independent proprietors, were more likely to leave the boats during loading times.

[a] Cooks, stewards, waiters, chambermaids, and porters
[b] Roustabouts, deckhands, firemen, and watchmen
[c] Engineers, captains, mates, clerks, and pilots
[d] Barbers, barkeepers, and carpenters
[e] Includes but is not confined to people born in Scotland, France, England, Spain, Portugal, Italy, and China.

TABLE A.3. Crews of Ninety-three St. Louis Steamboats, Occupational Rank by Race and Ethnicity, 1850[a]

	Cabin Crew	Deck Crew	Officers	Other	Total
Free black	199	24	3	4	230
	(31%)	(1%)	(>1%)	(8%)	(7%)
Native white	343	592	618	31	1,584
	(55%)	(33%)	(88%)	(62%)	(50%)
Irish	41	784	31	10	866
	(6%)	(44%)	(4%)	(20%)	(27%)
German	40	330	26	4	400
	(6%)	(18%)	(4%)	(8%)	(13%)
Other[b]	13	71	21	1	106
	(2%)	(4%)	(3%)	(2%)	(3%)
Total	636	1,801	699	50	3,186
	(100%)	(100%)	(100%)	(100%)	(100%)

Source: Manuscript Seventh Population Census of the United States, Free Schedule, St. Louis, Ward Four, 1850, Reel 417, National Archives, Washington, D.C.

Note: See Table A.2.

[a] For jobs included in each occupational rank, see Table A.2.
[b] For ethnicities included in this category, see Table A.2.

TABLE A.4. New Orleans River Workers, Race and Ethnicity by Occupational Rank, 1880[a]

	African American	Native White	Irish	German	Other[b]	Total
Cabin and deck crews	429 (99%)	109 (27%)	39 (78%)	11 (39%)	65 (71%)	653 (65%)
Officers	2 (1%)	289 (73%)	11 (22%)	17 (61%)	26 (29%)	345 (35%)
Total	431 (100%)	398 (100%)	50 (100%)	28 (100%)	91 (100%)	998 (100%)

Source: Manuscript Tenth Population Census of the United States, New Orleans, 1880, Reels 458–64, National Archives, Washington, D.C.

Note: See Table A.2.

[a] For jobs included in each occupational rank, see Table A.2.
[b] For ethnicities included in this category, see Table A.2.

TABLE A.5. St. Louis River Workers, Race and Ethnicity by Occupational Rank, 1880[a]

	African American	Native Whites	Irish	German	Other[b]	Total
Cabin and deck crews	700 (100%)	410 (51%)	68 (77%)	88 (83%)	59 (80%)	1,325 (75%)
Officers	0 (0%)	384 (49%)	20 (23%)	18 (17%)	14 (20%)	436 (25%)
Total	700 (100%)	794 (100%)	88 (100%)	106 (100%)	73 (100%)	1,761 (100%)

Source: Manuscript Tenth Population Census of the United States, St. Louis, 1880, Reels 718–36, National Archives, Washington, D.C.

Note: See Table A.2.

[a] For jobs included in each occupational rank, see Table A.2.
[b] For ethnicities included in this category, see Table A.2.

notes

ABBREVIATIONS

Arkansas Acts	*General Acts of Arkansas* (Little Rock, 1843)
FHS	Filson Historical Society, Louisville, Kentucky
HNOC	Historic New Orleans Collection, New Orleans, Louisiana
Kentucky Acts	*Kentucky Acts* (Frankfort, 1824, 1860, 1861)
LLMVC	Louisiana and Lower Mississippi Valley Collection, Louisiana State University Special Collections, Baton Rouge, Louisiana
Louisiana Acts	*Acts . . . of the Legislature of the State of Louisiana* (New Orleans, 1812–59)
LSCR	Louisiana Supreme Court Records, Special Collections, University of New Orleans, New Orleans, Louisiana
MDAH	Mississippi Department of Archives and History, Jackson, Mississippi
MHS	Missouri Historical Society, St. Louis, Missouri
Mississippi Acts	*Mississippi Laws* (Jackson, 1842, 1862)
Missouri Acts	*Laws of Missouri* (Jefferson City, 1841, 1843, 1859)
MSCR	Missouri Supreme Court Records, Missouri State Archives, Jefferson City, Missouri
NA	National Archives, Washington
NAGLR	National Archives–Great Lakes Region, Southern District of Illinois, Chicago, Illinois
NAGPR	National Archives–Great Plains Region, Eastern District of Missouri, Kansas City, Missouri
NASWR	National Archives–Southwest Region, Eastern District of Louisiana, Fort Worth, Texas
SHC	Southern Historical Collection, Wilson Library, University of North Carolina, Chapel Hill, North Carolina
SHSM	State Historical Society of Missouri, Columbia, Missouri
Tennessee Acts	*Public Acts of the State of Tennessee* (Nashville, 1833)

1. Twain, *Autobiography*, 291.

2. Twain, *Life on the Mississippi*, 118–19.

3. Osofsky, ed., *Puttin' on Ole Massa*, 187, 189.

4. For statistics on New Orleans steamboat commerce in 1860 see *Debow's Review* 31 (September 1861): 454–58. For the cotton crop see Moore, *Emergence of the Cotton Kingdom*, 285–86.

5. Letter signed by Edward Bates, *Debow's Review* 12 (May 1852): 569.

6. Blassingame, ed., *Slave Testimony*, 393.

7. Edwards, *Uncle Tom's Companions*, 92. New Orleans masters noticed this preference as well. The master of the slave John Scott testified in court that "he purchased him [Scott] to drive a dray, but the boy preferred working on steamboats." See also *McMaster v. Beckwith*, testimony of Matthew Maher, LSCR.

8. Blassingame, ed., *Slave Testimony*, 441.

9. *Trials and Confessions of Madison Henderson*, 8. This document is extremely rare. I have used the copy in Cornell University's Law School library. Not all slaves wanted to work on the river. For an example of a slave who did not want to be sold to a boat captain for fear of losing a favorable Nashville master see Israel Campbell, *Bond and Free*, 76.

10. See testimony of William Stone, 3744–45.

11. Louis C. Hunter, *Steamboats on the Western Rivers*, ch. 2.

12. Captain Basil Hall, *Travels in North America*, 368.

13. Western steamboats have been the subject of numerous histories. The best works include Twain, *Life on the Mississippi*; Habermehl, *Life on the Western Rivers*; Louis C. Hunter, *Steamboats on the Western Rivers*; Haites, Mak, and Walton, *Western River Transportation*; Haites and Mak, "Ohio and Mississippi River Transportation"; Haites and Mak, "Social Savings"; and Haites and Mak, "Steamboating on the Mississippi." See also Dayton, *Steamboat Days*; Petersen, *Steamboating on the Upper Mississippi*; and Merrick, *Old Times on the Upper Mississippi*. For pre-industrial flatboats and keelboats see Baldwin, *Keelboat Age*, and especially Allen, *Western Rivermen*.

14. Louis C. Hunter, *Steamboats on the Western Rivers*, ch. 2, esp. 90–91. For more detail on how the structure and mechanics of steamboats developed see Flexner, *Steamboats Come True*.

15. United States Treasury reports, which probably don't include all steamboats, list a total of 14,752 free workers on the rivers in 1851. See Louis C. Hunter, *Steamboats on the Western Rivers*, 443, 448.

16. Robert S. Starobin (*Industrial Slavery*, 30) argued that 10,000 bondsmen worked on the western rivers. Philip S. Foner and Ronald L. Lewis (*Black Worker to 1869*, 199) claim that 5,000 African Americans worked in internal navigation. Estimates of the total number of steamboats on the western rivers vary. Louis C. Hunter (*Steamboats on the Western Rivers*, 33, 443) estimates that there were 740 by

1850. Edward and Herbert Quick (*Mississippi Steamboatin'*, 170) claim there were a thousand Mississippi steamers in operation at midcentury.

17. See Seventh Population Census of the United States, Free Schedule, St. Louis, Ward Four, Reel 417, and Slave Schedule, St. Louis, Ward Four, Reel 424, NA.

18. Starobin, *Industrial Slavery*, introduction. For other studies of industrial slavery see Dew, *Bond of Iron*; Lewis, *Coal, Iron, and Slaves*; and Outland, "Slavery, Work, and the Geography."

19. Cecelski, *Waterman's Song*, xiii. W. Jeffrey Bolster (*Black Jacks*, 2) estimates that 20,000 African Americans, the vast majority of whom he claims were free blacks, worked on Atlantic ships.

20. Seventh Population Census of the United States, Free Schedule, St. Louis, Ward Four, Reel 417, and Slave Schedule, St. Louis, Ward Four, Reel 424, NA.

21. Louis C. Hunter, *Steamboats on the Western Rivers*, 442–43.

22. *Barry v. Kimball*, No. 4684, 12 La Ann 372 (1857), LSCR. Other examples of urban residence are common in the qualitative documentation from the period. See *United States v.* Louisville, testimony of the slave Judy Taylor, NAGLR. For slaves living in New Orleans see *McMaster v. Beckwith*, LSCR, and Grandy, *Narrative*, 30. For African Americans in St. Louis see Osofsky, ed., *Puttin' on Ole Massa*, narrative of William Wells Brown; *Trials and Confessions of Madison Henderson*; and *Ridgely v.* Reindeer, MSCR.

23. Unsigned letter to Mary Littrell, May 27, 1855, Mary A. Davis Papers, FHS; *United States v.* Louisville, testimony of Nelson Collins, NAGLR. For rural-living slaves see Beverly v. *Empire*, testimony of J. Leight [*sic*], LSCR; *United States v.* Black Hawk, testimony of Peter Stewart, NAGLR; and *United States v.* Louisville, testimony of William Richeson, NAGLR.

24. Testimony of Will Long, 2408.

25. Curry, *Free Black in Urban America*, 247.

26. This is an estimate based on census data. Occupational definitions in this census only sometimes identify river workers. Many river hands are often hidden by vague occupational titles such as "barber," "steward," "waiter," or "chambermaid." See Seventh Population Census of the United States, Pittsburgh, Reels 745–46; New Orleans, Reels 235–38; and St. Louis, Reels 415–18, NA. For a discussion of the problem of recording river workers in the census see Wright, *History and Growth of the United States Census*, 151.

27. Louis C. Hunter, *Steamboats on the Western Rivers*, 450. See also Foner and Lewis, *Black Worker to 1869*, 51.

28. For distinctions between the officers and the deck and cabin crews see Louis C. Hunter, *Steamboats on the Western Rivers*, 443. For examples of industries where slaves sometimes rose to more skilled positions see Dew, *Bond of Iron*, 107, and Outland, "Slavery, Work, and the Geography."

29. Twain, *Life on the Mississippi*, 37.

30. The 1850 St. Louis slave census does not provide occupational data that

would precisely document the positions that slaves filled. My assertion that, compared to other groups of free laborers, a disproportionate number of slaves worked on deck is based on travelers' observations, as well as the fact that steamboats in St. Louis that employed slaves generally listed far fewer free deck crew members than they would have needed.

31. Testimony of Henry Clay, in *American Slave*, 112.

32. Charles Mackay, *Life and Liberty in America*, 151.

33. Cunynghame, *Glimpse at the Great Western Republic*, 142.

34. Quick and Quick, *Mississippi Steamboatin'*, 236.

35. The eighty-five chambermaids enumerated in the 1850 St. Louis census do not reflect the total number of chambermaids employed on all boats. Many workers, some of whom may have been jailed, were apparently in St. Louis at the time of the enumeration. It is possible to tell how many slaves worked in this position because this was the only job women held on board. Thus all slave women included in the slave steamboat census filled this job. The large percentage of African American chambermaids among those enumerated reflects the disproportionate number of African American women in southern cities and their domination of domestic-labor jobs.

36. Thomas, *From Tennessee Slave*, 115. See also Quick and Quick, *Mississippi Steamboatin'*, 235–36.

37. *St. Louis Globe-Democrat*, January 8, 1893.

38. *United States v.* Louisville, testimony of Adam Cook, NAGLR. Early river historian John Habermehl (*Life on the Western Rivers*, 76) notes the importance of New Orleans as a center of slave leasings to steamboats. See also Louis C. Hunter, *Steamboats on the Western Rivers*, 449. For an example of a typical runaway advertisement see *Missouri Republican*, October 13, 1847.

39. *Pelham v.* Messenger, testimony of Frank Pelham, LSCR.

40. One free black hand recalled taking summers off. He remembered that the boat he ran on was a big one and "could not run in the summer" so he "lay around" until business picked up in the fall. See Blassingame, ed., *Slave Testimony*, 387. Winters were slower times in the industry as well. Northern rivers frequently froze, and many smaller rivers became too shallow for steamboats during this season. The rhythms of the agricultural cycle also caused a slack in trade at these times.

41. Entry for September 21, 1836, James Kennerly Diary, 1826–38, Journals and Diaries, MHS.

42. Entry for October 18, 1836, ibid.

43. Entries for February 17, May 4, and July 10, 1837, ibid.

44. *United States v.* Louisville, testimony of Joseph Jackson, NAGLR.

45. Testimony of Judy Taylor, ibid.

46. Drew, *Refugee*, 179.

47. *Adams v. Trabue*, testimony of William Pigman, LSCR.

48. *Frank Pelham v.* Messenger, testimony of J. T. Thompson, LSCR.

49. Account Book, 1830–60, James Rudd Papers, FHS. For other examples of

slaves working for several years on steamboats, see *Hennen v.* Doswell, testimony of Caruthers, LSCR; Clarke and Clarke, *Narratives of the Sufferings*, 81–83.

50. For work of African American sailors see Scott, "Common Wind"; Cecelski, "Shores of Freedom"; Cecelski, *Waterman's Song*; Bolster, *Black Jacks*; Farr, *Black Odyssey*; Putney, *Black Sailors*; Rediker, *Between the Devil and the Deep Blue Sea*; and Linebaugh and Rediker, *Many-Headed Hydra*. For work on river workers see Moore, "Simon Gray, Riverman"; Egerton, *Gabriel's Rebellion*; and Wood, *Women's Work, Men's Work*.

For an argument that stresses the local, neighborhood orientation of the slave community see Kaye, "Neighborhoods and Solidarity."

51. Starobin briefly discussed slave steamboat workers. See his *Industrial Slavery*, 30.

CHAPTER ONE

1. "Steamboat Stories," in William H. Tippitt Collection, MDAH. See also Quick and Quick, *Mississippi Steamboatin'*, 236.

2. Charles Latrobe, *Rambler in North America*, 299. Travelers also noticed white workers. For example, see Everest, *Journey*, 97.

3. Foster, *Way-side Glimpses*, 172.

4. Tixier, *Tixier's Travels*, 45.

5. See leasings for 1856–59, Account Book, 1830–60, James Rudd Papers, FHS.

6. Letter signed by James Lackland, September 1, 1846, Lackland Papers, MHS.

7. *United States v.* Louisville, testimony of William Richeson, NAGLR.

8. Time *v.* Parmelee, MSCR. In this Missouri Supreme Court case John Carlisle of St. Louis recalled his role as an agent. He told the court, "I then hired him [a slave David] to the *Harry of the West*. Miss Smith, the owner of the boy, was at that time at Cape Gerardeau [sic] in this state. I was acting as agent for Miss Smith, and had always hired negroes for her."

9. Letter signed H. G. Smith, n.d., Slaves and Slavery Collection, MHS. The letter likely dates from the late 1850s. See also *Charles Beardslee and Wife v. Parmelee*, MSCR.

10. See Lackland Letters, Folder 1, Lane Collection, Lackland Papers, MHS.

11. Osofsky, ed., *Puttin' on Ole Massa*, 208.

12. Document signed Elizabeth Pease, New Orleans, April 3, 1856, Slaves and Slavery Collection, MHS.

13. *United States v.* Louisville, testimony of Judy Taylor, NAGLR.

14. *Ridgely v.* Reindeer, testimony of Stephen Ridgely, MSCR.

15. *Frank Pelham v.* Messenger, testimony of J. Thompson, LSCR; *Barry v. Kimball*, No. 4684, 12 La Ann 372 (1857), testimony of John William, LSCR.

16. Clarke and Clarke, *Narratives of the Sufferings*, 82.

17. *Barry v. Kimball*, No. 4684, 12 La Ann 372 (1857), testimony of John William, LSCR.

18. Drew, *Refugee*, 178.

19. *Bryan v.* Aunt Letty, testimony of Thomas Baldwin, MSCR.

20. *McMaster v. Beckwith*, testimony of Solomon Lynchhart, LSCR. The court concurred with Lynchhart's assessment of Scott's masterless existence and reduced the fine for his escape.

21. Letter signed by James Lackland, July 18, 1846, Lackland Papers, MHS.

22. *Beardslee v. Perry*, testimony of John Carlisle, MSCR. See also *Rountree v.* Brilliant, LSCR.

23. *Pelham v.* Messenger, testimony of R. Fletcher, LSCR.

24. *Beardslee v. Perry*, testimony of John Carlisle, MSCR.

25. Letter signed by James Lackland, St. Louis, May 29, 1846, Lackland Papers, MHS.

26. Bolster, *Black Jacks*, ch. 7.

27. For an excellent summary of these laws see Tansey, "Out-of-State Free Blacks."

28. "An Act to Amend the Several Acts of this State in Relation to Free Negroes and Mulattoes," Act of February 26, 1842, *Mississippi Acts*, 1842, 65.

29. "An Act Concerning Free Negroes, Mulattoes, and Emancipation," Act of March 3, 1860, *Kentucky Acts*, 1860, 129. Arkansas legislators allowed nonresident free black steamboat workers to circulate through their cities and towns provided they did not stay for more than three months. See "An Act to Prohibit the Emigration and Settlement of Free Negroes, or Free Persons of Color, into This State," Act of January 20, 1843, *Arkansas Acts*, 1843, 63.

30. "An Act to Amend an Act Entitled 'An Act Concerning Free Negroes, Mulattoes, and Emancipation,'" Act of January 23, 1861, *Kentucky Acts*, 1861, 1. State lawmakers made an allowance for stewards, whose jobs often required them to leave boats. Free black stewards living in other states were allowed to leave boats and obtain provisions as long as they had a written pass from either their boat clerk or their captain.

31. "An Act More Effectively to Prevent Free Persons of Color from entering into This State, and for Other Purposes," Act of February 23, 1843, *Missouri Acts*, 1843, 66–67.

32. Carrierre, "Blacks in Pre–Civil War Memphis," 127–28.

33. "An Act to Repeal Part of an Act Entitled 'An Act Concerning Slaves,'" Act of December 1, 1859, *Missouri Acts*, 1859, 90–91. The 1855 statute was repealed (and described) in this 1859 law.

34. Blassingame, ed., *Slave Testimony*, 387.

35. Tansey, "Out-of-State Free Blacks," 378–81. For another analysis of police autonomy in New Orleans and their selective enforcement of the law see McGoldrick, "Policing of Slavery in New Orleans."

36. The narratives of William Wells Brown, Madison Henderson, Milton Clarke, Sella Martin, and others reveal significant time spent in the principal port cities of the western rivers. See Osofsky, *Puttin' on Ole Massa*, 183–95; *Trials and Confessions of Madison Henderson*, 24, 29, 31, 41–45, 57, 60, 61, 71–75; Clarke and Clarke, *Narratives of the Sufferings*, 81–82; and Blassingame, ed., *Slave Testimony*, 730–33.

37. *Trials and Confessions of Madison Henderson*, 43.

38. Drew, *Refugee*, 255.

39. Entry for March 22, 1864, Logbook of the *Ike Hammitt*, Inland Waterways Collection, Cincinnati Public Library, Cincinnati, Ohio.

40. Testimony of William McCarthy, 1375.

41. Wheeler, *Steamboatin' Days*, 103.

42. Louis C. Hunter, *Steamboats on the Western Rivers*, 34.

43. Blassingame, ed., *Slave Testimony*, 728.

44. Thomas, *From Tennessee Slave*, 109, 112–13.

45. Ibid., 108.

46. Goodrich, *Family Tourist*, 437.

47. Didimus, *New Orleans as I Found It*, 15.

48. Ibid., 1, 15.

49. *Rice v. Cade*, LSCR.

50. Latham, *Black and White*, 150. For stevedores in the postbellum period see Arnesen, *Waterfront Workers*.

51. *Pipkin v. Pipkin*, testimony of George Ramsey, LSCR.

52. Didimus, *New Orleans as I Saw It*, 16.

53. Ingraham, *Sunny South*, 344.

54. Wade, *Slavery in the Cities*, 29; Crété, *Daily Life in Louisiana*, 53.

55. Wade, *Slavery in the Cities*, 17–18; Blassingame, *Black New Orleans*, 1–2.

56. For the roots of free black society in New Orleans see Hanger, *Bounded Lives*. For the antebellum period see Blassingame, *Black New Orleans*, and Dabel, "My Ma Went to Work Early," 218–25.

57. For examples of steamboat slaves in New Orleans coffeehouses see *Barry v. Kimball*, No. 4684, 12 La Ann 372 (1857), testimony of Isole Darcole, LSCR, and *Hennen v. Doswell*, testimony of J. Y., LSCR.

58. *Immigrant of a Hundred Years Ago*, 36–37.

59. Tower, *Slavery Unmasked*, 337.

60. *Trials and Confessions of Madison Henderson*, 28.

61. *Immigrant of a Hundred Years Ago*, 36–37.

62. Thomas, *From Tennessee Slave*, 109. The best account of Congo Square's historical development is Jerah Johnson, "New Orleans's Congo Square," 117–53.

63. Redpath, *Roving Editor*, 162.

64. Ingraham, *Southwest*, 111; Crété, *Daily Life in Louisiana*, 43, 57; Tansey, "Out-of-State Free Blacks," 369–86. For an account of slave and free black steamboat workers in the Calaboose see *Trials and Confessions of Madison Henderson*, 42.

65. Crété, *Daily Life in Louisiana*, 94–95; Wade, *Slavery in the Cities*, 201.

66. Walter Johnson, *Soul by Soul*, 167–68.

67. Thomas, *From Tennessee Slave*, 110.

68. *Emmerling v. Beebe*, testimony of John Eaton, LSCR.

69. Olmsted, *Journey to the Seaboard Slave States*, 592; Wade, *Slavery in the Cities*, 151, 157; Niehaus, *Irish in New Orleans*, 54.

70. Louis C. Hunter, *Steamboats on the Western Rivers*, 662.

71. Roderick A. McDonald, "Independent Economic Production," 193. According to McDonald, sugar plantation slaves had regular contact with retail agents in St. Louis, Natchez, and New Orleans. Between 1844 and 1861, slaves on the Gay estate sent an average of four or five shipments of moss crop to western river cities. The slaves there also shipped molasses to St. Louis, for which they received eight to twelve dollars a barrel. When contracting goods, slaves paid shipping charges and even the sales commission of agents.

72. Tixier, *Tixier's Travels*, 41.

73. Charles Mackay, *Life and Liberty in America*, 255.

74. Ibid.

75. Martineau, *Retrospect of Western Travel*, 9.

76. Houstoun, *Hesperos*, 53.

77. Bremer, *Homes of the New World*, 187.

78. Nason, *Journal of a Tour*, 66.

79. Blassingame, ed., *Slave Testimony*, 433.

80. Ibid., 524.

81. Drew, *Refugee*, 192.

82. Ibid., 192.

83. Randolph B. Campbell, *Empire for Slavery*, 57–61.

84. Bolton, *Arkansas*, 127.

85. Krauthamer, "Blacks on the Borders," 38–41.

86. Randolph B. Campbell, *Empire for Slavery*, 57–61.

87. For a good description of this process in northeastern Louisiana see Joe Gray Taylor, *Negro Slavery in Louisiana*, 60–69. For the steamboat economy along the Yazoo see Owens, *Steamboats and the Cotton Economy*.

88. Allen, *Western Rivermen*, 124–29.

89. Morris, *Becoming Southern*, 121–22.

90. Hogan and Davis, eds., *William Johnson's Natchez*.

91. Morris, "Event in Community Organization."

92. Dew, "Black Ironworkers," 328.

93. Jordan, *Tumult and Silence at Second Creek*, 5, 206–10.

94. Bond, "'Every Duty Incumbent upon Them,'" 255. Beverly G. Bond of the University of Memphis graciously provided the names of the free black rivermen from her analysis of Memphis's 1860 free population census.

95. *Memphis Daily Appeal*, July 31, 1855.

96. Ibid., October 30, 1857.

97. While I have not seen textual evidence that the Jacob Burkle estate was a haven for runaway slaves, my inspection of the house at 826 North Second Street persuaded me that it was.

98. *Memphis Daily Appeal*, July 24, 1857.

99. For Memphis women see Bond, "'Every Duty Incumbent upon Them.'" For free black women in early New Orleans see Kimberly S. Hanger, *Bounded Lives*.

100. For masters leasing slaves to steamboats in order to disguise a sale see Osofsky, ed., *Puttin on Ole Massa*, 191–92, and *Sarah Hill v. James White*, testimony of

Oscar Hamilton, LSCR. For the river economy in Arkansas see McNeilly, *The Old South Frontier*, 1–5, 123–56, and Bolton, *Arkansas*, 125–44. For insightful descriptions of the river topography in Arkansas see Foti, "River's Gifts and Curses."

101. Davis, *Frontier Illinois*, 165–67. See also the Historic Illinois Preservation Society website for a general history at ‹http://www.state.il.us/hpa/lib/AfAmHist.htm› (December 2003).

102. Litwack, *North of Slavery*, ch. 3. For a more recent assessment of northern free black communities see Horton and Horton, *In Hope of Liberty*.

103. Stanley W. Campbell, *Slave Catchers*, 112.

104. Ibid., ch. 6.

105. Louis C. Hunter, *Steamboats on the Western Rivers*, 30, 47–49, 661. See also Mahoney, *River Towns in the Great West*, esp. chs. 3 and 4, and Adler, *Yankee Merchants*.

106. Fehrenbacher, *Slavery, Law, and Politics*, 121–30.

107. Seventh Population Census of the United States, Free Schedules, St. Louis, Reels 415–18, and Slave Schedules, 1850, St. Louis, Reel 424, NA; Frederick Way Jr., comp., *Way's Packet Directory*.

108. These men were listed in the Seventh Population Census (cited in the previous note) as both with a steamboat crew and living at a St. Louis residence.

109. Primm, *Lion of the Valley*, 165, 179.

110. Babcock, ed., *Memoir of John Mason Peck D.D.*, 90.

111. *Missouri Republican*, August 23, 1847; *St. Louis Globe-Democrat*, December 28, 1853.

112. Clamorgan, *Colored Aristocracy of St. Louis*, 51.

113. Osofsky, ed., *Puttin' on Ole Massa*, 207.

114. Clamorgan, *Colored Aristocracy of St. Louis*, 53.

115. Fehrenbacher, *Slavery, Law, and Politics*, 129.

116. Osofsky, ed., *Puttin' on Ole Massa*, 185–86. For an example of a mob of whites killing an African American boatman see *New Orleans Picayune*, June 29, 1849.

117. Herman, "Macintosh Affair"; Primm, *Lion of the Valley*, 175.

118. Thomas, *From Tennessee Slave*. For a detailed description of the African American community see Lovett, *African-American History of Nashville*, chs. 1–2.

119. Lovett, *African-American History of Nashville*, 6–16.

120. Coleman, *Slavery Times in Kentucky*, 43.

121. Hudson, "Crossing the 'Dark Line,'" 69.

122. Ibid., 44. For statistics on Louisville's slave and free black populations see Curry, *Free Black in Urban America*, appendix A. See also Burckin, "'Spirit of Perseverance.'"

123. Burckin, "'Spirit of Perseverance,'" 77.

124. Hodes, *White Women, Black Men*, 130.

125. Ibid., 129, 130.

126. Ibid., 130.

127. Coleman, *Slavery Times in Kentucky*, 44.

128. Stanley W. Campbell, *Slave Catchers*, 144–46.

129. For examples of slave boat workers working on levees in Illinois and Indiana see *Beverly v.* Empire, testimony of John Shade, LSCR, and *Trials and Confessions of Madison Henderson*, 19.

130. S. C. Slater to John Slater, July 3, 1848, Missouri History Papers, MHS. For discussion of the custom of jailing steamboat slaves in Covington and Louisville see *Beverly v.* Empire, testimony of John Shade, LSCR.

131. Blassingame, ed., *Slave Testimony*, 527, 525.

132. Ross, *Workers on the Edge*, 72. Ross details the impact of steamboats on the transformation of class relations in the city. See also Louis C. Hunter, *Steamboats on the Western Rivers*, 644.

133. Cheek and Cheek, "John Mercer Langston," 44–45. In 1804 and 1807 a series of Black Laws were passed by the state in an attempt to limit black migration to the state. The laws required blacks to post a $500 bond within twenty days of entering the state or face expulsion.

134. Francis Trollope, *Domestic Manners of the Americans*, 37.

135. Lafcadio Hearn, *Children of the Levee*, 11.

136. Henry Louis Taylor Jr. and Vicky Dula, "The Black Residential Experience and Community Formation in Antebellum Cincinnati," in Henry Louis Taylor Jr., ed., *Race and the City*, 100, 116–17.

137. Nikki Marie Taylor, "'Frontiers of Freedom,'" 19.

138. Hagedorn, *Beyond the River*.

139. Egerton, *Gabriel's Rebellion*, 151.

140. Ullman, *Martin R. Delany*, 27–28.

141. Ibid.

142. Sterling, *Making of an Afro-American*, 43.

143. Delany, *Blake*.

144. See, for instance, Van Deburg, *Slave Drivers*, ch. 2.

145. Wade, *Slavery in the Cities*, ch. 6.

CHAPTER TWO

1. Osofsky, ed., *Puttin' on Ole Massa*, 210.

2. Ibid., 216–18.

3. Bolster, *Black Jacks*, 75. For an interpretation that argues for even more harmonious race relations in the early eighteenth century see Rediker, *Between the Devil and the Deep Blue Sea*, ch. 4.

4. Houstoun, *Hesperos*, 44.

5. *Nicholas Decker et al. v. Duncan Carter*, NAGPR.

6. Cunynghame, *Glimpse at the Great Western Republic*, 143.

7. Lanman, *Adventures in the Wilds of the United States*, 167.

8. Entry on page 22, n.d., Mississippi River Travel Diary, DU.

9. Quick and Quick, *Mississippi Steamboatin'*, 251.

10. Blassingame, ed., *Slave Testimony*, 432.

11. Everest, *Journey*.

12. The privacy of cabin rooms gave travelers and officers ample opportunity for sexual advances. See Osofsky, ed., *Puttin' on Ole Massa*, 194.

13. Habermehl, *Life on the Western Rivers*, 84–85. Sung on the Mississippi, where chambermaids were overwhelmingly African American, the racial implications of this song would have been clear to all listeners.

14. In 1850, steamboat workers were officially deemed "inland mariners" by the U.S. government and were thus subject to maritime law. The 1835 statute prohibited officers "from malice, hatred, or revenge" and from beating, wounding, or imprisoning any member of the crew. I have researched federal admiralty records for the Eastern District of Louisiana, the Southern District of Illinois and the Eastern District of Missouri. In the 1850s, river workers sued somewhat frequently under the 1835 statute in federal court. I found no suits for flogging in any of these courts. See Macarthur, comp., *Seaman's Contract*. Early river historian John Habermehl claimed that slaves on steamboats were better treated than free workers. See Habermehl, *Life on the Western Rivers*, 76.

15. *McKinney v.* Yalla Busha, testimony of George Robertson, LSCR. For a case in which a free black traveler was whipped for allegedly stealing see *Hynes v. Kirkman*, LSCR. For other examples of African Americans committing suicide in order to avoid boat conditions see *Missouri Republican*, May 22, 1846, and *New Orleans Picayune*, July 22, 1849. White workers also killed themselves. See, for example, *Missouri Republican*, August 10, 1847.

16. Lakier, *Russian Looks at America*, 232.

17. *McKinney v.* Yalla Busha, testimony of John Littleton, LSCR.

18. *Barry v. Kimball*, No. 4684, 12 La Ann 372 (1857), testimony of John Byrne, LSCR.

19. *Pelham v.* Messenger, testimony of John Kennedy, LSCR.

20. For a discussion of rough culture see Peter Way, *Common Labour*.

21. *New Orleans Picayune*, June 9, 1839.

22. Ibid., February 14, 1864. For an account of a fight between a free black steward and a white worker see ibid., April 22, 1859.

23. Ibid., April 8, 1849; Cheek and Cheek, "John Mercer Langston," 45–46.

24. My research into antebellum newspapers confirms Louis C. Hunter's claim that interracial labor strikes did not generally occur on antebellum rivers. I have found no newspaper accounts of interracial strikes involving free blacks or slaves. Newspaper articles detailing strikes suggest that most were confined to the deck crew, where African Americans were less concentrated. For a typical example of a strike by deckhands see *St. Louis Globe-Democrat*, September 16, 1853. Louis C. Hunter (*Steamboats on the Western Rivers*, 474) documents one instance of an interracial strike in 1866 Cincinnati.

25. *Blair et al. v.* Aunt Letty, NAGPR.

26. Ibid., testimony of Robert Baldwin.

27. Ibid.

28. Ibid., testimony of John Blair and Robert Baldwin, NAGPR.

29. Habermehl, *Life on the Western Rivers*, 92–97. Habermehl describes how steamboat European immigrants gradually rejected class solidarity with African Americans in favor of racism. Racial tensions may have been more contentious in the upper South and lower North. For regional variations in race relations see Berlin, *Slaves Without Masters*, ch. 6, esp. 212–16.

30. Olmsted, *Cotton Kingdom*, 232.

31. Quick and Quick, *Mississippi Steamboatin'*, 235.

32. Louis C. Hunter, *Steamboats on the Western Rivers*, 272, 278; *New Orleans Picayune*, September 7, 1844; ibid., September 11, 1844; ibid., February 11, 1849; *Missouri Republican*, November 29, 1847.

33. When slaves died, their masters sometimes sued for negligence; see *Johnstone v. Arabia*, MSCR; and *Rice v. Cade*; *Morgan's Syndics v. Fiveash*; *Lacoste v. Sellick*; *Poree v. Cannon*; *England v. Gripon*; *Howes v. Red Chief*; *Huntington v. Ricard*; and *Barry v. Kimball*, all LSCR.

34. *Missouri Republican*, October 17, 1846. For an account of an African American steward's drowning death see *New Orleans Picayune*, December 4, 1849.

35. Entry for August 28, 1859, Sarah Lois Wadley Diary, vol. 1, SHC.

36. Starobin, *Industrial Slavery*, 72.

37. Louis C. Hunter, *Steamboats on the Western Rivers*, 290–98. For examples of African Americans killed in boiler explosions see *New Orleans Picayune*, April 26, 1859; ibid., November 16, 1849; and *Rountree v. Brilliant*.

38. Starobin, *Industrial Slavery*, 44.

39. Quick and Quick, *Mississippi Steamboatin'*, 321. Such explosions were caused by a variety of structural problems, including the lack of proper pressure gauges and defective plates and pumps, and a range of other design problems. Engineers seeking maximum speed were to blame in some instances since they sometimes allowed water levels to get too low in the boilers, causing a buildup in pressure.

40. Testimony of Betty Robertson, 356.

41. Louis C. Hunter, *Steamboats on the Western Rivers*, ch. 6, 656.

42. Ibid., 430–35.

43. Quoted in Starobin, *Industrial Slavery*, 65. In this case, the master thought that his slaves' sickness was caused by damp below-deck sleeping quarters. Illness struck all crew members, but slave and free rivermen received different treatment on shore. Federally funded marine hospitals, founded to help address the public health threats posed by maritime workers, covered only free workers. While there may have been exceptions, slave workers generally remained in the care of masters and private physicians. In some cases, officers took them to urban slave hospitals, though in these instances, masters were responsible for treatment costs.

44. *United States v.* Louisville, testimony of Judy Taylor, NAGLR.

45. Testimony of Elmo Steele, 2027.

46. Davies, *American Scenes*, 100. See also Houstoun, *Hesperos*, 54, and Bodichon, *American Diary*, 112–13. In the postwar period, a woman named Annie Carter reported a "special agreement" under which she performed the duties of a cham-

bermaid, as well as waiting and cooking. See *Norman Laughlin et al. v.* Robert Semple, NASWR.

47. Rosenberg, *Jenny Lind in America*, 163.

48. A. Oakey Hall, *Manhattaner in New Orleans*, 183; Charles Latrobe, *Rambler in North America*, 296.

49. Piercy, *Route from Liverpool*, 73.

50. McIlwaine, *Memphis Down in Dixie*, 191–92.

51. Foster, *Way-side Glimpses*, 172.

52. Gustavus A. Henry to Mrs. M. Henry, November 22, 1849, Gustavus A. Henry Papers, Box 1, Folder 1, SHC.

53. Osofsky, ed., *Puttin' on Ole Massa*, 187. See also Bodichon, *American Diary*, 112–13. Workers generally had to purchase their own clothes, which were more costly for cabin laborers than deck workers. See Habermehl, *Life on the Western Rivers*, 28.

54. Charles Latrobe, *Rambler in North America*, 296.

55. A. Oakley Hall, *Manhattaner in New Orleans*, 179.

56. Ibid., 179–80.

57. *Mary Johns v. Henry Brinker*, testimony of Joseph Jones, LSCR.

58. *Block v.* Trent, LSCR.

59. Habermehl, *Life on the Western Rivers*, 153. Deck passengers generally carried their own provisions.

60. Ibid., 59–63; Louis C. Hunter, *Steamboats on the Western Rivers*, 400–402; *Blair et al. v. Steamboat* Aunt Letty, NAGPR.

61. Wortley, *Travels in the United States*, 110.

62. Steele, *Summer Journey*, 211.

63. Russell, *My Diary North and South*, 178.

64. For the best description of chambermaid duties see *Mary Johns v. Henry Brinker*, LSCR, and Houstoun, *Hesperos*, 6–7. See also Sophie Pearson, unpublished manuscript "The Man—His Boats—the River," ch. 10, Box 3, Sophie Cooley Pearson Collection, LLMVC.

65. Gustavus A. Henry to Mrs. M. Henry, November 22, 1849, Gustavus A. Henry Papers, Box 1, Folder 1, SHC.

66. See *Wm. Patterson v.* Great Republic, NAGPR.

67. Woodson, "Negroes of Cincinnati." This article has been reprinted in Dabney, *Cincinnati's Colored Citizens*, 38.

68. Clamorgan, *Colored Aristocracy of St. Louis*, 58, 63.

69. Olmsted, *Journey to the Seaboard Slave States*, 565.

70. Testimony of Charles Williams, 183.

71. Russell, *My Diary North and South*, 183.

72. Houstoun, *Hesperos*, 160.

73. Thomas, *From Tennessee Slave*, 107.

74. Charles Latrobe, *Rambler in North America*, 289.

75. Habermehl, *Life on the Western Rivers*, 46.

76. Marryat, *Diary in America*, 367.

77. McIlwaine, *Memphis Down in Dixie*, 192.

78. Cunynghame, *Glimpse at the Great Western Republic*, 142. For an example from the immediate postwar period see Entry for June 5, [no year], Diary of Sallie Diana Smith, Trail Collection, Box 1, Folder 8, SHSM.

79. See steamboat crew lists, Seventh Population Census of the United States, St. Louis, Reel 417, NA. Barbers would have been among the black workers least tied to the boat—a fact that may be responsible for the small number of barbers recorded in the census. For more on how barbering was considered "nigger work" in the South see Berlin, *Slaves Without Masters*, 235–36.

80. Thomas, *From Tennessee Slave*, 85.

81. Hogan and Davis, eds., *William Johnson's Natchez*, 508, 743.

82. For barbers' tasks, and the shifting of workers between riverside barbershops and steamboats, see Hogan and Davis, eds., *William Johnson's Natchez*, and Blassingame, ed., *Slave Testimony*, testimony of Isaac Throgmorton, 432–33.

83. Tixier, *Tixier's Travels*, 45. See also Olmsted, *Journey to the Seaboard Slave States*, 564, and Louis C. Hunter, *Steamboats on the Western Rivers*, 391.

84. Charles Latrobe, *Rambler in North America*, 293.

85. Olmsted, *Cotton Kingdom*, 274. For a similar account of mealtime segregation see Buckingham, *Slave States of America*, 480–81. Buckingham noted that two free mulatto women who rode in the ladies cabin of his Alabama steamer were considered unfit to eat with either the African American servants or the rest of the passengers. Officers forced them to eat standing up in the kitchen.

86. Entry for February 5, 1860, Diary of 1860, James H. Otey Papers, Folder 49, Volume 12, SHC.

87. Wortley, *Travels in the United States*, 110.

88. Ehrenpreis, ed., *Happy Country*, 269–70.

89. Bremer, *Homes of the New World*, 194.

90. *New Orleans Picayune*, December 23, 1864.

91. Testimony of Will Long, 2409.

92. *St. Louis Globe-Democrat*, January 8, 1893.

93. See Blassingame, ed., *Slave Testimony*, testimony of Isaac Throgmorton, 702–35; narrative of William Wells Brown, in Osofsky, ed., *Puttin' on Ole Massa*; Clarke and Clarke, *Narratives of the Sufferings*; and testimony of Henry Crawhion, John Hatfield, Aaron Sidles, and John C—N in Drew, *Refugee*.

94. Drew, *Refugee*, 255–57.

95. Ralph, *Dixie*, 22.

96. For a general overview of a fireman's job see Quick and Quick, *Mississippi Steamboatin'*, 235. For the gradual conversion to coal fuel see Louis C. Hunter, *Steamboats on the Western Rivers*, 267–70. Wood was used more than coal on the antebellum rivers because good-quality coal was only readily available along the upper Ohio. The cheapness and efficiency of coal gradually encouraged a broader market to emerge, and by 1860, it was in widespread use throughout the western river system. For a description of firemen loading coal into coal hoppers near the

fires see Sophie Pearson, unpublished manuscript "The Man—His Boats—the River," ch. 8, Box 3, Sophie Cooley Pearson Collection, LLMVC.

97. Sophie Pearson, unpublished manuscript "The Man—His Boats—the River," ch. 8, Box 3, Sophie Cooley Pearson Collection, LLMVC.

98. Quick and Quick, *Mississippi Steamboatin'*, 179. Firemen on the lower Mississippi checked wood piles for snakes before loading.

99. Bremer, *Homes of the New World*, 174.

100. Olmsted, *Cotton Kingdom*, 272.

101. Charles Latrobe, *Rambler in North America*, 299. Antebellum traveler Alex Mackay (*Western World*, 48) noted the "frantic pace" of the work of African American firemen.

102. For descriptions of firemen's work see Louis C. Hunter, *Steamboats on the Western Rivers*, 453; Merrick, *Old Times on the Upper Mississippi*, 59–63; *John Gleason et al. v.* Urilda, NAGPR; *McKinney v.* Yalla Busha, LSCR; and Alex Mackay, *Western World*, 46–48.

103. Habermehl, *Life on the Western Rivers*, 87. Atlantic deep-sea merchant ships had very different hull designs than western steamboats. While Atlantic ships stored their cargo and shipped their passengers in large holds below water level, steamboats were designed for the shallow western rivers. They had flatter, broader-based hulls, which split cargo between deck and small holds, six to seven feet high.

104. Testimony of Berry Smith, 1981–82.

105. A complete record of a western river steamboat cargo, including individual shipments and their weight, is contained in the bills of lading for several runs of the Missouri River steamer the *Evening Star* in 1867. See Records of the *Evening Star*, Box 2, Folders 37–47, Trail Collection, SHSM.

106. Testimony of William Waymen, 4144. For other reports of plantation slaves working with steamboat hands see *Rice v. Cade*, LSCR, and Lanman, *Adventures in the Wilds of the United States*, 210.

107. Lanman, *Adventures in the Wilds of the United States*, 167. Olmsted found "negroes lying asleep, in all postures, upon the freight" (*Cotton Kingdom*, 273).

108. Beadle, *Trip to the United States*, 65.

109. Lanman, *Adventures in the Wilds of the United States*, 167.

110. Louis C. Hunter, *Steamboats on the Western Rivers*, 454. For other descriptions of roustabout work see also Sophie Pearson, unpublished manuscript "The Man —His Boats—the River," ch. 8, Box 3, Sophie Cooley Pearson Collection, LLMVC; "River-Boatmen of the Lower Mississippi"; *Williams v.* Jacob, NAGPR; *Bennett v.* Nashville, LSCR; *Rice v. Cade*, LSCR; and Houstoun, *Hesperos*, 54.

111. Testimony of Peter Barber, 25.

112. Lanman, *Adventures in the Wilds of the United States*, 167.

113. "River-Boatmen of the Lower Mississippi," 145.

114. Nichols, *Forty Years of American Life*, 153.

115. Habermehl, *Life on the Western Rivers*, 79.

116. Olmsted, *Journey to the Seaboard Slave States*, 564.

117. Olmsted, *Cotton Kingdom*, 215.

118. Flint, *Recollections of the Last Ten Years*. See also Quick and Quick, *Mississippi Steamboatin'*, 236.

119. Mahoney, *River Towns in the Great West*, 173–75. Mahoney also cites several travelers who noted the "profane" activities of boatmen.

120. The *New Orleans Picayune* reported on September 2, 1849, that "the amount of petit thieving which is daily done on the levee, cannot be appreciated by those who do not visit this great business mart."

121. Briggs, "Lawlessness in Cairo, Illinois," 73 n. 22.

122. Merrick, *Old Times on the Upper Mississippi*, 134. See also Mahoney, *River Towns in the Great West*, 173.

123. Habermehl, *Life on the Western Rivers*, 87; *England v. Gripon*, LSCR.

124. Lafcadio Hearn, *Children of the Levee*, 81.

125. William W. Pugh to Joseph W. Pugh, April 23, 1845, Records of Southern Antebellum Plantations, Series G, Part 1, Reel 5, Microfilm 2296.

126. *Barry v. Kimball*, No. 4684, 12 La Ann 372 (1857), testimony of Isole Darcole, LSCR; Grandfort, *New World*, 81.

127. Testimony of Ben Lawson, 245.

128. Letter from Rev. William Andrews, *Sailor's Magazine and Seamen's Friend* 32, no. 3 (November 1859): 88.

129. Letter from Rev. I. Dallas, ibid., 90.

130. Louis C. Hunter, *Steamboats on the Western Rivers*, 461.

131. Ibid., 461.

132. Habermehl, *Life on the Western Rivers*, 167.

133. Alex Mackay, *Western World*, 46.

134. Rediker, *Between the Devil and the Deep Blue Sea*, ch. 4.

135. Charles Latrobe, *Rambler in North America*, 299.

136. Ibid.

137. Lanman, *Adventures in the Wilds of the United States*, 167.

138. Francis Trollope, *Domestic Manners of the Americans*, 8.

139. Bremer, *America of the Fifties*, 262.

140. Quick and Quick, *Mississippi Steamboatin'*, 250–51.

141. Testimony of Robert Bryant, 65.

142. Habermehl, *Life on the Western Rivers*, 81.

143. Bodichon, *American Diary*, 113.

144. For a discussion of this phenomenon in the postbellum South see Tera Hunter, *To 'Joy My Freedom*.

145. Delany, *Blake*, 100.

146. This discussion draws on Levine, *Black Culture and Black Consciousness*, chs. 1–2.

147. Testimony of William H. McCarthy, 1373.

148. Quick and Quick, *Mississippi Steamboatin'*, 252.

149. Habermehl, *Life on the Western Rivers*, 82–85.

150. Wheeler, *Steamboatin' Days*, 25.

151. Habermehl, *Life on the Western Rivers*, 84.

152. Quick and Quick, *Mississippi Steamboatin'*, 249.

153. Testimony of William H. McCarthy, 1374.

154. Bremer, *America of the Fifties*, 262.

155. Olmsted, *Journey to the Seaboard Slave States*, 609.

CHAPTER THREE

1. Osofsky, ed., *Puttin' on Ole Massa*, 188.

2. Ibid., 192.

3. Ibid.

4. Ibid., 188.

5. Ibid.

6. J. J. Boyd to R. C. Ballard, April 20, 1853, Ballard Papers, Box 12, Folder 190, SHC.

7. Tadman, *Speculators and Slaves*, 45.

8. Pritchett, "Interregional Slave Trade."

9. C. M. Rutherford to R. C. Ballard, March 19, 1850, Ballard Papers, Box 9, Folder 149, SHC.

10. C. M. Rutherford to R. C. Ballard, December 23, 1832, Ballard Papers, Box 1, Folder 9, SHC.

11. James R. Franklin to R. C. Ballard, October 29, 1833, Ballard Papers, Box 1, Folder 11, SHC. Franklin was especially concerned that the Louisiana law of 1831, which prohibited the interstate slave trade, would hurt prices by causing an over-supply in Mississippi. The law was repealed in 1834. See Tadman, *Speculators and Slaves*, 86.

12. Bancroft, *Slave Trading in the Old South*, 128–29; Louis C. Hunter, *Steamboats on the Western Rivers*, 420–21. Hunter describes the cheapness of deck passage as one of the distinguishing features of western river travel.

13. C. M. Rutherford to R. C. Ballard, November 1, 1849, Ballard Papers, Box 9, Folder 144, SHC.

14. Coleman, *Slavery Times in Kentucky*, 157–60. Coleman places more emphasis on the importance of Robards than does Bancroft, who portrayed him as an agent for other dealers, in *Slave Trading in the Old South*, 132.

15. Sandweiss, ed., *Seeking St. Louis*, 153. The St. Louis *Reveille* published a glowing tribute to the building on October 15, 1848.

16. Bancroft, *Slave Trading in the Old South*, 140.

17. Quoted in ibid., 280; Charles Mackay, *Life and Liberty in America*, 249–50.

18. Berlin, *Generations of Captivity*, ch. 4.

19. Osofsky, ed., *Puttin' on Ole Massa*, 191–92.

20. Hagedorn, *Beyond the River*. For the sexual dynamics of the trade see Baptist, "'Cuffy,' 'Fancy Maids,' and 'One-Eyed Men.'"

21. J. J. Boyd to R. C. Ballard, January 1, 1853, Ballard Papers, Box 12, Folder 184, SHC; Boyd to Ballard, December 22, 1852, Box 11, Folder 183, ibid.

22. Olsofsky, ed., *Puttin' on Ole Massa*, 192.

23. Samuel R. Browning to R. Boyd, December 29, 1848, Archibald H. Boyd Papers, DU.

24. Unknown to R. C. Ballard, December 9, 1833, Ballard Papers, Box 1, Folder 12, SHC.

25. C. M. Rutherford to R. C. Ballard, June 1, 1832, Ballard Papers, Box 11, Folder 178, SHC.

26. Osofsky, ed., *Puttin' on Ole Massa*, 194–95.

27. For a description of the Forks of the Road slave market see Barnett and Burkett, "Forks of the Road Slave Market."

28. For efforts by slaves to influence their sales see Walter Johnson, *Soul by Soul*, 176–87.

29. See Seventh Population Census of the United States, Pittsburgh, Reels 745–46, NA. Less residentially stable rivermen were probably less likely to be enumerated in the census than those who were married or members of nuclear families. For problems in recording river workers see Wright, *History and Growth of the United States Census*.

These findings rely on Professor Larry Glasco's database for the 1850 Pittsburgh census. This census does not list relationships between household members, so marriage relationships had to be inferred. For the method used in my computation, see Miller, "Computerized Method of Determining Family Structure."

30. See "List of slaves owned by James Rudd," Account Book, 1830–60, James Rudd Papers, FHS. Family relationships are generally not explicitly stated in the account book. The relationships I cite here are based on the slaves' ages and Rudd's apparent practice of demarcating one family from another with double lines.

For an example of slave brothers who leased themselves to the same boats see *Strawbridge v. Turner*, testimony of George Kirkland, LSCR, and *John Buddy v. Vanleer*, testimony of John Lieber, LSCR. Blood-related free black workers also sometimes shipped together. For example, Lucinda Van Dugan and her daughter Amanda shipped as chambermaids on the *Robert Fulton* in 1850. See Seventh Population Census of the United States, St. Louis, Reel 417, NA.

31. Testimony of Mollie Hatfield, 950.

32. *United States v.* Louisville, testimony of Judy Taylor, NAGLR.

33. Testimony of Lee Hobby, 1739–41.

34. Olmsted, *Cotton Kingdom*, 270.

35. Habermehl, *Life on the Western Rivers*, 83.

36. Merrick, *Old Times on the Upper Mississippi*, 160.

37. Maud Cuney-Hare, *Negro Musicians*, 89.

38. *Ridgely v.* Reindeer, testimony of H. Moreland, MSCR.

39. *Tyson v. Ewing*, 3 J. J. Marsh. 185 (Ky, 1830).

40. *Trials and Confessions of Madison Henderson*, 29–30.

41. Blassingame, ed., *Slave Testimony*, 432.

42. Bolster, *Black Jacks*, 165. Bolster emphasizes that most deep-sea sailors and

whalemen did not form stable families in port. Coastal sailors, whose voyage lengths were more like those of steamboat workers, were more likely to support families.

43. Louis C. Hunter, *Steamboats on the Western Rivers*, 466.

44. Ibid., 465–66.

45. Ibid.

46. Account book, 1830–60, James Rudd Papers, FHS.

47. Letter signed by James Lackland, May 29 1846, Lackland Papers, MHS.

48. Cunynghame, *Glimpse at the Great Western Republic*, 143.

49. *Pelham v.* Messenger, testimony of Robert Fletcher, LSCR.

50. *Hennen v.* Doswell, testimony of Caruthers, LSCR.

51. Blassingame, ed., *Slave Testimony*, 441. The American Freedmen's Inquiry Commission was established during the Civil War to gather information about how to improve the condition of emancipated slaves.

52. *Bryan v.* Aunt Letty, testimony of Thomas Baldwin, MSCR.

53. *Spaulding v. Taylor et al.*, LSCR.

54. *United States v.* Louisville, testimony of Judy Taylor, NAGLR.

55. Louis Hughes, *Thirty Years a Slave*, 103.

56. Olmsted, *Journey to the Seaboard Slave States*, 564.

57. Account book, 1830–60, James Rudd Papers, FHS.

58. Letter signed by W. C. L., December 7, 1835, Lane Collection, MHS.

59. Letter signed by James Lackland, July 18 1846, Lackland Papers, MHS. For a description of slaves being paid "ordinary" wages rather than the full value of their Sunday hire see Murray, *Lands of the Slave and the Free*, 251.

60. Davies, *American Scenes*, 101.

61. Grandy, *Narrative*, 30.

62. Thomas, *From Tennessee Slave*, 108, 119. For another account of the custom of tipping see Potter, *Hairdresser's Experience*, 158.

63. Pope, *Early Days in Arkansas*, 7–8. John Habermehl (*Life on the Western Rivers*, 48, 155) wrote that "those who gave tips" were "sure to get the warmest buckwheat pancakes and the nicest fried eggs."

64. Olmsted, *Cotton Kingdom*, 272.

65. Testimony of Billy Slaughter, 179.

66. Habermehl, *Life on the Western Rivers*, 50–51.

67. Testimony of Lizzie Chandler, 41.

68. Steele, *Summer Journey*, 212.

69. There is an extensive literature on slaves producing goods during their own time and selling them. Most of this literature does not focus on maritime workers, however. For an important exception that illustrates the important role of river workers as traders in the Georgia low country see Wood, *Women's Work, Men's Work*, chs. 3–4.

70. Blassingame, ed., *Slave Testimony*, testimony of Cox, 390.

71. Ibid., testimony of Sella Martin, 728.

72. Quoted in Cheek and Cheek, "John Mercer Langston," 34.

73. Clarke and Clarke, *Narratives of the Sufferings*, 82.

74. Drew, *Refugee*, 192.

75. *Trials and Confessions of Madison Henderson*, 59.

76. Blassingame, ed., *Slave Testimony*, 728.

77. Cheek and Cheek, "John Mercer Langston," 34.

78. Blassingame, ed., *Slave Testimony*, 728.

79. *Trials and Confessions of Madison Henderson*, confession of Madison Henderson, 57. For other commentary on profits see Blassingame, ed., *Slave Testimony*, 389–90.

80. *McMaster v. Beckwith*, testimony of Daniel Tucker, LSCR; *Emmerling v. Beebe*, testimony of John Eaton, LSCR.

81. Clamorgan, *Colored Aristocracy of St. Louis*, 58 n. 74.

82. Ibid., 63 n. 105.

83. Ibid., n. 106.

84. Blassingame, ed., *Slave Testimony*, 389–90.

85. *Ridgely v.* Reindeer, testimony of Stephen Ridgely, MSCR.

86. Grandy, *Narrative*, 29–30.

87. Ibid., 30.

88. For studies emphasizing the efforts of freedpeople to reclaim kin ties in the Reconstruction era see Eric Foner, *Reconstruction*, and Gutman, *Black Family*. For the impact of the internal slave trade on slave communities see Stevenson, *Life in Black and White*, and Malone, *Sweet Chariot*.

89. Anthony Trollope, *North America*, 373.

90. I am indebted to Phillip D. Troutman for his concept of the slave grapevine. He read his paper, "Grapevine in the Slave Market: African American Geographic Literacy, Information, and Escape," at the Organization of American Historians Conference, April 2002. The best study of slave communication and the maritime world remains Scott, "Common Wind."

91. Pulszky and Pulszky, *White, Red, Black*, 241–42.

92. William W. Pugh to Joseph W. Pugh, April 23, 1845, Records of Southern Antebellum Plantations, Series G, Part 1, Reel 5, Microfilm 2296.

93. Clarke and Clarke, *Narratives of the Sufferings*, 74.

94. Ibid., 81.

95. Ibid.

96. Ibid.

97. Ibid.

98. Sally's narrative and its depiction of boatmen as carriers of information likely reflect actual events. While boat workers were central to networks of slave resistance in the West, they were not key figures in the raging sectional debates on slavery, within which slave narratives were written. Thus, although Aunt Sally's depictions of tyrannical masters and unending toil must be read critically, there was no immediate political motivation behind her descriptions of river networks. The role of these networks, at least in the context of Aunt Sally's narrative, is accurately depicted. For a broad discussion on the forces that shaped the writing of slave narratives, see Andrews, *To Tell a Free Story*.

99. *Aunt Sally.*

100. Ibid., chs. 1–9.

101. Ibid., 171–72.

102. Ibid., 172–73.

103. Frederick Way Jr., *Way's Packet Directory*, 303, lists a steamboat *Magnolia.* Way comments that the boat was built in 1852 and that it ran out of Mobile in the 1850s.

104. Horton, *Free People of Color*, 69.

105. Ibid.

106. Ibid.

CHAPTER FOUR

1. Osofsky, ed., *Puttin' on Ole Massa*, 187.

2. Ibid., 216.

3. This statement is based on the voluminous anecdotal evidence I have found. For the best analysis of slave runaways see Franklin and Schweninger, *Runaway Slaves*. This chapter places more importance on the Mississippi River system as a means of escape than do Franklin and Schweninger. I am also indebted to studies of slave escapes along the Atlantic seaboard. See Cecelski, *Waterman's Song*, ch. 5, and Waldstreicher, "Reading the Runaways." See also Bolster, *Black Jacks.*

4. Stephanie M. H. Camp ("'I Could Not Stay There'") convincingly argues that in contrast to male slaves, female slaves were more likely to be "truant" from plantations for only short periods of time.

5. Mentor, ed., "James Kirke Paulding," 328.

6. Lafcadio Hearn, *Children of the Levee*, 11.

7. Sprague, ed., *His Promised Land*, 48.

8. Osofsky, ed., *Puttin' on Ole Massa*, 72.

9. Sprague, ed., *His Promised Land*, 63.

10. Blockson, *Underground Railroad*, 31.

11. This statement, or a similar derivation of it, was common in river city runaway slave advertisements. See, for instance, Syndor, *Slavery in Mississippi*, 108.

12. *Eaton v. Vaughan*, MSCR.

13. Lawmakers in Mississippi, Arkansas, and Texas did not pass specific laws making it illegal for steamboat captains to carry fugitives out of these states. Supreme courts in these states may well have heard cases under more general statutes.

Louisiana laws regulating steamboat officers and owners changed slightly over time. See "An Act to Take the Most Effective Measures in Order to Prevent the Transportation or Carrying Away of Slaves out of This State . . . ," Act of February 13, 1816, *Louisiana Acts*, 1816, 8–14; "An Act to Amend the Act Entitled 'An Act to Take the Most Effective Measures in Order to Prevent the Transportation, or Carrying Away of Slaves out of State . . .' Approved 13 February 1816," Act of March 26, 1835, *Louisiana Acts*, 1835, 152–53; "An Act to Prevent the Carrying Away of Slaves, and for Other Purposes," Act of March 19, 1839, *Louisiana Acts*, 1839,

118–20; and "An Act . . . Passed for the Purpose of Preventing Slaves from Being Transported or Conducted out of This State," Act of March 25, 1840, *Louisiana Acts*, 1840, 89–91. For Missouri see "An Act Supplementary to an Act Entitled 'An Act Concerning Slaves,'" Act of February 13, 1841, *Missouri Acts*, 1841, 146–47. This act made it illegal for any "master, commander or [steamboat] owner . . . to transport any servant or slaves, from one point or place in this state to any other point . . . without the consent or permission of the person or persons to whom slave doth or right belong." For Kentucky see "An Act to Prevent the Masters of Vessels, and Others from Employing or Removing Persons of Colour from This State," Act of January 7, 1824, *Kentucky Acts*, 1824, 406–7; and "An Act to Amend an Act Entitled 'An Act to Prevent the Masters of Vessels, and Others from Employing or Removing Persons of Colour from This State,'" Act of February 12, 1828, *Kentucky Acts*, 1828, 178–79. This 1828 amendment made captains liable for Kentucky fugitives coming on board from the northern side of the Ohio River. For Tennessee see "Act to Amend the Act Entitled 'An Act More Effectively to Prevent the Owners of Steam Boats and Stages from Carrying off Slaves without the Knowledge or Consent of Their Masters,'" Act of November 12, 1833, *Tennessee Acts*, 1833, 75. For further discussion of these laws see Schafer, *Slavery, the Civil Law, and the Supreme Court*, 98–101.

14. Schafer, *Slavery, the Civil Law, and the Supreme Court of Louisiana*, 98–101.

15. *Perry v. Beardslee*, MSCR.

16. *Emmerling v. Beebe*, testimony of M. Bruno, LSCR.

17. Osofsky, ed., *Puttin' on Ole Massa*, 187, 189.

18. Delany, *Blake*, 100.

19. Blassingame, ed., *Slave Testimony*, 434. See also the narrative of John C— N in Benjamin Drew, *Refugee*, 192.

20. *Missouri Republican*, October 9, 1847.

21. *New Orleans Picayune*, November 18, 1854.

22. *Adams v. Trabue*, testimony of R. Cox, LSCR. See also *Beardslee v. Perry*, MSCR.

23. *New Orleans Picayune*, May 9, 1854.

24. *Meekin v. Thomas*, 17 B. Mon. 710 (Ky, 1857). For another account of a slave escaping at Cincinnati's levee see Drew, *Refugee*, 197.

25. Blassingame, ed., *Slave Testimony*, 732–33.

26. Ibid., 526–27.

27. Quick and Quick, *Mississippi Steamboating'*, 250.

28. For rural runaways, see *Feltus v. Anders*, LSCR; *Withers v. El Paso*, MSCR; *Price v. Thorton et al.*, MSCR; Drew, *Refugee*, 90; and *New Orleans Picayune*, May 9, 1854.

29. Osofsky, ed., *Puttin' on Ole Massa*, 148.

30. *Price v. Tatum*, testimony of John Thorp, MSCR. This case was published as *Price v. Thorton et al.*

31. Drew, *Refugee*, 90.

32. Malone, *Sweet Chariot*, 81.

33. Blassingame, ed., *Slave Testimony*, 723.

34. Tregilis, *River Roads to Freedom*.

35. Several examples of such escapes exist in Kentucky court reports. See *Edwards v. Vail*, 3 J. J. Marsh 595 (Ky, 1830); *Church v. Chambers*, 3 Dana 274 (Ky, 1835); *Gordon v. Longest*, 16 Peters 97 (Ky, 1842); *McFarland v. McKnight*, 6 B. Mon. 500 (Ky, 1846).

36. *Eaton v. Vaughan*, testimony of John Nichols, MSCR. In this case, a runaway slave received help from a free black woodcutter who was known to be his longtime friend. See also Joe Gray Taylor, *Negro Slavery in Louisiana*, 191, and Orville W. Taylor, *Negro Slavery in Arkansas*, 218–19.

37. Joe Gray Taylor, *Negro Slavery in Louisiana*, 190; Wade, *Slavery in the Cities*, ch. 8.

38. Quoted in Wade, *Slavery in the Cities*, 215.

39. Ibid., 220.

40. Drew, *Refugee*, 130.

41. *New Orleans Picayune*, September 18, 1849.

42. Hogan and Davis, eds., *William Johnson's Natchez*, 401.

43. *Buel v.* New York, testimony of James Powell, LSCR.

44. *Strawbridge v. Turner*, testimony of F. Bernardy, LSCR.

45. *New Orleans Picayune*, September 18, 1849.

46. Sprague, ed., *His Promised Land*, 35.

47. For a discussion of routine efforts to prevent the shipment of runaways see *Withers v.* El Paso, testimony of Henry Thornburgh, T. Groom, and W. McCreight [*sic*], MSCR.

48. Osofsky, ed., *Puttin' on Ole Massa*, 151.

49. Drew, *Refugee*, 130.

50. Ibid., 170.

51. Sprague, ed., *His Promised Land*, 39.

52. For an example of stealing passes see Blassingame, ed., *Slave Testimony*, 730.

53. *New Orleans Picayune*, October 17, 1854.

54. Thomas, *From Tennessee Slave*, 113–14.

55. Louis Hughes, *Thirty Years a Slave*, 105. Other rural slaves obtained passes in the countryside. See *Eaton v. Vaughan*, testimony of John Nichols and George Ward, MSCR; and *Price v. Tatum*, testimony of John Thorp and W. Hackley, MSCR.

56. Louis Hughes, *Thirty Years a Slave*, 105.

57. Drew, *Refugee*, 130.

58. *New Orleans Picayune*, May 9, 1854.

59. Blassingame, ed., *Slave Testimony*, 237. Runaway slave ads sometimes mentioned a forged steamboat pass. For example, see *Missouri Republican*, July 31, 1847.

60. For an example of a slave steamboatman being hired as a free man see *Emmerling v. Beebe*, LSCR.

61. *McMaster v. Beckwith*, testimony of Solomon Lynchhart, LSCR. For other examples of slave boat workers leasing themselves to certain boats against the wishes

of their master see *Hennen v.* Doswell, LSCR; *Bryan v.* Aunt Letty, MSCR; and *Rountree v.* Brilliant.

62. *Ridgely v.* Reindeer, testimony of Stephen Ridgely, MSCR.

63. Ibid., testimony of George Strong, MSCR.

64. *Palfrey v. Kerr et al.*, testimony of Stephen Aldrich, MSCR.

65. Osofsky, ed., *Puttin' on Ole Massa*, 149.

66. *Hurst v. Wallace*, testimony of David Hiner, LSCR.

67. *Buel v.* New York, 32.

68. Clarke and Clarke, *Narratives of the Sufferings*, 83.

69. Mooney, *Slavery in Tennessee*, 53.

70. Blassingame, ed., *Slave Testimony*, 462.

71. *Owen v. Brown*, testimony of William Frillings, LSCR.

72. *Eaton v. Vaughan*, testimony of William Gearhartt [*sic*], MSCR.

73. *Price v. Tatum*, testimony of William Hubbell, MSCR.

74. Sprague, ed., *His Promised Land*, 63.

75. *Williamson v. Norton*, LSCR.

76. *Spaulding v. Taylor et al.*, testimony of O. Bird, LSCR.

77. Ibid., testimony of William Hubbell. This sentence was underlined in the original document.

78. Melville, *Confidence-Man*, 18.

79. Louis Hughes, *Thirty Years a Slave*, 80, 87.

80. Sprague, ed., *His Promised Land*, 39–40.

81. *St. Louis Globe-Democrat*, October 7, 1853.

82. Green, *Narrative*, 33.

83. *Hurst v. Wallace*, testimony of David Hiner, LSCR. Such stories are frequently cited and probably exaggerated in Levi Coffin's history of the Underground Railroad, *Reminiscences of Levi Coffin*. See also Joe Gray Taylor, *Negro Slavery in Louisiana*, 188.

84. Drew, *Refugee*, 170.

85. Levi Coffin's history of the Underground Railroad (*Reminiscences of Levi Coffin*, 389) cites an example of a helpful captain. See also *Burke, f.w.c., v. Clarke*.

86. Osofsky, ed., *Puttin' on Ole Massa*, 332.

87. In one Missouri case, boat officers admitted that the practice of subcontracting labor made them ignorant of the status of African American workers. See *Blair et al. v.* Aunt Letty, NAGPR. For family connections securing illegal hires see *Goldenbow v. Wright*, LSCR.

88. Osofsky, ed., *Puttin' on Ole Massa*, 151.

89. Ibid.

90. Ibid. For a story of a cook helping a slave boy to ride upriver see testimony of Holt Collier, 450.

91. Parker identified the person who captured him as a "white mate," clearly contrasting his race with that of the deckhand who helped him (Sprague, ed., *His Promised Land*, 44).

92. Ibid., 43.

93. *Owen v. Brown*, testimony of Richard Bows, LSCR.

94. Reported in Davies, *American Scenes*, 86. For another example of slaveholders' fear of African American boat workers aiding escapees see *Hill v. White*, testimony of R. Northern, LSCR.

95. *New Orleans Picayune*, May 4, 1844.

96. Ibid., July 18, 1841.

97. Tower, *Slavery Unmasked*, 242.

98. *Withers v. El Paso*, testimony of Thomas Groom, MSCR.

99. Ibid., testimony of Henry Thornburgh.

100. Coffin, *Reminiscences of Levi Coffin*, 458.

101. *New Orleans Picayune*, May 14, 1844.

102. *New Orleans Picayune*, August 22, 1841. For an example of a *St. Louis Gazette* editorial on the need to ban the employment of free black steamboat workers on the western rivers see its reprint in the *Boston Liberator*, October 15, 1841.

103. *Emmerling v. Beebe*, testimony of Pierre De Laronde and Michael Partit, LSCR.

104. *Marciacq v. H. M. Wright*.

105. Pickard, ed., *Kidnapped and the Ransomed*, 240.

106. *Buel v. New York*, testimony of James Pedis, LSCR.

107. *Hennen v. Doswell*, testimony of J. Y., LSCR.

108. Sprague, ed., *His Promised Land*, 60.

109. *Withers v. El Paso*, testimony of Henry Thornburgh, MSCR.

110. Ibid., testimony of Woolford McCamunt.

111. Drew, *Refugee*, 53.

112. Louis Hughes, *Thirty Years a Slave*, 81.

113. Ibid., 87–88.

114. *Feltus v. Anders*, LSCR.

115. Ibid., testimony of Samuel Foster.

116. Ibid.

117. Sprague, ed., *His Promised Land*, 41–42.

118. *Eaton v. Vaughan*, MSCR.

119. Blassingame, ed., *Slave Testimony*, 730.

120. Ibid., 731.

121. Ibid.

122. Osofsky, ed., *Puttin' on Ole Massa*, 83.

123. Ibid., 84.

124. Ibid., 150.

125. Ibid.

126. Drew, *Refugee*, 188.

127. *Hurst v. Wallace*, LSCR.

128. *Price v. Tatum*, MSCR.

129. *Slatter v. Holton*, testimony of Henry Peterson, LSCR.

130. The captain's inaction likely stemmed from his lack of legal liability. He had not shipped Thorton out of Louisiana but instead had taken him on from another boat, the *Henry Clay*, when that boat ran aground on a sandbar.

131. Sprague, ed., *His Promised Land*, 36–37.

132. Blassingame, ed., *Slave Testimony*, 733.

133. Osofsky, ed., *Puttin' on Ole Massa*, 84.

134. Green, *Narrative*, 34.

135. Catterall, *Judicial Cases*, 428–29.

136. Nikki Marie Taylor, "'Frontiers of Freedom,'" 65–70.

137. James Oliver Horton and Stacy Flaherty, "Black Leadership," in Henry Louis Taylor Jr., ed., *Race and the City*, 75–77.

138. Cheek and Cheek, "John Mercer Langston," 44.

139. Drew, *Refugee*, 256. For another case in which a northern African American man, who was likely a boatman, helped a slave elude bounty hunters see Sprague, ed., *His Promised Land*, 132–34.

140. Drew, *Refugee*, 256.

141. Ibid., 257.

142. Hagedorn, *Beyond the River*, 232–37.

143. Ullman, *Martin R. Delany*, 27–28.

144. Blassingame, ed., *Slave Testimony*, 733–34.

145. Olsofsky, ed., *Puttin' on Ole Massa*, 223.

CHAPTER FIVE

1. *Missouri Daily Republican*, July 10, 1841. See also *St. Louis Daily New Era*, July 10, 1841.

2. Thompson, *Tradesman's Travels*, 157.

3. For the best case study of slaves and the law see Schafer, *Becoming Free, Remaining Free*. See also Seematter, "Trials and Confessions." Seematter deserves considerable credit for bringing the long-neglected narrative to public attention. Her interpretation of the narrative, however, is less than sympathetic to the men's lives and actions. Her main argument is that the men's trial and execution represents a triumph for law and order. She favors the men's formal trial to the vigilante justice that flourished in the city's early years.

   This chapter draws on a large literature on slave theft. See Hindus, *Prison and Plantation*; Schwartz, *Twice Condemned*; Genovese, *Roll, Jordan, Roll*, 599–609; Starobin, *Industrial Slavery*, 78–80; and Lichtenstein, "'That Disposition to Theft,'" 413–40. For discussion of how this alternative morality was challenged in the postbellum period, see Hahn, "Hunting, Fishing, and Foraging"; Wiener, *Social Origins of the New South*; and Reidy, *From Slavery to Agrarian Capitalism*. Free blacks were also frequent lawbreakers in the Old South. Leonard Curry (*Free Black in Urban America*, ch. 7) illustrates that they were particularly likely to be prosecuted over property crimes.

4. *Louisville Journal*, April 23, 1841.

5. *Trials and Confessions of Madison Henderson.*

6. *Missouri Republican*, July 24, 1841.

7. For a broader discussion of how the confessional genre relates to other slave narratives, see Andrews, *To Tell a Free Story*, 39–44.

8. Berlin, *Slaves Without Masters*, 186.

9. *Missouri Republican*, July 14, 1841.

10. Ibid.

11. Ibid.

12. Catalogue and Record of Colored Students, 1834–1972, Mudd Library, Special Collections, Oberlin, Ohio.

13. Gara, *Liberty Line*; Franklin and Schweninger, *Runaway Slaves.*

14. *Boston Liberator*, July 9, 1841. The article originally appeared in the *Christian Watchmen.*

15. *St. Louis Daily New Era*, July 8, 1841.

16. *New Orleans Picayune*, July 29, 1841.

17. *Missouri Republican*, July 24, 1841.

18. *Oxford English Dictionary*, 2nd ed., s.v. "Rascal."

19. Melville, *Confidence-Man*, 20.

20. Dr. Samuel Cartwright, "Diseases and Peculiarities of the Negro Race," *Debow's Review of the South and West* 11, no. 3 (New Orleans, 1851), 333.

21. Ibid., 334.

22. Ibid., 333.

23. Ibid.

24. *Trials and Confessions of Madison Henderson*, 20, 23.

25. *Boston Liberator*, August 20, 1841.

26. The figure of the rascal has been left out of discussions of nineteenth-century masculinity. For discussions of black masculinity in this period see Hine and Jenkins, eds., *"Manhood Rights."*

27. Levine, *Black Culture and Black Consciousness*, ch. 2, esp. 102–33.

28. Ibid., 407–20, esp. 410–11. See also Roberts, *From Trickster to Badman*, ch. 5.

29. *Trials and Confessions of Madison Henderson*, 13.

30. Ibid., 14.

31. Ibid., 13.

32. Ibid., 37–42.

33. Ibid., 39.

34. Ibid., 40.

35. Ibid.

36. Ibid., 42–43.

37. Ibid., 43.

38. Ibid., 49.

39. Ibid., 49–51.

40. Ibid., 50.

41. Ibid., 49.

42. Ibid., 50.

43. *Boston Liberator*, August 20, 1841.

44. *Trials and Confessions of Madison Henderson*, 50.

45. Ibid., 50.

46. Ibid., 65.

47. Hinks, ed., *David Walker's Appeal*; Bolster, *Black Jacks*, 197–200.

48. *Trials and Confessions of Madison Henderson*, 52–55.

49. Ibid., 59. For more on Brown's Methodism see *Missouri Republican*, July 10, 1841.

50. *Trials and Confessions of Madison Henderson*, 49.

51. Ibid., 28.

52. Ibid.

53. Ibid.

54. Ibid., 48.

55. Ibid., 28.

56. Ibid., 42.

57. Ibid.

58. Ibid., 17, 57.

59. Ibid., 24, 29, 31, 41–45, 57, 60, 61, 71–75. For editorial comment on Seward's job working on the steamboat *Agnes* see *New Orleans Bee*, May 11, 1841.

60. *Trials and Confessions of Madison Henderson*, 24, 29, 41–43, 57.

61. Mahoney, *River Towns in the Great West*, 173–75.

62. News articles from New Orleans and St. Louis illustrate what was undoubtedly a pattern of crime in other western cities. See, for instance, *New Orleans Picayune*, September 4, 1839, April 8, 1849, May 30, 1844, August 9, 1854, and August 3, 1854; *Missouri Republican*, August 18, 1845, October 3, 1846, and October 5, 1846; and *St. Louis Globe-Democrat*, December 28, 1853.

63. *Louisville Journal*, April 23, 1841.

64. Reprinted in the *New Orleans Picayune*, April 27, 1841.

65. *Trials and Confessions of Madison Henderson*, 29.

66. Ibid., 72.

67. Ibid., 42.

68. Ibid., 29, 73.

69. Ibid., 64.

70. Ibid., 76.

71. Ibid., 28.

72. Ibid., 20.

73. Ibid., 21.

74. Ibid. Such activities were common in western cities. In one typical case, a local slave picked up a load of provisions from the steamboat *Uncle Sam* by falsely representing himself to the boat's steward as a servant of a local merchant. *See New Orleans Picayune*, April 8, 1849.

75. *Trials and Confessions of Madison Henderson*, 56.

76. *New Orleans Picayune*, July 29, 1841. See also *Missouri Republican*, July 10, 1841.

77. *Trials and Confessions of Madison Henderson*, 14–19. It is important to note that Henderson was not always indifferent to the plight of other slaves. "I never willingly engaged in any robbery where there was a negro slave entrusted with the custody of the property," he said, "for I could not bear to get them in trouble when I knew they had so few means of protection; and whenever anything of the kind is done, and slaves are about, they are certain to be suspected" (ibid., 28–29).

78. Ibid., 71.

79. Ibid.

80. Ibid., 60.

81. Ibid., 76.

82. Ibid., 57.

83. Ibid.

84. Ibid., 57–58. For corroboration of these events see *Galena Gazette*, July 17, 1841.

85. *Trials and Confessions of Madison Henderson*, 58.

86. Ibid., 31, 60, 73–74. See *Galena Gazette*, July 17, 1841.

87. *Trials and Confessions of Madison Henderson*, 60.

88. Ibid., 73.

89. Ibid., 60.

90. Ibid., 59.

91. That the men thought the time was right is inferred from comments made by Brown and Seward. Brown said that "on Friday night the *Missouri* came up and it was said that Mr. Collier [a partner in the Pettus bank] had brought up a large amount of money." Seward commented that they met Henderson that night on the *Missouri* when it docked on the levee (ibid., 61, 74).

92. Ibid., 33–34, 46, 61–62, 75; *Missouri Republican*, April 20, 1841; *St. Louis Daily New Era*, April 20, 1841.

93. *Missouri Argus*, April 19, 1841.

94. *St. Louis Daily New Era*, April 19, 1841.

95. Ibid., April 20, 1841.

96. *Missouri Republican*, April 30, 1841.

97. The *Cincinnati Daily Gazette* reported on May 17, 1841, that the crimes created a "high degree of excitement throughout the whole western and south western country."

98. *Trials and Confessions of Madison Henderson*, 35, 47, 63, 76.

99. *Missouri Republican*, May 1, 1841; *New Orleans Picayune*, May 9, 1841.

100. *St. Louis Daily New Era*, May 5, 1841; *Missouri Republican*, May 6, 1841.

101. *Trials and Confessions of Madison Henderson*, 76; *Louisville Journal*, May 8, 1841; *Cincinnati Daily Gazette*, May 6, 1841.

102. *Trials and Confessions of Madison Henderson*, 76.

103. Ibid., 35; *Missouri Republican*, May 10, 1841.

104. *Trials and Confessions of Madison Henderson*, 63.

105. Ibid., 47.

106. Ibid.

107. *National Anti-Slavery Standard*, July 15, 1841.

108. *Trials and Confessions of Madison Henderson*, 35.

109. *Missouri Republican*, May 25, 1841.

110. For a good overview of procedures in felony slave cases see Thomas D. Morris, *Southern Slavery and the Law*, 239–48.

111. *New Orleans Picayune*, June 3, 1841.

112. *St. Louis Daily New Era*, May 25, 1841. Coverage of the men's trials filled St. Louis newspapers from May 10 to June 7. Unfortunately, the St. Louis Circuit Court Project has not found the transcripts of the trial in St. Louis Circuit Court.

113. *Missouri Republican*, May 25, 1841.

114. Ibid., July 2, 1841.

115. *Boston Liberator*, August 20, 1841.

116. *Missouri Republican*, July 10, 1841. See also *St. Louis Daily New Era*, July 10, 1841.

117. For more on the display of the men's heads see Seematter, "Trials and Confessions," 46.

118. "The Abolitionists and the Negroes," *St. Louis Penant*, quoted in *Boston Liberator*, June 4, 1841.

119. *St. Louis Daily New Era*, May 1, 1841.

120. Ibid.

121. *Missouri Republican*, May 5, 1841.

122. *St. Louis Daily New Era*, May 1, 1841; *Missouri Argus*, July 30, 1841.

123. *New Orleans Bee*, July 14, 1841.

124. Reprinted in the *Boston Liberator*, October 15, 1841.

125. *New Orleans Picayune*, August 22, 1841.

126. *New Orleans Bee*, April 23, 1841.

127. See "An Act More Effectively to Prevent Free Persons of Color from Entering into This State, and for Other Purposes," Act of February 23, 1843, *Missouri Acts*, 1843, 66–67.

128. For an excellent summary of this law see Tansey, "Out-of-State Free Blacks," 372.

129. *New Orleans Bee*, July 14, 1841.

130. *New Orleans Picayune*, August 22, 1841. "An Act to Amend the Several Acts of this State in Relation to Free Negroes and Mulattoes," Act of February 26, 1842, *Mississippi Acts*, 1842, 67.

131. "An Act to Amend the Several Acts of this State in Relation to Free Negroes and Mulattoes," Act of February 26, 1842, *Mississippi Acts*, 1842, 67.

132. Johnson is quoted in Berlin, *Slaves Without Masters*, 332–33. For reaction to the St. Louis events and confirmation of the men's Mississippi operations see *Natchez Free Trader*, July 29, 1841.

133. Berlin, *Slaves Without Masters*, 332–33.

134. *Colored American*, May 15, 1841.

CHAPTER SIX

1. Haskins, *First Black Governor*, chs. 1–4.
2. The evidence from Union naval operations on the western front support Ira Berlin's argument that slaves were "the prime movers in the emancipation drama." See Berlin, "Who Freed the Slaves?" 291.
3. Ramold, *Slaves, Sailors, Citizens*, ch. 1.
4. Historians have recently begun to focus their attention on the role of African American steamboat workers in the Civil War. See Bennett, "'Frictions'"; Roca, "Presence and Precedents"; Brewer, "African American Sailors"; and, especially, Ramold, *Slaves, Sailors, Citizens*.
5. Musicant, *Divided Waters*, 74; Roca, "Presence and Precedents," 103.
6. Musicant, *Divided Waters*, 74.
7. Roca, "Presence and Precedents," 108.
8. Testimony of George Taylor Burns, 29–30.
9. Louis C. Hunter, *Steamboats on the Western Rivers*, 559. For the Confederate navy, see Luraghi, *History of the Confederate Navy*, 159.
10. Louis C. Hunter, *Steamboats on the Western Rivers*, 547–49; Anderson, *By Sea and by River*, chs. 6–9.
11. For the Confederate Constitution see *Mississippi Acts*, "Constitution of the Confederate States of America," December 1862, 62–63.
12. For payment practices on Confederate boats see *William Ward v.* Shreveport and *Alhambra Reeder v.* Shreveport, NAGPR.
13. Confederate captains were occasionally taken north for prosecution on treason charges to the Southern District of Illinois. See, for instance, *United States v.* Louisville and *United States v.* Black Hawk, NAGLR.
14. *United States v.* Louisville, NAGLR.
15. Blassingame, ed., *Slave Testimony*, testimony of a colored man, 387.
16. The trial of the *Shreveport* crew and the several officers who participated in the revolt is one of the few nineteenth-century mutiny prosecutions I found record of. The men were found not guilty, and, in separate wage suits, they won $800 in back wages. Relevant testimony exists for both the circuit court case (mutiny criminal trial) and the district case (civil trial over wages). See *William Ward v.* Shreveport and *Alhambra Reeder v.* Shreveport, NAGPR. For a decision in the mutiny case see United States District Court Records, Law Record C, Eastern District Law, Equity, and Criminal Files, 588–92, NAGPR.
17. Brewer, "African American Sailors," 285.
18. Ramold, *Slaves, Sailors, Citizens*, 37–45. The War Department did not grant the navy control of the western river fleet until October 1, 1862. For the idiosyncratic command structures of Union operations on the western rivers, see Chester G. Hearn, *Ellet's Brigade*.
19. *United States v.* Louisville, NAGLR.
20. McIlwaine, *Memphis Down in Dixie*, 211.

21. Bennett, "'Frictions,'" 118–45.

22. "Life of Peter Boyd," Folder 1, Slaves and Slavery Collection, MHS.

23. Ramold, *Slaves, Sailors, Citizens*, 63–64.

24. Roca, "Presence and Precedents," 108.

25. The experiences of these workers have not been adequately incorporated into studies of the Reconstruction era. Whereas river historian Louis Hunter refers to these workers briefly, calling them "socially handicapped" and "tractable" (*Steamboats on the Western Rivers*, 451, 478), most historians of emancipation have not considered them at all. The literature focuses almost entirely on the story of agricultural workers withdrawing from plantation gang labor, setting up family economies, and gradually becoming enmeshed in various forms of tenant farming or sharecropping. For leading examples see Mandle, *Not Slave, Not Free*; Ransom and Sutch, *One Kind of Freedom*; Saville, *Work of Reconstruction*; Higgs, *Competition and Coercion*; Jones, *Slavery and Freedom*; Jones, *Dispossessed*; and Jaynes, *Branches without Roots*. This literature is so well developed that historians can now begin to conceptualize commercial occupational experiences. For industrial work in the Reconstruction period see Fink and Reed, eds., *Race, Class, and Community*. The best is Rachleff, *Black Labor in Richmond*. Rachleff's analysis, however, is less concerned with changing relations in the workplace than with broader community activism. Tera Hunter (*To 'Joy My Freedom*) discusses the changing nature of employer-employee relations in domestic work.

26. McIlwaine, *Memphis Down in Dixie*, 211.

27. Lafcadio Hearn, *Children of the Levee*, 62.

28. Blassingame, ed., *Slave Testimony*, 600.

29. Testimony of Peter Corn, 91.

30. Testimony of Peter Brown, 314.

31. McIlwaine, *Memphis Down in Dixie*, 218–19. The author, and her research assistant, William McCaskill, interviewed captains and roustabouts on the Memphis docks. For similar comments see testimony of Primus Smith in Blassingame, ed., *Slave Testimony*, 600; testimony of Boston Blackwell, 171; and testimony of George Bollinger, 38.

32. See, for instance, Litwack, *Been in the Storm So Long*; Foner, *Reconstruction*; Robinson, "Difference Freedom Made"; McKenzie, *One South or Many?*; and Cohen, *At Freedom's Edge*.

33. Blassingame, ed., *Slave Testimony*, 600.

34. Testimony of Tony Piggy, 346.

35. Testimony of Boston Blackwell, 171.

36. Testimony of George Bollinger, 38.

37. Ralph, *Dixie*, 25.

38. For discussion of the increasing number of African Americans in roustabout positions see Lafcadio Hearn, *Children of the Levee*, 63.

39. Hesse-Wartegg, *Travels on the Lower Mississippi*, 27–28.

40. "Address by Captain L. V. Cooley before the Tulane Society of Economics

New Orleans, April 11, 1911," Box 3, Folder 4, Sophie Cooley Pearson Collection, LLMVC.

41. Quoted in Arnesen, *Waterfront Workers of New Orleans*, 104. See Julian Ralph, "The Old Way to Dixie," *Harper's* 76 (January 1893): 175.

42. Ralph, *Dixie*, 21.

43. G. W. Nichols, "Down the Mississippi," *Harper's* 41 (November 1870): 844.

44. For this term see Newcomb Family Genealogy List, Box 9, George Merrick Papers, Wisconsin Historical Society, Madison, Wisconsin.

45. Nichols, "Down the Mississippi," 844.

46. Hesse-Wartegg, *Travels on the Lower Mississippi*, 27.

47. Testimony of Boston Blackwell, 171.

48. Botkin, ed., *Treasury of Mississippi River Folklore*, 250.

49. Unknown to John W. Tobin, October 18, 1870, Folder 54, Mss 249, John W. Tobin Collection, HNOC.

50. Chinese laborers were used in small numbers on the postbellum rivers. See news clipping titled "Steamboats, 1870, 1871, 1872," from Little Rock, Arkansas, dated June 19, 1870, in William Tippitt Scrapbook, vol. 1, Memphis Public Library, Memphis History Room, Memphis, Tennessee.

51. *Memphis New Scimitar*, August 28, 1908, in Thomas P. Leathers Jr. Scrapbook, microfilm no. z1662; *Memphis Avalanche*, October 28, 1871, in William H. Tippitt Collection, microfilm no. 1430, MDAH.

52. Mary Wheeler's transcription of songs from old African American roustabouts in the 1920s is a vibrant window into the culture of the postbellum steamboat workplace. Through song, African Americans commented on the world around them in ways that were sometimes playful, sometimes critical, but always distinctive of the African American working class. See Wheeler, *Steamboatin' Days*.

53. Testimony of Ishe Webb, 79–80.

54. Unknown, at Ouachita River, Lower Plantation, to John F. Tobin, New Orleans, June 11, 1873, Folder 54, John W. Tobin Collection, HNOC.

55. Ibid., January 27, 1874.

56. One white steamboat engineer reported with exasperation that African American roustabouts on his boat told him that "no white man" could make them work faster. See *Charles Fisher et al. v. Carrie A. Thorn*, testimony of G. W. Shields, NASWR.

57. Quoted in Arnesen, *Waterfront Workers of New Orleans*, 105. Sometimes roustabouts jumped ship in the middle of voyages. See *Vicksburg Herald*, April 24, 1875.

58. See *Charles Fisher et al. v. Carrie A. Thorn*, testimony of G. W. Shields, NASWR.

59. Louis C. Hunter, *Steamboats on the Western Rivers*, 474.

60. *M. Smith et al. v.* Thompson Dean, NASWR.

61. "River-Boatmen of the Lower Mississippi," 145; Lafcadio Hearn, *Children of the Levee*, 63.

62. Surrency, *History of the Federal Courts*, 148; Louis C. Hunter, *Steamboats on the Western Rivers*, 474–75. Admiralty jurisdiction was clearly extended by the Supreme Court in The *Eagle*, 8 Wall. 15 (U.S. 1868). Several earlier cases, however, beginning with Genessee Chief *v. Fitzhugh et al.*, 12 How. 443, 454 (U.S. 1851), suggest that the extension began earlier. Both the federal courts in the Southern District of Illinois and the Eastern District of Louisiana began hearing admiralty cases by the late 1850s.

63. *Norman Laughlin et al. v.* Robert Semple, testimony of Annie Carter, NASWR. For similar examples of postwar wage cases in Louisiana see *George Sanders et al. v.* Clarksville, NASWR, and *John T. Brenck et al. v.* Susie Silver, NASWR.

64. *Norman Laughlin et al. v.* Robert Semple, testimony of Annie Carter, NASWR.

65. *Joseph Brady v.* Carrie Converse, NASWR.

66. Sixteen cases were officially discontinued. One hundred and twenty-two disappeared from court records after their initial filing, so their outcomes are unknown. These cases were most likely not pursued due to out-of-court settlement or more likely the failure of plaintiffs to continue prosecution. Civil cases were often slow to go to court, and the combination of poverty and mobility made it difficult for workers to follow through with initial filings.

67. Lafcadio Hearn, *Children of the Levee*, 63. Louis Hunter (*Steamboats on the Western Rivers*, 475) argues that boat owners originally supported the extension of admiralty laws to the western rivers because they thought the new requirements for shipping papers, which were required under admiralty law, would alleviate the problem of workers quitting. They soon regretted having to use shipping papers, however, because the documents prevented them from dismissing workers at will, a loss that outweighed the benefits of a more stable labor force.

68. Testimony of George Arnold, 5.

69. See Circuit Court Records, 1847–55, NASWR.

70. While Atlantic sailors were allowed to sue in this court as well, all but two of these suits involved river steamboats, a fact that may reflect a greater severity in the discipline on inland steamboats compared with Atlantic ships.

71. *Wm. Scott v. Samuel White*, NASWR.

72. *Gloster Hill v. A. Jumel [sic]*, NASWR.

73. *Alexander White v.* Frank Paragold *[sic]*, NASWR.

74. I was able to trace only a small number of individuals because many names on the census roll were illegible and I did not count names in the court records that matched more than one person in the census roll.

75. *United States v.* Henry Tete, NASWR.

76. *United States v.* Hy Pizzati, NASWR.

77. *United States v.* John H. Hanna, NASWR.

78. *United States v.* Warren, NASWR.

79. *United States v.* Frank Paragold *[sic]*, NASWR.

80. *Martin Self v.* Bart Able, NASWR. See also *Isaac Shook v.* Garry Owen, NASWR.

81. *Mamie May v. Phillip Crooks*, NASWR.

82. Minute Book 23, ibid.

83. Creighton, *Rites and Passages*, 106–7.

84. For verdicts see Complete Record of the Eastern District of Louisiana, RG 21, NASWR.

85. Fourteen cases disappeared from court records after they had been filed.

86. *Mary Johns v. Henry J. Brinker*, LSCR.

87. Ibid.

88. Ibid., testimony of Mary Johns.

89. Ibid.

90. Ibid., testimony of William Davis.

91. In court testimony she also claimed to have launched a federal district court case to recover lost wages. I have not found this case in federal court records. See ibid., testimony of Mary Johns.

92. Ibid.

93. Ibid. The custom was to employ two chambermaids on large steamboats.

94. Ibid.

95. Ibid.

96. George W. Healy III, "Remedies for Maritime Personal Injury and Wrongful Death in American Law: Sources and Development," 68 *Tulane Law Review* 311 (1994), in Robert M. Javis, ed., *An Admiralty Law Anthology* (Anderson Publishing, 1995), 63–65.

97. *Henry Reed v.* Bart Able, NASWR.

98. *Robert Kyle v.* Exporter, NASWR.

99. *Peter Dyer v. Thomas Leathers et al.*, testimony of Peter Dyer, LSCR.

100. Ibid., testimony of George Harris.

101. Ibid., testimony of Peter Dyer.

102. Botkin, ed., *Treasury of Mississippi River Folklore*, 254–55.

103. Ibid.

104. Ralph, *Dixie*, 23–24.

105. The Federal Civil Rights Act of March 1, 1875, required that "all persons within the jurisdiction of the United States shall be entitled to the full and equal enjoyment of the accommodations, advantages, facilities, and privileges of inns, public conveyances on land or water, theaters, and other places of public amusement . . . [subject] only to the conditions and limitations established by law, and applicable alike to citizens of every race and color, regardless of any previous condition of servitude." For newspaper articles reporting lawsuits in which boat owners won because they offered "separate but equal" accommodations to African American travelers see Steamboat Newspaper Clippings, 1873–76, William H. Tippitt Scrapbook, vol. 2, Memphis History Room, Memphis Public Library, Memphis, Tennessee. See, especially, undated article for 1875 describing a Greenville, Mississippi, suit. See also *Memphis Avalanche*, May 24, 1875. For examples of other suits under this legislation see the National Archives–Great Lakes Region's *Beacon* 4, no. 3 (January/February 1995). This publication describes two Evansville, Indiana, suits. For a Louisiana case see *United States v.* John C. Mitchell, NASWR. Unlike

the Mississippi cases, in which defendants won outright, the two Evansville cases and the Louisiana case never received decisions. They were all continued on court docket books for several years until they disappeared. For more discussion of African American steamboat passengers see Louis C. Hunter, *Steamboats on the Western Waters*, 391 n. 3.

The Federal Civil Rights Act of 1875 was deemed unconstitutional in 1883. The practice of providing "separate but equal" steamboat accommodations, however, appears to have been well established by this time.

106. My interpretation of the gains made by steamboat travelers through segregation supports Howard Rabinowitz's arguments in "From Exclusion to Segregation." It is unclear to what extent the situation was different on northern rivers. For another important Iowa case in which the court upheld an African American woman's right to sit at an integrated cabin table, see *Coger v. The North West. Union Packet Company* (December 1873). More research is needed to determine what impact this ruling had on upper Mississippi steamboats.

107. Rivington, *Reminiscences of America*, 219.

108. Ralph, *Dixie*, 17.

EPILOGUE

1. The public-use sample for the 1880 census is a nationwide 1 percent sample of all enumerated individuals. For this analysis and those that follow, I selected all individuals with river occupations from the following states: Pennsylvania, Ohio, Kentucky, Tennessee, Indiana, Illinois, Missouri, Wisconsin, Minnesota, Arkansas, Mississippi, and Louisiana. I then eliminated river workers living in counties in eastern Pennsylvania and those adjoining the Great Lakes from the sample.

The data utilized in this book were made available (in part) by the Inter-University Consortium for Political and Social Research. Steven Ruggles and Russell R. Menard originally collected the data. Neither the collectors of the data nor the consortium bear any responsibility for the analysis or the interpretations presented here. See Steven Ruggles and Russell R. Menard, Census of the Population, 1880 [United States]: Public Use Sample [Computer File] (Minneapolis, Minn.: University of Minnesota, Department of History, Social Science Research Laboratory [producer], 1994; Ann Arbor, Mich.: Inter-University Consortium for Political and Social Research [distributor], 1995).

Government-compiled census statistics for 1879 indicate that 15,833 people worked on steamboats in the western region in that year (Louis C. Hunter, *Steamboats on the Western Rivers*, 443). Historian George Merrick noted regional variation in the employment of African Americans. He recalled that the upper Mississippi had mostly white laborers but that "when [they] ran through to St. Louis the white fellows gradually drifted away and soon [they] had only colored labor." See "The History of the Diamond Jo Line," Box 14, George Merrick Papers, Wisconsin Historical Society, Madison, Wisconsin.

2. Bolster, *Black Jacks*, ch. 8.

3. Thirty-three out of forty-three African American river workers recorded in the census sample lived in these cities.

4. Tenth Population Census of the United States, St. Louis, Reels 718–36, and New Orleans, Reels 458–64, NA. John Blassingame's analysis of the same New Orleans census found a larger steamboat group. He found 1,694 steamboat workers (2.8 percent of the total employed male population in the city), of which 595 were African Americans (35.1 percent of the total number of boat workers). He found that nearly 800 freedpeople worked on steamboats in 1870. See Blassingame, *Black New Orleans*, appendix, table 8.

5. For statistics on urban populations in 1880 see Larsen, *Rise of the Urban South*.

6. "Constitution and By-laws of the St. Louis Harbor No. 28, American Association of Masters and Pilots of Steam Vessels, St. Louis, Mo, 1893," Edmund Gray Collection, Western Historical Manuscript Collection, Ellis Library, University of Missouri–Columbia. The generational mobility of European immigrants in the broader economy is clearly reflected in the western river labor force. See Griffen and Griffen, *Natives and Newcomers*.

7. Tenth Population Census of the United States, St. Louis, Reels 718–36, NA.

8. Ibid., New Orleans, Reels 458–64.

9. *Southwestern Christian Advocate*, November 8, 1900.

10. Charles B. Spahr, "America's Working People," *Outlook*, May 6, 1899, 35.

11. For declining real wages see Louis C. Hunter, *Steamboats on the Western Rivers*, 466. It was not uncommon for deckhands to receive a dollar a day in wages as late as the early twentieth century—the same wage that free boatmen received at midcentury. Tight competition within the industry, and the challenge of the railroad, encouraged owners to drive down wages and cut costs. The characterization of river work as "nigger" labor throughout the western river region coincided with the declining economic status of these jobs.

12. *Southwestern Christian Advocate*, November 8, 1900. For other examples see Arnesen, *Waterfront Workers of New Orleans*, 105.

13. Arnesen, *Waterfront Workers of New Orleans*.

14. Lafcadio Hearn, *Children of the Levee*, 81.

15. John Edmund Boland Recollections, Box 1, Folder 4, Sophie Cooley Pearson Collection, LLMVC.

16. Ibid.

17. For a discussion of this transformation see Cronon, *Nature's Metropolis*.

18. Louis C. Hunter, *Steamboats on the Western Rivers*, 660–62, chs. 12 and 14.

19. Ibid., 563.

20. Ibid., 662.

21. Painter, *Exodusters*, ch. 15.

22. By the 1920s, newspaper articles were reflecting on the decline of an American icon—the death of the "negro roustabout." See *Memphis Evening Appeal*, April 14, 1927; and *Memphis New Scimitar*, article clipping for 1929, in William H. Tip-

pitt Collection, microfilm no. 1430, MDAH. For commentary from black river workers on the decline of the industry see testimony of Charity Anderson, 16, and testimony of Shadrach Cyrus, 546.

23. Chevan, "Riverboat Music."
24. Viorst, *Fire in the Streets*, 21.
25. Arnesen, *Brotherhoods of Color*, 2.

bibliography

MANUSCRIPT COLLECTIONS

Baton Rouge, Louisiana
    Louisiana and Lower Mississippi Valley Collections, Louisiana State University Special Collections
        Sophie Cooley Pearson Collection, 1843–1973, MS 3237
Chapel Hill, North Carolina
    University of North Carolina, Wilson Library, Southern Historical Collection
        Rice C. Ballard Papers, 1882–88, MS 4850
        Gustavus A. Henry Papers, 1804–52, MS 1431
        James H. Otey Papers, 1800–1863, MS 568
        Sarah Lois Wadley Diary, Volume 1, MS 1258
Cincinnati, Ohio
    Cincinnati Public Library, Inland Waterways Collection
        Logbook of the *Ike Hammitt*, July 10, 1863–March 21, 1867
Columbia, Missouri
    State Historical Society of Missouri
        E. B. Trail Collection, 1884–1965, MS 2071
    University of Missouri–Columbia, Ellis Library, Western Historical Manuscript Collection
        Edmund Gray Collection, 1831–1955, MS C3611
Durham, North Carolina
    Rare Book, Manuscript, and Special Collections Library, Duke University
        Archibald H. Boyd Papers, 1841–97
        Mississippi River Travel Diary, 1838, MS 2994
Jackson, Mississippi
    Mississippi Department of Archives and History
        William H. Tippitt Collection
Louisville, Kentucky
    Filson Historical Society
        Mary A. Davis Papers, 1855–98, MSS CA
        James Rudd Papers, 1789–1867

Madison, Wisconsin
  Wisconsin Historical Society
    George Byron Merrick Papers, 1838–1934
Memphis, Tennessee
  Memphis History Room, Memphis Public Library
    William H. Tippitt Scrapbooks
Nashville, Tennessee
  Tennessee State Library and Archives
    Diaries, etc.
New Orleans, Louisiana
  Historic New Orleans Collection, Williams Research Center
    Tobin Collection, 1860–1943, MSS 249
Oberlin, Ohio
  Mudd Library, Special Collections
    Catalogue and Record of Colored Students, 1834–1972
St. Louis, Missouri
  Missouri Historical Society
    William Clark Breckenridge Papers, 1752–1927
    James Kennedy Diary, 1826–38
    James C. Lackland Papers
    William Carr Lane Collection
    Slaves and Slavery Collection
    Missouri History Collection
Washington, D.C.
  National Archives
    Manuscript Seventh Population Census of the United States, Slave and
      Free, 1850
    Manuscript Tenth Population Census of the United States, 1880

NEWSPAPERS AND PERIODICALS

Boston Liberator
Cincinnati Daily Gazette
Colored American
Debow's Review of the South and West
Galena Gazette
Harper's New Monthly Magazine
Louisville Journal
Memphis Avalanche
Memphis Daily Appeal
Memphis Evening Appeal
Memphis News Scimitar
Missouri Argus

Missouri Republican
Natchez Free Trader
National Anti-Slavery Standard
New Orleans Bee
New Orleans Picayune
The Sailors Magazine and Seamen's Friend
St. Louis Daily New Era
St. Louis Daily Republican
St. Louis Globe-Democrat
Southwestern Christian Advocate
Vicksburg Herald

STATE SUPREME COURT RECORDS

Jefferson City, Missouri
  Missouri Supreme Court Records, Missouri State Archives
    Beardslee v. Perry, No. 45A, Box 48, 14 Mo 88 (1851)
    Beardslee and Wife v. Parmelee, No. 20, Box 20, 10 Mo 586 (1847)
    Bryan v. Aunt Letty, No. 13, Box 588 (1856)
    Eaton v. Vaughan, No. 18, Box 41, 9 Mo 743 (1846)
    Johnstone v. Arabia, No. 3, Box 584, 24 Mo 86 (1853)
    Palfrey v. Kerr et al., No 1783, 8 Mart (N.S.) 503 (1830)
    Price v. Thorton et al., No. 18, Box 43, 10 Mo 135 (1846)
    Ridgely v. Reindeer, No. 6, Box 596, 27 Mo 442 (1858)
    Time *v. Parmelee*, No. 20, Box 20, 10 Mo 586 (1847)
    Withers v. El Paso, No. 23, Box 72, 24 Mo 204 (1857)
New Orleans, Louisiana
  Louisiana Supreme Court Records, Special Collections, University of New
    Orleans
    Adams v. Trabue, No. 6833, Unreported (La, 1855)
    Barry v. Kimball, No. 3500, 10 La Ann 787 (1857); No. 4684, 12 La Ann
      372 (1857)
    Bennett v. Nashville, No. 5210, Unreported (1854)
    Beverly v. Empire, No. 6323, 15 La Ann 432 (1860)
    Block v. Trent, No. 855, 18 La Ann 664 (1866)
    John Buddy v. Vanleer, No. 1901, 6 La Ann 34 (1851)
    Buel v. New York, No. 3689, 17 La 541 (1841)
    Burke, f.w.c., v. Clarke, No. 3112, 11 La 206 (1837)
    Peter Dyer v. Thomas Leathers et al., No. 4380, 28 La Ann 6 (1876)
    Emmerling v. Beebe, No. 3642, 15 La 251 (1840)
    England v. Gripon, No. 6316, 15 La Ann 304 (1860)
    Feltus v. Anders, No. 4576, 5 Rob 7 (La, 1843)
    Goldenbow v. Wright, 13 La 371 (1839)
    Hennen v. Doswell, No. 2735, Unreported (1853)

Howes v. Red Chief, Nos. 5944, 6487, 15 La Ann 321 (1860)
Huntington v. Ricard, No. 2288, 6 La Ann 806 (1851)
Hurst v. Wallace, No. 2402, 5 La 98 (1833)
Hynes v. Kirkman, No. 2039, 4 La 47 (1832)
Mary Johns v. Henry Brinker, No. 5399, 30 La Ann 241 (1878)
Sarah Hill v. James White, No. 4489, 11 La Ann 170 (1856)
Lacoste v. Sellick, No. 6101, 1 La Ann 336 (1846)
J. L. Marciacq v. H. M. Wright, *Captain and Owners,* No. 4645, 13 La Ann 27 (1858)
McKinney v. Yalla Busha, No. 602, Unreported (1848)
McMaster v. Beckwith, No. 2017, 2 La 329 (1831)
Morgan's Syndics v. Fiveash, No. 1700, 7 Mart (n.s. 410) (La, 1829)
Owen v. Brown, No. 4927, 12 La Ann 172 (1857)
Pelham v. Messenger, No. 6629, 16 La Ann 99 (1861)
Pipkin v. Pipkin, No. 2809, 7 La Ann 617 (1852)
Poree v. Cannon, No. 6006, 14 La Ann 501 (1859)
Rice v. Cade, 10 La Ann 288 (1836)
Rountree v. Brilliant, No. 2804, 8 La Ann 289 (1853)
Slatter v. Holton, No. 3894, 19 La 39 (1841)
Spaulding v. Taylor et al., No. 5628, 1 La Ann 195 (1846)
Strawbridge v. Turner and Woodruff et al., No. 2803, 8 La 537 (1835)
Succession of Parker, No. 6868, 17 La Ann 28 (1865)
Williamson v. Norton, No. 2427, 7 La Ann 393 (1852)

STATE LAWS

Acts . . . of the Legislature of the State of Louisiana. New Orleans, 1812–59.
General Acts of Arkansas. Little Rock, 1843.
Kentucky Acts. Frankfort, 1824, 1860, 1861.
Laws of Missouri. Jefferson City, 1841, 1843, 1859.
Mississippi Laws. Jackson, 1842, 1862.
Public Acts of the State of Tennessee (Nashville, 1833.

FEDERAL COURT RECORDS

Chicago, Illinois
   National Archives–Great Lakes Region, Southern District of Illinois
      United States v. Louisville, No. 346, Unreported (1863)
      United States v. Black Hawk, No. 392, Unreported (1863)
Fort Worth, Texas
   National Archives–Southwest Region, Eastern District of Louisiana
      Joseph Brady v. Carrie Converse, No. 9738, Unreported (1871)
      John T. Brenck et al. v. Susie Silver, No. 10822, Unreported (1876)
      Gloster Hill v. A. Jumel [sic], No. 9287, Unreported (1869)

Robert Kyle v. Exporter, No. 10190, Unreported (1873)

Norman Laughlin et al. v. Robert Semple, No. 10725, Unreported (1872)

Mamie May v. Phillip Crooks, No. 9668, Unreported (1871)

Henry Reed v. Bart Able, No. 10827, Unreported (1876)

George Sanders et al. v. Clarksville, No. 10832, Unreported (1876)

Wm. Scott v. Samuel White, No. 9096, Unreported (1868)

Martin Self v. Bart Able, No. 8846, Unreported (1867)

Charles Fisher et al. v. Carrie A. Thorn, No. 9770, Unreported (1871)

Isaac Shook v. Garry Owen, No. 10737, Unreported (1876)

M. Smith et al. v. Thompson Dean, No. 10722, Unreported (1876)

United States v. John C. Mitchell, No. 364, Unreported (1875)

United States v. Frank Paragold *[sic]*, No. 1333, Unreported (1880)

United States v. Henry Tete, No. 1286, Unreported (1879)

United States v. Hy Pizzati, No. 2101, Unreported (1879)

United States v. John H. Hanna, No. 1283, Unreported (1882)

United States v. Warren, No. 1920, Unreported (1888)

Alexander White v. Frank Paragold *[sic]*, No. 10131, Unreported (1873)

Kansas City, Missouri

National Archives–Great Plains Region, Eastern District of Missouri

Blair et al. v. Aunt Letty, No. 183, Box 5, Unreported (1857)

Nicholas Decker et al. v. Duncan Carter, No. 646, Unreported (1859).

John Gleason et al. v. Urilda, No. 1519, Unreported (1868)

Henry James v. Cora, No. 1162, Unreported (1866)

Wm. Patterson v. Great Republic, No. 1563, Unreported (1869)

Alhambra Reeder v. Shreveport, No 872, Unreported (1861)

William Ward v. Shreveport, No. 862, Unreported (1861)

Williams v. Jacob, No. 1773, Unreported (1870)

SLAVE NARRATIVES

Aunt Sally; or, The Cross the Way of Freedom; a Narrative of the Slave-Life and Purchase of the Mother of Rev. Isaac Williams of Detroit, Michigan. Cincinnati: American Reform Tract, 1858.

Bibb, Henry. *Narrative of the Life and Adventures of Henry Bibb, an American Slave, Written by Himself.* New York: the Author, 1849.

Blassingame, John W., ed. *Slave Testimony: Two Centuries of Letters, Speeches, Interviews and Autobiographies.* Baton Rouge: Louisiana State University Press, 1977.

Brown, William Wells. *Narrative of William Wells Brown, a Fugitive Slave. Written by Himself.* Boston: American Anti-Slavery Society, 1847.

Campbell, Israel. *Bond and Free; or, Yearnings for Freedom, from the Green Brier House, Being the Story of My Life in Bondage.* Philadelphia: Israel Campbell, 1861.

Clarke, Lewis, and Milton Clarke. *Narratives of the Sufferings of Lewis and Milton*

Clarke: Sons of a Soldier of the Revolution, During a Captivity of More than Twenty Years Among the Slaveholders of Kentucky, One of the So Called Christian States of North America. New York: Arno Press, 1969.

Drew, Benjamin. *The Refugee: A North-Side View of Slavery.* Reading, Mass.: Addison-Wesley Publishing Company, 1969.

Grandy, Moses. *Narrative of the Life of Moses Grandy, Late a Slave in the United States of America.* Boston: Oliver Johnson, 1844.

Green, J. D. *Narrative of the Life of J. D. Green, a Runaway Slave from Kentucky Containing an Account of His Three Escapes in 1839, 1846, and 1848.* Huddersfield: Henry Fielding, 1864.

Hughes, Louis. *Thirty Years a Slave: From Bondage to Freedom.* Milwaukee: South Side Printing Company, 1897.

Osofsky, Gilbert, ed. *Puttin' on Ole Massa: The Slave Narratives of Henry Bibb, Williams Wells Brown, and Solomon Northrup.* New York: Harper and Row, 1969.

Pickard, Kate E., ed. *The Kidnapped and the Ransomed: The Narrative of Peter and Vena Still after Forty Years of Slavery.* Lincoln: University of Nebraska Press, 1995.

Sprague, Stuart Seely, ed. *His Promised Land: The Autobiography of John P. Parker, Former Slave and Conductor on the Underground Railroad.* New York: W. W. Norton, 1996.

Thomas, James P. *From Tennessee Slave to St. Louis Entrepreneur: The Autobiography of James Thomas.* Edited by Loren Schweninger. Columbia: University of Missouri Press, 1984.

Trials and Confessions of Madison Henderson, alias Blanchard, Alfred Amos Warrick, James W. Seward, and Charles Brown, Murderers of Jesse Baker and Jacob Weaver: as Given by Themselves and Likeness of Each, Taken in Jail Shortly after Their Arrest. St. Louis: Chambers and Knapp, Republican Office, 1841.

SLAVE TESTIMONY

Testimony of Charity Anderson. In *The American Slave: A Composite Autobiography.* Edited by George P. Rawick. Supplement, Series 1, Volume 1, Alabama Narratives. Westport, Conn.: Greenwood Press, 1972.

Testimony of Jim Archer. In *The American Slave: A Composite Autobiography.* Edited by George P. Rawick. Supplement, Series 1, Volume 6, Mississippi Narratives, Part 1. Westport, Conn.: Greenwood Press, 1977.

Testimony of George Arnold. In *The American Slave: A Composite Autobiography.* Edited by George P. Rawick. Volume 6, Indiana Narratives. Westport, Conn.: Greenwood Press, 1972.

Testimony of Peter Barber. In *Mother Wit: The Ex-Slave Narratives of the Louisiana Writers' Project.* Edited by Ronnie W. Clayton. New York: Peter Lang, 1990.

Testimony of Henry Barnes. In *The American Slave: A Composite Autobiography.*

Edited by George P. Rawick. Supplement, Series 1, Volume 1, Alabama Narratives. Westport, Conn.: Greenwood Press, 1977.

Testimony of Bettie Massingale Bell. In *The American Slave: A Composite Autobiography*. Edited by George P. Rawick. Supplement, Series 1, Volume 1, Alabama Narratives. Westport, Conn.: Greenwood Press, 1977.

Testimony of Boston Blackwell. In *The American Slave: A Composite Autobiography*. Edited by George P. Rawick. Volume 8, Arkansas Narratives, Part 1 and 2. Westport, Conn.: Greenwood Publishing, 1972.

Testimony of George Bollinger. In *The American Slave: A Composite Autobiography*. Edited by George P. Rawick. Volume 11, Arkansas Narratives, Part 7, and Missouri Narratives. Westport, Conn.: Greenwood Press, 1972.

Testimony of Bernice Bowden. In *The American Slave: A Composite Autobiography*. Edited by George P. Rawick. Volume 16, Kansas, Kentucky, Maryland, Ohio, Virginia, and Tennessee Narratives. Westport, Conn.: Greenwood Press, 1972.

Testimony of Mack Brantley. In *The American Slave: A Composite Autobiography*. Edited by George P. Rawick. Volume 8, Arkansas Narratives, Part 1 and 2. Westport, Conn.: Greenwood Publishing, 1972.

Testimony of Peter Brown. In *The American Slave: A Composite Autobiography*. Edited by George P. Rawick. Volume 8, Arkansas Narratives, Part 1 and 2. Westport, Conn.: Greenwood Publishing, 1972.

Testimony of Robert Bryant. In *The American Slave: A Composite Autobiography*. Edited by George P. Rawick. Series 2, Volume 11, Arkansas Narratives, Part 7, and Missouri Narratives. Westport, Conn.: Greenwood Press, 1972.

Testimony of George Taylor Burns. In *The American Slave: A Composite Autobiography*. Edited by George P. Rawick. Supplement, Series 1, Volume 5, Indiana and Ohio Narratives. Westport, Conn.: Greenwood Press, 1977.

Testimony of Uncle Richard Carruthers. In *The American Slave: A Composite Autobiography*. Edited by George P. Rawick. Volume 3, Texas Narratives, Part 2. Westport, Conn.: Greenwood Press, 1972.

Testimony of Lizzie Chandler. In *Mother Wit: The Ex-Slave Narratives of the Louisiana Writers' Project*. Edited by Ronnie W. Clayton. New York: Peter Lang, 1990.

Testimony of Henry Clay. In *The American Slave: A Composite Autobiography*. Edited by George P. Rawick. Supplement, Series 1, Volume 12, Oklahoma Narratives. Westport, Conn.: Greenwood Press, 1977.

Testimony of Henry Clay. In *The WPA Oklahoma Slave Narratives*. Edited by T. Lindsay Baker and Julie P. Baker. Norman: University of Oklahoma Press, 1996.

Testimony of Aunt Clussey. In *The American Slave: A Composite Autobiography*. Edited by George P. Rawick. Supplement, Series 1, Volume 1, Alabama Narratives. Westport, Conn.: Greenwood Press, 1972.

Testimony of Holt Collier. In *The American Slave: A Composite Autobiography*.

Edited by George P. Rawick. Supplement, Series 1, Volume 7, Mississippi
Narratives, Part 1. Westport, Conn.: Greenwood Press, 1977.

Testimony of Peter Corn. In *The American Slave: A Composite Autobiography*.
Edited by George P. Rawick. Series 2, Volume 11, Missouri Narratives. Westport, Conn.: Greenwood Press, 1972.

Testimony of Lauana Creel. In *The American Slave: A Composite Autobiography*.
Edited by George P. Rawick. Volume 6, Alabama and Indiana Narratives. Westport, Conn.: Greenwood Press, 1972.

Testimony of Kate Curry. In *The American Slave: A Composite Autobiography*.
Edited by George P. Rawick. Volume 4, Texas Narratives, Part 3. Westport,
Conn.: Greenwood Publishing, 1972.

Testimony of Shadrach Cyrus. In *The American Slave: A Composite Autobiography*. Edited by George P. Rawick. Supplement, Series 1, Volume 7, Mississippi
Narratives, Part 2. Westport, Conn.: Greenwood Press, 1977.

Testimony of Clara Davis. In *The American Slave: A Composite Autobiography*.
Edited by George P. Rawick. Supplement, Series 1, Volume 1, Alabama Narratives. Westport, Conn.: Greenwood Press, 1977.

Testimony of Mrs. Cora Carroll Gilliam. In *The American Slave: A Composite
Autobiography*. Edited by George P. Rawick. Supplement, Series 2, Volume 1,
Alabama, Arizona, Arkansas, District of Columbia, Florida, Georgia, Indiana,
Kansas, Maryland, Nebraska, New York, North Carolina, Oklahoma, Rhode
Island, South Carolina, and Washington Narratives. Westport, Conn.: Green-
wood Press, 1979.

Testimony of Mollie Hatfield. In *The American Slave: A Composite Autobiography*.
Edited by George P. Rawick. Supplement, Series 1, Volume 8, Mississippi
Narratives, Part 3. Westport, Conn.: Greenwood Press, 1977.

Testimony of Celia Henderson. In *The American Slave: A Composite Autobiography*. Edited by George P. Rawick. Supplement, Series 1, Volume 5, Indiana and
Ohio Narratives. Westport, Conn.: Greenwood Press, 1977.

Testimony of Henry Henderson. In *The WPA Oklahoma Slave Narratives*. Edited
by T. Lindsay Baker and Julie P. Baker. Norman: University of Oklahoma
Press, 1996.

Testimony of W. E. Hobbs. In *The American Slave: A Composite Autobiography*.
Edited by George P. Rawick. Supplement, Series 2, Volume 1, Alabama, Ari-
zona, Arkansas, District of Columbia, Florida, Georgia, Indiana, Kansas,
Maryland, Nebraska, New York, North Carolina, Oklahoma, Rhode Island,
South Carolina, and Washington Narratives. Westport, Conn.: Greenwood
Press, 1979.

Testimony of Lee Hobby. In *The American Slave: A Composite Autobiography*.
Edited by George P. Rawick. Supplement, Series 2, Volume 5, Texas Narratives, Part 4. Westport, Conn.: Greenwood Publishing, 1972.

Testimony of Lizzie Jackson. In *The WPA Oklahoma Slave Narratives*. Edited by
T. Lindsay Baker and Julie P. Baker. Norman: University of Oklahoma Press, 1996.

Testimony of Mary Kindred. In *The American Slave: A Composite Autobiography*. Edited by George P. Rawick. Supplement, Series 2, Volume 6, Texas Narratives, Part 5. Westport, Conn.: Greenwood Press, 1979.

Testimony of Julia King. In *The American Slave: A Composite Autobiography*. Edited by George P. Rawick. Volume 16, Kansas, Kentucky, Maryland, Ohio, Virginia, and Tennessee Narratives. Westport, Conn.: Greenwood Press, 1972.

Testimony of Ben Lawson. In *The WPA Oklahoma Slave Narratives*. Edited by T. Lindsay Baker and Julie P. Baker. Norman: University of Oklahoma Press, 1996.

Testimony of Little Annie. In *The American Slave: A Composite Autobiography*. Edited by George P. Rawick. Supplement, Series 2, Volume 6, Texas Narratives, Part 5. Westport, Conn.: Greenwood Press, 1979.

Testimony of Will Long. In *The American Slave: A Composite Autobiography*. Edited by George P. Rawick. Supplement, Series 2, Volume 6, Texas Narratives, Part 5. Westport, Conn.: Greenwood Press, 1979.

Testimony of Louis Love. In *The American Slave: A Composite Autobiography*. Edited by George P. Rawick. Volume 7, Texas Narratives, Part 6. Westport, Conn.: Greenwood Press, 1972.

Testimony of John Majors. In *The American Slave: A Composite Autobiography*. Edited by George P. Rawick. Volume 7, Texas Narratives, Part 6. Westport, Conn.: Greenwood Press, 1972.

Testimony of Andy McAdams. In *The American Slave: A Composite Autobiography*. Edited by George P. Rawick. Volume 7, Texas Narratives, Part 6. Westport, Conn.: Greenwood Press, 1972.

Testimony of William H. McCarthy. In *The American Slave: A Composite Autobiography*. Edited by George P. Rawick. Supplement, Series 1, Volume 9, Mississippi Narratives, Part 4. Westport, Conn.: Greenwood Press, 1977.

Testimony of Henry Louis McGaffey. In *The American Slave: A Composite Autobiography*. Edited by George P. Rawick. Supplement, Series 1, Volume 9, Mississippi Narratives, Part 4. Westport, Conn.: Greenwood Press, 1977.

Testimony of Isaam Morgan. In *The American Slave: A Composite Autobiography*. Edited by George P. Rawick. Supplement, Series 1, Volume 1, Alabama Narratives. Westport, Conn.: Greenwood Press, 1977.

Testimony of Polk Nelson. In *The American Slave: A Composite Autobiography*. Edited by George P. Rawick. Supplement, Series 1, Volume 5, Indiana and Ohio Narratives. Westport, Conn.: Greenwood Press, 1977.

Testimony of Tony Piggy. In *The American Slave: A Composite Autobiography*. Edited by George P. Rawick. Volume 10, Arkansas Narratives. Westport, Conn.: Greenwood Press, 1972.

Testimony of Betty Robertson. In *The WPA Oklahoma Slave Narratives*. Edited by T. Lindsay Baker and Julie P. Baker. Norman: University of Oklahoma Press, 1996.

Testimony of Billy Slaughter. In *The American Slave: A Composite Autobiography*.

Edited by George P. Rawick. Series 1, Volume 6, Alabama and Indiana Narratives. Westport, Conn.: Greenwood Press, 1972.

Testimony of Berry Smith. In *The American Slave: A Composite Autobiography*. Edited by George P. Rawick. Supplement, Series 1, Mississippi Narratives, Part 5. Westport, Conn.: Greenwood, 1977.

Testimony of Jordan Smith. In *The American Slave: A Composite Autobiography*. Edited by George P. Rawick. Supplement, Series 2, Volume 9, Texas Narratives, Part 8. Westport, Conn.: Greenwood Press, 1979.

Testimony of Elmo Steele. In *The American Slave: A Composite Autobiography*. Edited by George P. Rawick. Supplement, Series 1, Volume 10, Mississippi Narratives, Part 5. Westport, Conn.: Greenwood Press, 1977.

Testimony of William Stone. *The American Slave: A Composite Autobiography*. Edited by George P. Rawick. Supplement, Series 2, Volume 9, Texas Narratives, Part 8. Westport, Conn.: Greenwood Press, 1979.

Testimony of Ruby Pickens Tartt. In *The American Slave: A Composite Autobiography*. Edited by George P. Rawick. Volume 6, Alabama and Indiana Narratives. Westport, Conn.: Greenwood Press, 1972.

Testimony of Samuel S. Taylor. In *The American Slave: A Composite Autobiography*. Edited by George P. Rawick. Volume 11, Arkansas Narratives, Part 7, and Missouri Narratives. Westport, Conn.: Greenwood Press, 1972.

Testimony of James V. In *The American Slave: A Composite Autobiography*. Edited by George P. Rawick. Volume 16, Kansas, Kentucky, Maryland, Ohio, Virginia, and Tennessee Narratives. Westport, Conn.: Greenwood Publishing, 1972.

Testimony of Lucinda Vann. In *The WPA Oklahoma Slave Narratives*. Edited by T. Lindsay Baker and Julie P. Baker. Norman: University of Oklahoma Press, 1996.

Testimony of Virginia Washington. In *The American Slave: A Composite Autobiography*. Edited by George P. Rawick. Supplement, Series 1, Volume 5, Indiana and Ohio Narratives. Westport, Conn.: Greenwood Press, 1977.

Testimony of William Waymen. In *The American Slave: A Composite Autobiography*. Edited by George P. Rawick. Supplement, Series 2, Volume 10, Texas Narratives, Part 9. Westport, Conn.: Greenwood Press, 1979.

Testimony of Ishe Webb. In *The American Slave: A Composite Autobiography*. Edited by George P. Rawick. Series 2, Volume 11, Arkansas Narratives, Part 7. Westport: Greenwood Press, 1972.

Testimony of Charles Williams. In *The American Slave: A Composite Autobiography*. Edited by George P. Rawick. Supplement, Series 2, Volume 1, Alabama, Arizona, Arkansas, District of Columbia, Florida, Georgia, Indiana, Kansas, Maryland, Nebraska, New York, North Carolina, Oklahoma, Rhode Island, South Carolina, and Washington Narratives. Westport, Conn.: Greenwood Press, 1979.

Abbott, John S. C. *South and North; or, Impressions Received During a Trip to Cuba and the South*. New York: Negro Universities Press, 1969.

Beadle, Charles. *A Trip to the United States in 1887*. London: J. S. Virtue and Company, n.d.

Bodichon, Barbara Leigh Smith. *An American Diary, 1857–1858*. Edited by Joseph W. Reed Jr. London: Routledge and Kegan Paul, 1972.

Bremer, Fredrika. *America of the Fifties: The Letters of Fredrika Bremer*. Edited by Adolph B. Brenson. New York: The American-Scandinavian Foundation, 1924.

———. *The Homes of the New World: Impressions of America*. Vol. 2. Translated by Mary Howitt. New York: Harper and Bros., 1853.

Buckingham, J. S., Esq. *The Slave States of America*. Vol. 1. New York: Negro Universities Press, 1968.

Burckin, Alexander I. "'A Spirit of Perseverance': Free African-Americans in Late Antebellum Louisville." *The Filson Club Historical Quarterly* 70, no. 1 (January 1996): 61–81.

Chambers, William. *Things as They Are in America*. New York: Negro Universities Press, 1968.

Chevalier, Michael. *Society, Manners and Politics in the United States: Being a Series of Letters on North America*. Boston: Weeks, Jordan and Company, 1839.

Cunynghame, Lieut.-Col. Arthur. *A Glimpse at the Great Western Republic*. London: Richard Bentley, 1851.

Davies, Ebenezer. *American Scenes and Christian Slavery: A Recent Tour of Four Thousand Miles in the United States*. London: John Snow, 1849.

Didimus, H. *New Orleans as I Found It*. New York: Harper and Bros., 1845.

Ehrenpreis, Anne Henry, ed. *Happy Country This America: A Travel Diary of Henry Arthur Bright*. Columbus: Ohio State University Press, 1978.

Everest, Rev. Robert. *A Journey through the United States and Part of Canada*. London: John Chapman, 1855.

Featherstonhaugh, G. W. *Excursion through the Slave States*. New York: Negro Universities Press, 1968.

Flint, Timothy. *Recollections of the Last Ten Years, Passed in Occasional Residences and Journeyings in the Valley of the Mississippi*. New York: Knopf, 1932.

Foster, Lillian. *Way-side Glimpses, North and South*. New York: Negro Universities Press, 1969.

Goodrich, C. A. *The Family Tourist. A Visit to the Principal Cities of the Western Continent: Embracing an Account of Their Situation, Origin, Plan, Extent, Inhabitants, Manners, Customs, and Amusements, and Public Works, Institutions, Edifices, &c.* Hartford: Case, Tiffany and Company, 1848.

Grandfort, Marie Fontenay de. *The New World*. Translated by Edward C. Wharton. New Orleans: Sherman, Wharton, and Company, 1855.

Gurney, Joseph John. *A Journey in North America: Described in Familiar Letters to Amelia Opie*. New York: Da Capo Press, 1973.

Hall, A. Oakey. *The Manhattaner in New Orleans; or, Phases of "Crescent City" Life*. New York: J. S. Redfield, 1851.

Hall, Captain Basil. *Travels in North America, in the Years 1827 and 1828*. Vol. 3. Edinburgh: Cadell and Company, 1829.

Hesse-Wartegg, Ernst von. *Travels on the Lower Mississippi, 1879–1880*. Translated and edited by Frederic Trautmann. Columbia: University of Missouri Press, 1990.

Houstoun, Mrs. *Hesperos; or, Travels in the West*. London: John W. Parker, 1850.

An Immigrant of a Hundred Years Ago: A Story of Someone's Ancestor. Hattiesburg, Miss.: The Book Farm, 1941.

Ingraham, J. H. *The Southwest: By a Yankee*. Vol. 1. New York: Harper and Bros., 1835.

———. *The Sunny South; or, The Southerner at Home, Embracing Five Years' Experience of a Northern Governess in the Land of Sugar and Cotton*. New York: Negro Universities Press, 1968.

Lakier, Aleksandr Borisovich. *A Russian Looks at America: The Journey of Aleksandr Borisovich Lakier in 1857*. Translated and edited by Arnold Schrier Joyce Story. Chicago: University of Chicago Press, 1979.

Lanman, Charles. *Adventures in the Wilds of the United States and British American Provinces*. Vol. 2. Philadelphia: John W. Moore, 1856.

Latham, Henry. *Black and White: A Journal of Three Months' Tour in the United States*. London: Macmillan and Co., 1867.

Latrobe, Benjamin Henry. *The Journal of Latrobe*. New York: Burt Franklin, 1971.

Latrobe, Charles. *Rambler in North America*. New York: Harper and Bros., 1835.

Mentor, Lee Williams, ed. "James Kirke Paulding on the Mississippi, 1842." *Journal of Mississippi History* 10 (October 1948): 317–44.

Mackay, Alex. *The Western World; or, Travels in the United States in 1846–1847*. Vol. 3. London: Richard Bentley, 1849.

Mackay, Charles. *Life and Liberty in America; or, Sketches of a Tour in the United States and Canada in 1857–1858*. New York: Harper and Bros., 1859.

Marryat, Frederick. *A Diary in America: With Remark on Its Institutions*. Edited by Sydney Jackman. New York: Knopf, 1962.

Martineau, Harriet. *Retrospect of Western Travel*. Vol. 2. London: Saunders and Otley, 1838.

Murray, Henry. *Lands of the Slave and the Free*. London: John W. Parker, 1855.

Nason, Daniel. *Journal of a Tour from Boston to Savannah, Thence to Havana, in the Island of Cuba, with Occasional Notes during a Short Residence in Each Place: Thence to New Orleans and Several Western Cities*. Cambridge, Mass.: Daniel Nason, 1849.

Nichols, Thomas Low. *Forty Years of American Life, 1821–1861*. New York: Stackpole Sons, 1937.

Olmsted, Frederick Law. *The Cotton Kingdom: A Traveler's Observations on Cotton and Slavery in the American Slave States, 1853–1861*. Edited by Arthur Schlesinger. New York: Da Capo Press, 1996.

————. *Journey to the Seaboard Slave States*. New York: Mason Bros., 1861.

Piercy, Frederick Hawkins. *Route from Liverpool to Great Salt Lake Valley*. Edited by Fawn M. Brody. Cambridge, Mass.: Belknap Press of Harvard University Press, 1962.

Pope, Judge William. *Early Days in Arkansas: Being for the Most Part the Personal Recollections of an Old Settler*. Little Rock: Frederick Allsopp, 1895.

Potter, Eliza. *A Hairdresser's Experience in High Life*. New York: Oxford University Press, 1991.

Pulszky, Francis, and Theresa Pulszky. *White, Red, Black: Sketches of Society in the United States during the Visit of Their Guest*. Vol. 2. New York: Redfield, 1853.

Ralph, Julian. *Dixie; or, Southern Scenes and Sketches*. New York: Harper and Bros., 1895.

Redpath, James. *The Roving Editor; or, Talks with Slaves in the Southern States*. Edited by John R. McKivigan. University Park: Pennsylvania State University Press, 1996.

Rivington, W. J. *Reminiscences of America in 1869*. London: Sampson, Low and Marston, 1870.

Rockland, Michael Aaron, ed. *Sarmiento's Travels in the United States in 1847*. Princeton: Princeton University Press, 1970.

Rose, George M. A. *The Great Country; or, Impressions of America*. London: Tinsley Brothers, 1868.

Rosenberg, C. G. *Jenny Lind in America*. New York: Stringer and Townsend, 1851.

Russell, William Howard. *My Diary North and South*. Edited by Eugene H. Berwanger. Philadelphia: Temple University Press, 1988.

Steele, Mrs. *A Summer Journey in the West*. New York: John S. Taylor, 1841.

Thompson, William. *A Tradesman's Travels, in the United States and Canada in the Years 1840, 41, & 42*. Edinburgh: Oliver and Boyd, 1842.

Tixier, Victor. *Tixier's Travels on the Osage Prairies*. Edited by John Francis McDermott. Norman: University of Oklahoma Press, 1940.

Tower, Rev. Philo. *Slavery Unmasked: Being a Truthful Narrative of a Three Years' Residence and Journeying in Eleven Southern States: To Which Is Added the Invasion of Kansas, Including the Last Chapter of Her Wrongs*. New York: Negro Universities Press, 1969.

Trollope, Anthony. *North America*. New York: Knopf, 1951.

Trollope, Francis. *Domestic Manners of the Americans*. Vol. 1. New York: Howard, Wilford, Bell, 1904.

Wortley, Lady Emmerline Stuart. *Travels in the United States, etc., during 1849 and 1850*. New York: Harper and Bros., 1851.

MISCELLANEOUS PRIMARY SOURCES

"The River-Boatmen of the Lower Mississippi." *Annual Reports of the Supervising Surgeon General*. New Orleans: Marine Hospital Service, 1873.

Adler, Jeffrey S. *Yankee Merchants and the Making of the Urban West: The Rise and Fall of Antebellum St. Louis.* Cambridge: Cambridge University Press, 1991.

Allen, Michael. *Western Rivermen, 1763–1861: Ohio and Mississippi Boatmen and the Myth of the Alligator Horse.* Baton Rouge: Louisiana State University Press, 1990.

Anderson, Bern. *By Sea and by River: The Naval History of the Civil War.* New York: De Capo Press, 1962.

Andrews, William L. *To Tell a Free Story: The First Century of Afro-American Autobiography, 1760–1865.* Urbana: University of Illinois Press, 1988.

Arnesen, Eric. *Brotherhoods of Color: Black Workers and the Struggle for Racial Equality.* Cambridge, Mass.: Harvard University Press, 2001.

———. *Waterfront Workers of New Orleans: Race, Class, and Politics, 1863–1923.* Urbana: University of Illinois Press, 1994.

Babcock, Rufus, ed. *Memoir of John Mason Peck D.D., Edited from His Journals and Correspondences.* Carbondale: University of Southern Illinois Press, 1965.

Baldwin, Leland. *The Keelboat Age on the Western Waters.* Pittsburgh: University of Pittsburgh Press, 1941.

Bancroft, Frederic. *Slave Trading in the Old South.* Baltimore: J. H. Furst and Company, 1931.

Baptist, Edward E. "'Cuffy,' 'Fancy Maids,' and 'One-Eyed Men': Rape, Commodification, and the Domestic Slave Trade in the United States." *American Historical Review* 106, no. 5 (December 2001): 1619–50.

Barnett, Jim, and H. Clark Burkett. "The Forks of the Road Slave Market at Natchez." *Journal of Mississippi History* 63, no. 3 (Fall 2001): 169–88.

Beckles, Hilary McD. "An Economic Life of Their Own: Slaves as Commodity Producers and Distributors in Barbados." *Slavery and Abolition* 12 (May 1991): 31–48.

Bennett, Michael J. "'Frictions': Shipboard Relations between White and Contraband Sailors." *Civil War History* 47, no. 2 (June 2001): 118–45.

Berlin, Ira. *Generations of Captivity: A History of African-American Slaves.* Cambridge, Mass.: Belknap Press of Harvard University Press, 2003.

———. *Slaves Without Masters: The Free Negro in the Antebellum South.* New York: Vintage Books, 1976.

———. "Who Freed the Slaves? Emancipation and Its Meaning." In *Major Problems in the Civil War and Reconstruction.* 2nd ed., edited by Michael Perman. Boston: Houghton Mifflin, 1998.

Berlin, Ira, and Philip D. Morgan, ed. *The Slaves' Economy: Independent Production by Slaves in the Americas.* Portland, Ore.: Frank Case, 1991.

Blassingame, John W. *Black New Orleans, 1860–1880.* Chicago: University of Chicago Press, 1973.

———. *The Slave Community: Plantation Life in the Antebellum South.* Oxford: Oxford University Press, 1972.

Blockson, Charles. *The Underground Railroad*. New York: Prentice Hall, 1987.

Bolster, W. Jeffrey. *Black Jacks: African American Seamen in the Age of Sail*. Cambridge, Mass.: Harvard University Press, 1997.

Bolton, S. Charles. *Arkansas, 1800–1860: Remote and Restless*. Fayetteville: University of Arkansas Press, 1998.

Bond, Beverly G. "'Every Duty Incumbent upon Them': African-American Women in Nineteenth-Century Memphis." *Tennessee Historical Quarterly* 59, no. 4 (2000): 254–72.

Botkin, B. A., ed. *A Treasury of Mississippi River Folklore: Stories, Ballads, Traditions and Folkways of the Mid-American River Country*. New York: Crown Publishers, 1955.

Brewer, Charles. "African American Sailors and the Unvexing of the Mississippi River." *Prologue* 30, no. 1 (Spring 1998): 279–86.

Briggs, Harold E. "Lawlessness in Cairo, Illinois, 1848–1858." *Mid-America: An Historical Review* 33 (April 1951): 67–88.

Camp, Stephanie M. H. "'I Could Not Stay There': Enslaved Women, Truancy and the Geography of Everyday Forms of Resistance in the Antebellum Plantation South." *Slavery and Abolition* 23, no. 3 (December 2002): 1–20.

Campbell, John. "As 'a Kind of Freeman'?: Slaves' Market-Related Activities in the South Carolina Upcountry, 1800–1860." *Slavery and Abolition* 12 (May 1991): 131–69.

Campbell, Randolph B. *An Empire for Slavery: The Peculiar Institution in Texas, 1821–1865*. Baton Rouge: Louisiana State University Press, 1989.

Campbell, Stanley W. *The Slave Catchers: Enforcement of the Fugitive Slave Act*. Chapel Hill: University of North Carolina Press, 1968.

Capers, Gerald M. *The Biography of a River Town*. Chapel Hill: University of North Carolina Press, 1939.

Carrierre, Marious, Jr. "Blacks in Pre–Civil War Memphis." In *Black Communities and Urban Development in America: A Ten Volume Collection of Articles Surveying the Social, Political, Economic, and Cultural Development of Black Urban Communities*, edited with an introduction by Kenneth L. Kusmer, Vol. 2. New York: Garland Publishing, 1991.

Catterall, Helen. *Judicial Cases Concerning Slavery and the Negro*. Vol. 1. New York: Octagon Books, 1968.

Cecelski, David S. "The Shores of Freedom: The Maritime Underground Railroad in North Carolina, 1800–1861." *North Carolina Historical Review* 71 (April 1994): 174–206.

———. *The Waterman's Song: Slavery and Freedom in Maritime North Carolina*. Chapel Hill: University of North Carolina Press, 2001.

Chambers, H. A. *The Treasury of Negro Spirituals*. New York: Emerson Books, 1959.

Cheek, William, and Aimee Lee Cheek. "John Mercer Langston and the Cincinnati Riot of 1841." In *Race and the City: Work, Community, and Protest in Cincinnati, 1820–1970*, edited by Henry Louis Taylor Jr., 29–69. Chicago: University of Illinois Press, 1994.

Chevan, David. "Riverboat Music from St. Louis and the Streckfus Steamboat Line." *Black Music Research Journal* 9 (Fall 1989): 153–80.

Clamorgan, Cyprian. *The Colored Aristocracy of St. Louis*. Edited with an introduction by Julie Winch. Columbia: University of Missouri Press, 1999.

Coffin, Levi. *Reminiscences of Levi Coffin: The Reputed President of the Underground Railroad*. New York: Augustus M. Kelley, 1968.

Cohen, William. *At Freedom's Edge: Black Mobility and the Southern Quest for Racial Control, 1861–1915*. Baton Rouge: Louisiana State University Press, 1991.

Coleman, J. Winston. *Slavery Times in Kentucky*. Chapel Hill: University of North Carolina Press, 1940.

Creighton, Margaret S. *Rites and Passages: The Experience of American Whaling, 1830–1870*. Cambridge: Cambridge University Press, 1995.

Crété, Liliane. *Daily Life in Louisiana, 1815–1830*. Translated by Patrick Gregory. Baton Rouge: Louisiana State University Press, 1981.

Cronon, William. *Nature's Metropolis: Chicago and the Great West*. New York: W. W. Norton, 1991.

Cuney-Hare, Maud. *Negro Musicians and Their Music*. New York: Da Capo Press, 1974.

Curry, Leonard P. *The Free Black in Urban America, 1800–1850*. Chicago: University of Chicago Press, 1981.

Dabel, Jane E. "'My Ma Went to Work Early Every Morn': Color, Gender, and Occupation in New Orleans, 1840–1860." *Louisiana History* 41, no. 2 (Spring 2000): 217–29.

Dabney, Wendell Phillips. *Cincinnati's Colored Citizens*. New York: Negro Universities Press, 1970.

Davis, James E. *Frontier Illinois*. Bloomington: Indiana University Press, 1998.

Dayton, Fred Erving. *Steamboat Days*. New York: Tudor Publishing, 1939.

Delany, Martin R. *Blake; or, The Huts of America*. With an introduction by Floyd J. Miller. Boston: Beacon Press, 1970.

Dew, Charles B. "Black Ironworkers and the Slave Insurrection Panic of 1856." *Journal of Southern History* 61 (August 1975): 321–39.

———. *Bond of Iron*. New York: W. W. Norton, 1994.

Douglas, Hurt R. *Agriculture and Slavery in Missouri's Little Dixie*. Columbia: University of Missouri Press, 1992.

Edwards, J. Passmore. *Uncle Tom's Companions: Facts Stranger Than Fiction. A Supplement to Uncle Tom's Cabin: Being Startling Incidents in the Lives of Celebrated Fugitive Slaves*. London: Edwards and Company, 1852.

Egerton, Douglas R. *Gabriel's Rebellion: The Virginia Slave Conspiracies of 1800 and 1802*. Chapel Hill: University of North Carolina Press, 1993.

Farr, James Barker. *Black Odyssey: The Seafaring Traditions of Afro-Americans*. New York: Peter Lang, 1989.

Fehrenbacher, Don E. *Slavery, Law, and Politics: The Dred Scott Case in Historical Perspective*. New York: Oxford University Press, 1981.

Fields, Barbara Jeanne. *Slavery and Freedom on the Middle Ground*. New Haven: Yale University Press, 1985.

Fink, Gary, and Merl Reed, eds. *Race, Class, and Community in Southern Labor History*. Tuscaloosa: University of Alabama Press, 1994.

Flexner, James Thomas, *Steamboats Come True: American Inventors in Action*. New York: Fordham University Press, 1944.

Foner, Eric. *Reconstruction: America's Unfinished Revolution, 1863–1877*. New York: Harper and Row, 1988.

Foner, Philip S., and Ronald L. Lewis. *The Black Worker to 1869*. Philadelphia: Temple University Press, 1978.

Fox-Genovese, Elizabeth. *Within the Plantation Household: Black and White Women of the Old South*. Chapel Hill: University of North Carolina Press, 1988.

Franklin, John Hope, and Loren Schweninger. *Runaway Slaves: Rebels on the Plantation*. New York: Oxford University Press, 1999.

Gara, Larry. *The Liberty Line: The Legend of the Underground Railroad*. Lexington: University of Kentucky Press, 1976.

Genovese, Eugene. *Roll, Jordan, Roll: The World the Slaves Made*. New York: Vintage Books, 1976.

Goldin, Claudia Dale. *Urban Slavery in the American South, 1820–1860: A Quantitative History*. Chicago: University of Chicago Press, 1976.

Griffen, Clyde, and Sally Griffen. *Natives and Newcomers: The Ordering of Opportunity in Mid-Nineteenth-Century Poughkeepsie*. Cambridge, Mass.: Harvard University Press, 1978.

Gutman, Herbert. *The Black Family in Slavery and Freedom*. New York: Pantheon, 1976.

Habermehl, John. *Life on the Western Rivers*. Pittsburgh: McNary and Simpson, 1901.

Hagedorn, Ann. *Beyond the River: The Untold Story of the Underground Railroad*. New York: Simon and Schuster, 2002.

Hahn, Stephen. "Hunting, Fishing, and Foraging: Common Rights and Class Relations in the Post-Bellum South." *Radical History Review* 26 (November 1982): 37–64.

Haites, Erik F., and James Mak. "Ohio and Mississippi River Transportation, 1810–1860." *Explorations in Economic History* 8 (Winter 1970): 153–80.

———. "Social Savings Due to Western River Steamboats," *Research in Economic History* 3 (1978): 263–304.

———. "Steamboating on the Mississippi: A Purely Competitive Industry." *Business History Review* 45 (Spring 1971): 52–78.

Haites, Erik F., James Mak, and Gary M. Walton. *Western River Transportation*. Baltimore: Johns Hopkins University Press, 1975.

Hanger, Kimberly S. *Bounded Lives, Bounded Places: Free Blacks in Colonial New Orleans, 1769–1803*. Durham, N.C.: Duke University Press, 1997.

Hartman, Saidiya V. *Scenes of Subjection: Terror, Slavery, and Self-Making in Nineteenth-Century America*. Oxford: Oxford University Press, 1997.

Haskins, James. *The First Black Governor*. Trenton, N.J.: Africa World Press, 1996.

Hearn, Chester G. *Ellet's Brigade: The Strangest Outfit of All*. Baton Rouge: Louisiana State University Press, 2000.

Hearn, Lafcadio. *Children of the Levee*. Edited by O. W. Frost. Lexington: University of Kentucky Press, 1957.

Henderson, James A. "Reminiscences of the Rivers." *Western Pennsylvania Historical Magazine* 12 (October 1929): 230–41.

Herman, Janet S. "The Macintosh Affair." *Missouri Historical Society Bulletin* 26 (January 1970): 123–43.

Higgs, Robert. *Competition and Coercion: Blacks in the American Economy*. Cambridge: Cambridge University Press, 1977.

Hindus, Michael S. *Prison and Plantation: Crime, Justice and Authority in Massachusetts and South Carolina, 1767–1878*. Chapel Hill: University of North Carolina Press, 1980.

Hine, Darlene Clarke, and Earnestine Jenkins, eds. *"Manhood Rights": The Construction of Black Male History and Manhood, 1750–1870*. Vol. 1 of *A Question of Manhood: A Reader in U.S. Black Men's History and Masculinity*. Bloomington: University of Indiana Press, 1999.

Hinks, Peter P., ed. *David Walker's Appeal to the Coloured Citizens of the World*. University Park: Pennsylvania State University Press, 2000.

Hodes, Martha. *White Women, Black Men: Illicit Sex in the Nineteenth-Century South*. New Haven: Yale University Press, 1997.

Hogan, William Ransom, and Edwin Adams Davis, eds. *William Johnson's Natchez*. Baton Rouge: Louisiana State University Press, 1993.

Horton, James Oliver. *Free People of Color: Inside the African American Community*. Washington: Smithsonian Institution Press, 1993.

Horton, James Oliver, and Lois E. Horton. *In Hope of Liberty: Culture, Community and Protest among Northern Free Blacks, 1700–1860*. New York: Oxford University Press, 1997.

Howard, Leslie. *This Species of Property: Slave Life and Culture in the Old South*. New York: Oxford University Press, 1976.

Hudson, J. Blaine. "Crossing the 'Dark Line': Fugitive Slaves and the Underground Railroad in Louisville and North-Central Kentucky." *Filson History Quarterly* 75, no. 1 (Winter 2001): 33–83.

Hughes, Jon Christopher, ed. *Period of the Gruesome*. Lanham, Maryland: University Press of America, 1990.

Hunter, Louis C. *Steamboats on the Western Rivers: An Economic and Technological History*. Cambridge, Mass.: Harvard University Press, 1949.

Hunter, Tera W. *To 'Joy My Freedom: Southern Black Women's Lives and Labors after the Civil War*. Cambridge, Mass.: Harvard University Press, 1997.

Ignatiev, Noel. *How the Irish Became White*. New York: Routledge, 1995.

Jaynes, Gerald David. *Branches without Roots: The Genesis of the Black Working Class in the American South, 1862–1882*. New York: Oxford University Press, 1986.

Johnson, Jerah. "New Orleans's Congo Square: An Urban Setting for Early Afro-American Culture Formation." *Louisiana History* 32 (Spring 1991): 117–57.

Johnson, Michael P. "Runaway Slaves and the Slave Communities in South Carolina, 1799 to 1830." *William and Mary Quarterly* 38 (July 1981): 418–41.

Johnson, Walter. *Soul by Soul: Life Inside the Antebellum Slave Market*. Cambridge, Mass.: Harvard University Press, 1999.

Jones, Jacqueline. *The Dispossessed: America's Underclass from the Civil War to the Present*. New York: Basic Books, 1992.

Jordan, Winthrop. *Tumult and Silence at Second Creek: An Inquiry into a Civil War Conspiracy*. Baton Rouge: Louisiana State University Press, 1993.

Katznelson, Ira, and Aristide R. Zolberg, eds. *Working Class Formation: Nineteenth-Century Patterns in Western Europe and the United States*. Princeton: Princeton University Press, 1986.

Kaye, Anthony E. "Neighborhoods and Solidarity in the Natchez District of Mississippi: Rethinking the Antebellum Slave Community." *Slavery and Abolition* 23, no. 1 (April 2002): 1–24.

Kelman, Ari. *A River and Its City: The Nature of Landscape in New Orleans*. Berkeley: University of California Press, 2003.

Larsen, Lawrence H. *The Rise of the Urban South*. Lexington: University of Kentucky Press, 1985.

Levine, Lawrence. *Black Culture and Black Consciousness: Afro-American Folk Thought from Slavery to Freedom*. Oxford: Oxford University Press, 1977.

Lewett, Bobby L. *The African-American History of Nashville, Tennessee, 1780–1930*. Fayetteville: University of Arkansas Press, 1999.

Lewis, Ronald L. *Coal, Iron, and Slaves: Industrial Slavery in Maryland and Virginia, 1715–1865*. Westport, Conn.: Greenwood Press, 1979.

Lichtenstein, Alex. "'That Disposition to Theft, with Which They Have Been Branded': Moral Economy, Slave Management, and the Law." *Journal of Social History* 21 (Spring 1988): 413–35.

Linebaugh, Peter, and Marcus Rediker. "The Many-Headed Hydra: Sailors, Slaves and the Atlantic Working Class in the Eighteenth Century." *Journal of Historical Sociology* 3 (September 1990): 225–52.

———. *The Many-Headed Hydra: Sailors, Slaves, Commoners, and the Hidden History of the Revolutionary Atlantic*. Boston: Beacon Press, 2002.

Litwack, Leon. *Been in the Storm So Long: The Aftermath of Slavery*. New York: Knopf, 1979.

———. *North of Slavery: The Negro in the Free States*. Chicago: University of Chicago Press, 1961.

Lofton, John. *Denmark Vesey's Revolt*. Kent, Ohio: Kent State University Press, 1964.

Luraghi, Raimondo. *A History of the Confederate Navy*. Annapolis: Naval Institute Press, 1996.

Macarthur, Walter, comp. *The Seaman's Contract: 1790–1918, A Complete Reprint of the Laws Relating to United States Seamen*. San Francisco: James H. Barry Co., 1919.

Mahoney, Timothy R. *River Towns in the Great West: The Structure of Provincial Urbanization in the American Midwest, 1820–1870*. Cambridge: Cambridge University Press, 1990.

Malone, Ann Patton. *Sweet Chariot: Slave Family and Household Structure in Nineteenth-Century Louisiana*. Chapel Hill: University of North Carolina Press, 1992.

Mandle, Jay. *Not Slave, Not Free: The African American Economic Experience after the Civil War*. Durham, N.C.: Duke University Press, 1992.

McDonald, Roderick A. "Independent Economic Production by Slaves on Antebellum Louisiana Sugar Plantations." *Slavery and Abolition* 12, no. 1 (May 1991): 182–208.

McGoldrick, Stacy K. "The Policing of Slavery in New Orleans, 1852–1860." *Journal of Historical Sociology* 14, no. 4 (December 2001): 397–417.

McIlwaine, Shields. *Memphis Down in Dixie*. New York: E. P. Dutton, 1948.

McKenzie, Robert Tracy. *One South or Many? Plantation Belt and Upcountry in Civil War–Era Tennessee*. Cambridge: Cambridge University Press, 1994.

McNeilly, Donald P. *The Old South Frontier: Cotton Plantations and the Formation of Arkansas Society, 1819–1861*. Fayetteville: University of Arkansas Press, 2000.

Melville, Herman. *The Confidence-Man: His Masquerade*. With an introduction by Stephen Matterson. New York: Penguin Books, 1990.

Merrick, George Byron. *Old Times on the Upper Mississippi: The Recollections of a Steamboat Pilot from 1854 to 1863*. Cleveland: Arthur H. Clarke, 1909.

Mintz, Sidney W. "The Jamaican Internal Marketing Pattern: Some Notes and Hypothesis." *Social and Economic Studies* 4 (1955): 93–103.

Mooney, Chase C. *Slavery in Tennessee*. Bloomington: Indiana University Press, 1957.

Moore, John Hebron. *The Emergence of the Cotton Kingdom in the Old Southwest: Mississippi, 1770–1860*. Baton Rouge: Louisiana State University Press, 1988.

———. "Simon Gray, Riverman: A Slave Who Was Almost Free." *Mississippi Valley Historical Review* 49 (December 1962): 474–84.

Morgan, Philip D. "The Ownership of Property by Slaves in the Mid-Nineteenth Century Lowcountry." *Journal of Southern History* 49 (1983): 399–420.

———. "Work and Culture: The Task System and the World of Lowcountry Blacks, 1700–1880." *William and Mary Quarterly* 39 (October 1982): 563–99.

Morgan, Philip D., and Ira Berlin, eds. *Cultivation and Culture: Labor and the Shaping of Black Life in the Americas*. Charlottesville: University of Virginia, 1993.

Morris, Christopher. *Becoming Southern: The Evolution of a Way of Life, Warren County and Vicksburg, Mississippi, 1770–1860*. New York: Oxford University Press, 1995.

————. "An Event in Community Organization: The Mississippi Slave Insurrection of 1835." *Journal of Social History* 22, no. 1 (1988): 93–112.

Morris, Thomas D. *Southern Slavery and the Law, 1619–1860*. Chapel Hill: University of North Carolina Press, 1996.

Musicant, Ivan. *Divided Waters: The Naval History of the Civil War*. New York: HarperCollins, 1995.

Niehaus, Earl F. *The Irish in New Orleans, 1800–1860*. Baton Rouge: Louisiana State University Press, 1965.

Outland, Robert B., III. "Slavery, Work, and the Geography of the North Carolina Naval Stores Industry, 1835–1860." *Journal of Southern History* 62 (February 1996): 27–57.

Owens, Harry P. *Steamboats and the Cotton Economy: River Trade in the Yazoo-Mississippi Delta*. Jackson: University of Mississippi Press, 1990.

Painter, Nell Irvin. *Exodusters: Black Migration to Kansas after Reconstruction*. New York: W. W. Norton, 1976.

Petersen, William J. *Steamboating on the Upper Mississippi*. Iowa City: State Historical Society of Iowa, 1968.

Petit, Eber. *Sketches in the History of the Underground Railroad*. New York: Freeport, 1971.

Primm, James Neal. *Lion in the Valley: St. Louis, Missouri, 1764–1980*. St. Louis: Missouri Historical Society, 1981.

Pritchett, Jonathan B. "The Interregional Slave Trade and the Selection of Slaves for the New Orleans Market." *Journal of Interdisciplinary History* 28, no. 1 (Summer 1997): 57–85.

Putney, Martha S. *Black Sailors: Afro-American Merchant Seamen and Whalemen Prior to the Civil War*. Westport, Conn.: Greenwood Press, 1987.

Quick, Herbert, and Edward Quick. *Mississippi Steamboatin': A History of Steamboating on the Mississippi and Its Tributaries*. New York: Henry Holt, 1926.

Rabinowitz, Howard N. "From Exclusion to Segregation: Southern Race Relations, 1865–1890." *Journal of American History* 63 (September 1976): 325–50.

Rachleff, Peter. *Black Labor in Richmond, 1865–1890*. Urbana: University of Illinois Press, 1989.

Ramold, Steven J. *Slaves, Sailors, Citizens: African Americans in the Union Navy*. Dekalb: Northern Illinois University Press, 2002.

Ransom, Roger, and Richard Sutch. *One Kind of Freedom: The Economic Consequences of Emancipation*. Cambridge: Cambridge University Press, 1977.

Rediker, Marcus. *Between the Devil and the Deep Blue Sea: Merchant Seamen, Pirates, and the Anglo-American Maritime World, 1700–1750*. Cambridge: Cambridge University Press, 1987.

Reidy, Joseph P. *From Slavery to Agrarian Capitalism in the Cotton Plantation South: Central Georgia, 1800–1880*. Chapel Hill: University of North Carolina Press, 1992.

Roberts, John W. *From Trickster to Badman: The Black Folk Hero in Slavery and Freedom*. Philadelphia: University of Pennsylvania Press, 1989.

Robinson, Armstead. "The Difference Freedom Made." In *The State of Afro-American History: Past, Present, Future*, edited by Darlene Clark Hine. Baton Rouge: Louisiana State University, 1986.

Roca, Steven Louis. "Presence and Precedents: The USS Red Rover during the American Civil War, 1861–1865." *Civil War History* 44, no. 2 (June 1998): 91–110.

Roediger, David R. *The Wages of Whiteness*. New York: Verso, 1991.

Ross, Steven J. *Workers on the Edge: Work, Leisure, and Politics in Industrializing Cincinnati, 1788–1890*. New York: Columbia University Press, 1985.

Sandweiss, Lee Ann, ed. *Seeking St. Louis: Voices from a River City, 1670–2000*. St. Louis: Missouri Historical Society Press, 2000.

Saville, Julie. *The Work of Reconstruction: From Slave to Free Labor in South Carolina, 1860–1870*. Cambridge: Cambridge University Press, 1994.

Schafer, Judith Kelleher. *Becoming Free, Remaining Free: Manumission and Enslavement in New Orleans, 1846–1862*. Baton Rouge: Louisiana State University Press, 2003.

———. *Slavery, the Civil Law, and the Supreme Court of Louisiana*. Baton Rouge: Louisiana State University, 1994.

Schwartz, Philip. *Twice Condemned: Slaves and the Criminal Laws of Virginia, 1705–1865*. Baton Rouge: Louisiana State University Press, 1988.

Schweninger, Loren. "The Underside of Slavery: The Internal Economy, Self Hire, and Quasi-Freedom in Virginia, 1780–1865." *Slavery and Abolition* 12 (September 1991): 1–22.

Seematter, Mary. "Trials and Confessions: Race and Justice in Antebellum St. Louis." *Gateway Heritage* 12 (Fall 1991): 36–46.

Seibert, William. *The Underground Railroad from Slavery to Freedom*. New York: Macmillan, 1898.

Share, Allen J. *Cities in the Commonwealth: Two Centuries of Urban Life in Kentucky*. Lexington: University of Kentucky Press, 1981.

Sigafoos, Robert A. *Cotton Row to Beale Street: A Business History of Memphis*. Memphis: Memphis State University Press, 1979.

Starobin, Robert. *Industrial Slavery in the Old South*. New York: Oxford University Press, 1970.

Sterling, Dorothy. *The Making of an Afro-American: Martin R. Delany, 1812–1885*. New York: Doubleday, 1925.

Stevenson, Brenda E. *Life in Black and White: Family and Community in the Slave South*. New York: Oxford University Press, 1997.

Still, William. *The Underground Railroad*. Philadelphia: Porter and Coates, 1872.

Surrency, Erwin C. *History of the Federal Courts*. London: Oceana Publications, 1987.

Syndor, Charles Sackett. *Slavery in Mississippi*. Gloucester, Mass.: Peter Smith, 1965.

Tadman, Michael. *Speculators and Slaves: Masters, Traders, and Slaves in the Old South*. Madison: University of Wisconsin Press, 1989.

Tansey, Richard. "Out-of-State Free Blacks in Late Antebellum New Orleans." *Louisiana History* 22 (Fall 1981): 369–86.

Taylor, Henry Louis, ed. *Race and the City: Work, Community, and Protest in Cincinnati, 1820–1970.* Urbana: University of Illinois Press, 1993.

Taylor, Joe Gray. *Negro Slavery in Louisiana.* Baton Rouge: Thos. J. Moran, 1963.

Taylor, Orville W. *Negro Slavery in Arkansas.* Durham, N.C.: Duke University Press, 1958.

Tregilis, Helen Cox. *River Roads to Freedom: Fugitive Slave Notices and Sheriff Notices Found in Illinois Sources.* Bowie, Md.: Heritage Books, 1988.

Trotter, Joe W. *Black Milwaukee: The Making of an Industrial Proletariat, 1915–1945.* Urbana: University of Illinois, 1985.

Turner, Mary, ed. *From Chattel Slaves to Wage Slaves: The Dynamics of Labour Bargaining in the Americas.* Bloomington: University of Indiana Press, 1995.

Twain, Mark. *The Autobiography of Mark Twain.* New York: Harper and Bros., 1959.

———. *Life on the Mississippi.* New York: Harper and Bros., 1969.

Ullman, Victor. *Martin R. Delany: The Beginnings of Black Nationalism.* Boston: Beacon Press, 1971.

Van Deburg, William L. *The Slave Drivers: Black Agricultural Labor Supervisors in the Antebellum South.* Westport, Conn.: Greenwood Press, 1979.

Viorst, Milton. *Fire in the Streets: America in the Sixties.* New York: Simon and Schuster, 1979.

Wade, Richard. *Slavery in the Cities: The South, 1820–1860.* New York: Oxford University Press, 1964.

Waldstreicher, David. "Reading the Runaways: Self-Fashioning, Print Culture, and Confidence in Slavery in the Eighteenth-Century Mid-Atlantic." *William and Mary Quarterly* 56 (April 1999): 243–72.

Way, Frederick, Jr., comp. *Way's Packet Directory, 1848–1994: Passenger Steamboats of the Mississippi River System Since the Advent of Photography in Mid-Continent America.* Athens: Ohio University Press, 1994.

Way, Peter. *Common Labour: Workers and the Digging of North American Canals, 1780–1860.* Cambridge: Cambridge University Press, 1993.

Wheeler, Mary. *Steamboatin' Days: Folk Songs of the River Packet Era.* Baton Rouge: Louisiana State University Press, 1944.

White, Deborah Grey. *Ar'n't I a Woman? Female Slaves in the Plantation South.* New York: W. W. Norton, 1985.

White, Newman I. *American Negro Folk-songs.* Hatboro, Pa.: Folklore Associates, 1965.

Whitman, T. Stephen. "Industrial Slavery at the Margin: The Maryland Chemical Works." *Journal of Southern History* 59 (February 1993): 31–62.

Wiener, Jonathan M. *Social Origins of the New South: Alabama, 1860–1885.* Baton Rouge: Louisiana State University, 1978.

Wood, Betty. *Women's Work, Men's Work: The Informal Slave Economies of Lowcountry Georgia.* Athens: University of Georgia Press, 1995.

Wood, Peter. *Black Majority: Negroes in Colonial South Carolina from 1670 through the Stono Rebellion*. New York: W. W. Norton, 1974.

Woodson, Carter G. "Negroes of Cincinnati Prior to the Civil War." *Journal of Negro History* 1 (January 1916): 1–22.

Wright, Carroll D. *The History and Growth of the United States Census, Prepared for the Senate Committee on the Census*. Washington: Government Printing Office, 1900.

DISSERTATIONS

Krauthamer, Barbara. "Blacks on the Borders: African-Americans' Transition from Slavery to Freedom in Texas and the Indian Territory, 1836–1907." Ph.D. diss., Princeton University, 2000.

Miller, Buffington Clay. "A Computerized Method of Determining Family Structure from Mid-Nineteenth-Century Census Data." M.A. Thesis, University of Pennsylvania, Moore School of Electrical Engineering, 1972.

Scott, Julius Sherrard. "The Common Wind: Currents of Afro-American Communication in the Era of the Haitian Revolution." Ph.D. diss., Duke University, 1986.

Taylor, Nikki Marie. "'Frontiers of Freedom': The African American Experience in Cincinnati, 1802–1862." Ph.D. diss., Duke University, 2001.

index

Bright, Henry Arthur, 68–69
Brotherhood of Sleeping Car Porters, 179
Brown, Charles, 94, 124, 137; and abolitionist connections, 127–28, 138, 146; confessions of, 126; early life of, 127–28, 133–34; flight/capture of, after murders, 142–43; lawlessness of, 139, 175; and Pettus Bank robbery, 140–42; positions held on boats, 135; religion of, 133–34. *See also* Madison Henderson Gang; Rascals
Brown, William Wells, 15, 22, 53, 54, 123; as antislavery activist, 3, 149; escape of, 82, 101, 103, 104, 123; and family ties, 5, 81–82, 90, 99–100; final destination of, 120, 121; mobility of, 5, 19, 190 (n. 36); *Narrative of William Wells Brown, A Fugitive Slave*, 3; observing slave transportation, 5, 81, 86–88; in St. Louis, 11, 43; as steamboat waiter, 3, 62
Burkle, Jacob, 37–38, 192 (n. 97)

Cabin crew, 3, 13–14, 20, 55, 59–70, 80; cabin watchmen, 64; dress, 62, 197 (n. 53); music of, 69–70; porters, 64; reading/information networks of, 69, 70; stewards, 66–67, 94–95, 111; wages and tips, 13, 14, 91, 93, 94–95; waiters, 62–64. *See also* Chambermaids
Cairo, Ill., 39–40, 118
Calaboose jail, 29–30, 132, 136
Campbell, Stanley, 39
Canada: as escaped slave destination, 101, 120, 121
Cartwright, Samuel, 129
Chambermaids, 10, 13, 15–16, 188 (n. 35); after emancipation, 163–66; dress, 62; duties, 65–66; and family ties, 38, 89, 90, 96, 151; helping

slaves escape, 111, 112; sexual violence against, 55, 164, 195 (nn. 12, 13); wages and tips, 91, 92, 93
Chambers, Adam B., 126–30, 140, 144
Charleville, Peter, 94, 136, 142
Chevan, David, 178
Cincinnati, 194 (nn. 132, 133); abolitionists in, 20, 47, 48, 119, 133; African Americans in, 12, 47–48, 119; population of, 47; racial violence in, 48, 57; slave escapes at levee at, 101, 104, 107, 119
Civil Rights Act (1866), 162, 168
Civil Rights Act (1875), 168, 219–20 (n. 105)
Civil War, 149–54; African Americans in Confederate navy, 150, 151–52; African Americans in Mississippi Squadron, 150, 152, 153–54, 169, 215 (nn. 2, 4); and contrabands, 152–54; and free black river workers, dangers for, 152; and Mississippi River, use of by slaves to escape during, 149–50; steamboat workers during, 151–54; Union navy victory on Mississippi, 151; and worsened conditions for river slaves, 151–52, 154
Clamorgan, Cyprian, 43, 95; *Colored Aristocracy of St. Louis*, 66, 94
Clarke, Milton, 22, 94, 97, 179
Colored American, The, 147
Compromise of 1820, 40
Confederate Mississippi River Defense Fleet, 150, 151, 151–52, 215 (n. 13)
Confiscation Acts (1861 and 1862), 152
Cook, George, 21, 22
Cooks, 62, 64, 66
Cooley, Stoughton, 171, 172, 174, 176, 177
Cotton, 6, 42; plantation slaves' work with, 35; stacking of on deck, 6, 70, 73, 74; transport of slaves on boats to work with, 83

Court cases, 56; Dred Scott case, 40–41, 43, 85; filed by Atlantic mariners, 163, 218 (n. 70); filed by emancipated river workers, 154, 159–68, 218 (nn. 66, 70), 219–20 (n. 105); involving slave escapes, 23, 46–47, 103, 104, 108, 114–15, 190 (n. 20); lack of by freed river workers in late nineteenth century, 174; treason cases against Confederate navy captains, 151, 215 (n. 13); of Union black crew revolts, 152, 215 (n. 16)

Crooks, Phillip, 162–63

Cumberland River, 44–45, 105

Cunynghame, Arthur, 13, 54

Dancing, 29, 77

Davis, Jefferson, 103

Deckhands, 14, 70–78; culture of, 75–78; dancing, 77; dress, 70–71, 197 (n. 53); duties, 71, 73; firemen, 56, 59, 71, 91, 198–99 (nn. 96, 98, 101); more slaves than free blacks as, 13, 20, 80, 187–88 (n. 30); night watch, 74, 199 (n. 107); racial violence against, 54–55, 56–58; segregation of, 74–75; singing of, 54–55, 77–79, 89, 157, 217 (n. 52); wages, 91, 221 (n. 11). *See also* Roustabouts

Delany, Martin, 49, 77, 95, 120; *Blake; or, The Huts of America*, 50, 104

Disease, 59, 87, 196 (n. 43)

Draymen, 27–28

Drowning, 6, 56, 58, 87

Dyer, Peter, 166–67

Emancipation, and steamboat culture, 154–69; abuse of workers by mates, 156, 161, 162–68; African Americans as roustabouts, 155–62, 166–68, 171–73, 179, 217 (n. 56), 221 (n. 4), 221–22 (n. 22); African Americans excluded from being officers, 173; African Americans' real names,

use of, 157; chambermaids, 163–66; changes with freedom, 168–69; Chinese laborers, employment of, 157, 217 (n. 50); cities lived in, 173, 221 (nn. 3, 4); compensation for injuries from work, 166–68; continued segregation, 159; court cases brought by river workers, 154, 159–68, 218 (nn. 66, 70), 219–20 (n. 105); decline of numbers of workers, 171, 220 (n. 1); Exodusters, 177–78; first paid work for freed blacks, 155; harshness of work, 155–56, 175, 217 (n. 57); labor strikes, 158–59, 175; lawbreaking, 175; legal protection under maritime law, 161–62, 195 (n. 14), 218 (n. 67); race relations, 158–59; slowdowns, as protest of conditions, 156–57, 158; struggles to improve conditions, 154–55, 161–62, 169, 175, 216 (n. 25); wages, 157–61

Emancipation Proclamation, 152

Ennis (betrayer of Madison Henderson gang), 136, 140–41, 143

Exodusters, 177–78

Farragut, David, 151

Firemen, 56, 59, 198–99 (nn. 96, 98, 101); duties, 71; wages, 91

Flatboats, 9

Flogging, 56, 103, 123; after emancipation, 161, 162

Free blacks: in Arkansas, 38; as Atlantic sailors, 10, 59, 131, 132, 172, 187 (n. 19); average age of steamboat worker, 11; barbers, 36, 45, 67–68, 70; as cabin crew, 13, 66, 69, 70, 80, 91, 93, 182–83; as chambermaids, 38, 163–66; in Cincinnati, 48, 119, 194 (n. 133); dangers of reenslavement during Civil War, 152; as deckhands, 182–83; as deckhands, vs. number of slaves as, 13, 20, 80, 187–

88 (n. 30); employment prospects on steamboats, 15, 188 (n. 40); helping slaves escape, 45, 101–2, 109, 111, 112, 113, 119, 207 (n. 36), 209 (n. 102); hysteria about dangers of, after Madison Henderson Gang executions, 145–46; influence on river slaves, 23–24, 25–26, 28, 30–31, 35–36; and information networks, 70, 82, 97; legal jailing of "foreign" in slave states, 24–25, 146; legal protection against racial violence for, 56, 195 (n. 14); legal restrictions on in free states, 39, 40, 194 (n. 133); legal restrictions on in slave states, 23–25, 190 (nn. 29, 30); literacy of, 69, 131, 144; in Louisville, 45; in Memphis, 37, 38; mobility of, as steamboat workers, 19, 25, 36, 41–42, 50, 51, 82, 95; and names, demand for use of real, 69, 157; in New Orleans, 24, 25, 28–31; papers verifying, 107; as passengers on steamboats, 61, 198 (n. 85); percentage of steamboat workers, 12, 181–83; protection against racial violence under maritime law for, 55–56; and river trading, 93–94; in St. Louis, 41–42; in Tennessee, 44; women, 38, 198 (n. 85). *See also* African Americans; Emancipation, and steamboat culture; Steamboat workers

Fugitive Slave Acts (1793 and 1850), 39, 47, 118. *See also* Slave escapes

Fulton, Robert, 9

Gabriel's Rebellion, 36
Gambling, 43, 76
Garner, Margaret, 46–47
Green, J. D., 111, 119

Habermehl, John, 76
Hatfield, John, 26, 70, 119

Hearn, Lafcadio, 102, 155, 161, 175
Hemp, 46
Henderson, Madison, 124, 175; exploits of, 137–40; flight/capture of, after murders, 142–43; helping slaves escape, 138, 213 (n. 77); intelligence of, 129, 131, 137; life story of, 127, 131; lifestyle of, 8, 90, 94, 134, 137; mobility of, 134–35; and Pettus Bank robbery, 123, 140–42; and rascality, own view of, 129, 131, 140; trial and execution of, 123–26, 143–44. *See also* Madison Henderson Gang; Rascals
Henry, Gustavus, 62, 66
Hesse-Wartegg, Ernst von, 156
Hodes, Martha, 45
Holmes, James, 66, 95
Horton, James Oliver, 99
Hudson, J. Blaine, 45
Hughes, Louis, 92, 110, 115
Hunter, Louis C., 12

Illinois River, 120
Ironclads, 150–51

Jackson, Andrew, 44–45
Jackson, Joseph, 15, 151–52
Johns, Mary, 163–66
Johnson, William, 36, 68, 106, 146
Jordan, Winthrop D., 36

Kay, John, 37
Keelboats, 9
Kentucky River, 46

Labor strikes, 175; and need for racial harmony, 57, 158–59, 195 (n. 24)
Lackland, James, 21, 22, 23, 91, 92
Latrobe, Charles, 62, 71, 77
Leah's black boardinghouse, St. Louis, 90, 136, 141
Legislation: restricting free blacks in free states, 39, 40, 194 (n. 133); re-

stricting free blacks in slave states, 23–25, 190 (nn. 29, 30)

Levees: police on, 118; slave escapes on crowded, 101, 104, 106, 107, 119; workers on, 16, 27–28, 43, 47

Lexington, slave market at, 84–85

Lincoln, Abraham, 151

Long, Will, 12, 70

Louisville, 12, 45–46, 84

Louisville Journal, 126, 135

Lowry, Adam, 86, 87

Mackay, Charles, 13, 31, 32, 86

Madison Henderson Gang: attempts to escape from jail, 144; and Badman tradition, 130–31, 134, 147; and counterfeiting, 137–38; exploits of, 7–8, 126, 137–40; family ties of, 137; flight/capture of, after murders, 142–43; formation of, 136; life stories of in form of confessions, 126–28; lifestyle of members of, 134, 136; mobility of, 134–37; and Pettus Bank robbery, 140–42, 213 (n. 91); rascality of, 125–26, 129–30, 131, 135–37, 144, 175; reaction to executions of, 145–46, 147; trials and executions of, 123–26, 143–44, 214 (n. 112); and trickster tradition of Africa, 130, 134, 147. *See also* Rascals

Mamie May v. Phillip Crooks, master and captain of the Ozark, 162–63

Maritime law: protection for emancipated blacks under, 161–62, 195 (n. 14), 218 (n. 67); protection for free blacks under, 55–56

Martin, Sella, 26, 94, 104, 116, 121

May, Mamie, 162–63

Melody, George, 126

Melville, Herman, 129; *Confidence-Man*, 110

Memphis, 37–38, 86, 136

Merrick, George, 75–76

Militia Act (1862), 152

Mississippi River: African American culture around, 16–17, 31–33, 34–35; African Americans linked by, 19–20, 26, 50–51, 80; cities/rivers of river system steamboats worked, 9, 19; and Exodusters, 177–78; modern-day barges on, 178–79; as symbol of freedom, 3–5, 8, 26, 102; as symbol of freedom, change after Civil War, 175–79; transport of cotton on, 6, 70, 73, 74; use of by slaves to escape, 6–7, 101–3, 104–5, 106, 205 (n. 3); use of by slaves to escape, during Civil War, 149–50; use of by slaves to improve conditions, 7–8, 17, 95–96

Mississippi Squadron, 153, 215 (n. 18); African Americans serving with, 150, 152, 153–54, 169, 215 (nn. 2, 4); contrabands enlisting in, 152, 153–54, 215 (nn. 2, 4); victory of, 151

Missouri Republican, 128, 142, 143, 144, 145

Missouri River, 19, 42, 66, 81, 94, 109, 116, 117

Morrison, Tony, 46; *Beloved*, 47

Murrell, John, 36

Music, 29, 69–70, 178. *See also* Singing

Nash, James, 66

Nashville, 44

Natchez, 35–36, 88

National Anti-Slavery Standard, 143

Native Americans, and slaves, 33–34

New Orleans: African American culture of, 26–31; American District of, 30; Calaboose jail, 29–30, 132, 136; French Quarter of, 28–30; as hub of steamboat world, 26–27; interracial mixing in, 30–31; and jailing of free blacks, 24, 25; levee life

188 (n. 40); segregation on, of passengers, 61, 168, 198 (n. 85), 220 (n. 106); segregation of workers on, 68, 74–75, 159; sentimentalizing of, 3, 53, 178; slaves stowing away on to escape, 109–11, 115–16, 117–18; slave transportation on, 5, 81, 83–84, 85–88; technology of, 8–10; transport of cotton on, 6, 70, 73, 74

Steamboats, plying the pan-Mississippi world: *Agnes*, 136, 139, 140; *Aunt Letty*, 57–58; *Autocrat*, 41–42; *Charles Rebstock*, 164; *Die Vernon*, 42, 153; *Fidele* (fictional), 110, 129; *Iowa*, 42; *Kansas*, 42; *Louisville*, 22, 151, 152; *Magnolia*, 98, 110, 111, 205 (n. 103); *Mary Louisa*, 164, 165; *Missouri*, 109, 141; *Morton*, 66, 95; *Natchez*, 68, 166; *New York*, 106, 109; *Osark*, 162–63; *Pennsylvania*, 6; *Pike No. 3*, 111, 119; *Providence*, 156, 168; *Robert E. Lee*, 155; *Robert Semple*, 159, 160; *St. Ange*, 42; *St. Louis*, 42; *Shreveport*, 152, 215 (n. 16); *Tobacco Plant*, 23, 91

Steamboat workers: after emancipation, 154–69; and alcohol, 30–31, 42, 75–76, 157; average age of, 11, 173; barbers, 10, 13, 44, 45, 59, 67–68, 70, 90, 106, 198 (n. 79); buying freedom for family members, 95–96; cabin crew, 3, 20, 55, 59–70, 80, 91, 93, 182–84, 197 (n. 53); chambermaids, 10, 13, 15–16, 65–66, 92, 111, 112, 163–66, 188 (n. 35); chambermaids, and family ties, 38, 89, 90, 96, 151; chambermaids, sexual violence against, 55, 164, 195 (nn. 12, 13); cooks, 62, 64, 66; culture of, 75–79; deckhands, 13, 14, 20, 54–55, 56–58, 70–78, 80, 91, 182–84, 187–88 (n. 30), 221 (n. 11); and diseases, 59, 87, 196 (n. 43); eth-nicities of, 10, 20, 181–84; European immigrants, 28–29, 58, 68, 75, 196 (n. 29); and family ties, 42, 81–82, 88–91, 95–100, 202 (nn. 29, 30); firemen, 56, 59, 71, 91, 198–99 (nn. 96, 98, 101); hazards faced by, 6, 58–59, 79, 166; helping slaves escape, 101–2, 111–13, 208 (n. 87, 90, 91); and information networks, 7, 70, 82, 96, 97, 102, 204 (n. 98); and labor strikes, 57, 158–59, 175, 195 (n. 24); lawlessness of, 75–76, 135, 200 (nn. 119, 120), 212 (n. 62); and lawmakers' fears of, 36, 145–46; mobility of, 5, 19, 21–22, 25–26, 36, 41–42, 50–51, 82, 95, 104, 134–35, 190 (n. 36); and night watch, 74, 199 (n. 107); numbers of, 10, 181–84, 186–87 (n. 16); racial violence against, 54–58, 67, 156, 161, 162–68; religious activities, 76–77; river trading by, 93–94; segregation of, 68, 74–75, 159; slaves and free blacks connected as, 16–18, 19–20; and slowdowns as protest of conditions, 68–69, 156–57, 158, 217 (n. 56); variety of, 54, 61, 80; wages, 91–93, 94–95, 157–61, 221 (n. 11); white workers' strife with blacks, 57–58, 67, 74–75, 196 (n. 29). *See also* Emancipation, and steamboat culture

Stewards, 66–67; acquiring produce along river, 67; helping slaves escape, 111; wages and tips, 13, 91, 93, 94–95

Stowe, Harriet Beecher: *Uncle Tom's Cabin*, 88

Streckfus line, 178

Sugar plantations, 31–33, 192 (n. 71); and access to the Mississippi, 31; transport of slaves on boats to work on, 83

Sydney, Allen, 104, 120